GREAT CAMPAIGNS

THE MIDWAY CAMPAIGN

Naval aviation was the key to victory in the Pacific War.

GREAT CAMPAIGNS SERIES

GREAT CAMPAIGNS

THE MIDWAY CAMPAIGN

December 7, 1941 - June 6, 1942

REVISED AND EXPANDED EDITION

Jack Greene

COMBINED BOOKS
Pennsylvania

PUBLISHER'S NOTE

Combined Books, Inc., is dedicated to publishing books of distinction in history and military history. We are proud of the quality of writing and the quantity of information found in our books. Our books are manufactured with style and durability and are printed on acid-free paper. We like to think of our books as soldiers: not infantry grunts, but well dressed and well equipped avant garde. Our logo reflects our commitment to the modern and yet historic art of bookmaking.

We would like to hear from our readers and invite you to write to us at our offices in Pennsylvania with your reactions, queries, comments, even complaints. All of your correspondence will be answered directly by a member of the Editorial Board or by the author.

We encourage all of our readers to purchase our books from their local booksellers, and we hope that you let us know of booksellers in your area that might be interested in carrying our books. If you are unable to find a book in your area, please write to us.

For information, address:
COMBINED BOOKS, INC.
151 East 10th Avenue
Conshohocken, PA 19428

Library of Congress Cataloging-in-Publication Data
Greene, Jack.
  The Midway campaign, December 7, 1941-June 6, 1942 / Jack Greene.
    p. cm.
  Includes bibliographical references (p.) and index.
  ISBN 0-938289-11-X : $22.95
  1. Midway, Battle of, 1942. I. Title.
  D774.M5G74   1994
  940.54'26—dc20   94-41332
                                            CIP
Combined Books Edition   1   2   3   4   5

First published in the USA in 1988 as *War at Sea* (Gallery Books, NY) and revised and expanded in 1995 by Combined Books, Inc. This revised edition, now called *The Midway Campaign*, is distributed in North America by Stackpole Books, Inc., 5067 Ritter Road, Mechanicsburg, PA 17055, and distributed internationally by Greenhill Books, Lionel Leventhal Limited, Park House, 1 Russell Gardens, London NW11 9NN.

Printed in United States of America.
Maps by Beth Queman.

Contents

Maps

Preface to the Series

*J*onathan Swift termed war "that mad game the world so loves to play." He had a point. Universally condemned, it has nevertheless been almost as universally practiced. For good or ill, war has played a significant role in the shaping of history. Indeed, there is hardly a human institution which has not in some fashion been influenced and molded by war, even as it helped shape and mold war in turn. Yet the study of war has been as remarkably neglected as its practice commonplace. With a few outstanding exceptions, the history of wars and of military operations has until quite recently been largely the province of the inspired patriot or the regimental polemist. Only in our times have serious, detailed and objective accounts come to be considered the norm in the treatment of military history and related matters.

Yet there still remains a gap in the literature, for there are two types of military history. One type is written from a very serious, highly technical, professional perspective and presupposes that the reader is deeply familiar with the background, technology and general situation. The other is perhaps less dry, but merely lightly reviews the events with the intention of informing and entertaining the layperson. The qualitative gap between the last two is vast. Moreover, there are professionals in both the military and academia whose credentials are limited to particular moments in the long, sad history of war, and there are interested readers who have more than a passing understanding of the field; and then there is the concerned citizen, interested in understanding the military phenomena in an age of unusual violence and unprecedented armaments. It is to bridge the gap between the two types of military history, and to reach the professional and the serious amateur and the concerned citizen alike, that this series, GREAT CAMPAIGNS, is designed. Each volume in GREAT CAMPAIGNS is thus not merely an account of a particular military operation, but it is a unique reference to the theory and practice of war in the period in question.

The GREAT CAMPAIGNS series is a distinctive contribution to the study of war and of military history, which will remain of value for many years to come.

To Alessandro Massignani, long time friend, fellow student of history, and Bersagliere.

ABBREVIATIONS USED

AA = Anti-aircraft
AP = Armored Piercing
APD = Fast Attack Transport (often an older converted DD)
ASW = Anti-submarine Warfare
AT = Anti-tank
BB = Battleships
BC = Battlecruiser
CA = Heavy Cruiser (7.5"-8" guns)
CL = Light Cruiser (6.1" guns or less)
CNO = Chief of Naval Operations
CV = Aircraft Carrier
CVE = Escort Aircraft Carrier
CVL = Light Aircraft Carrier
DD = Destroyer
DP = Dual purpose guns - AA as well as surface combat capable
HE = High Explosive
HFA = Heavy Field Artillery
IHQ = Japanese Imperial Headquarters
IJA = Imperial Japanese Army
IJN = Imperial Japanese Navy
MG = Machine Gun
OB = Order of Battle
RAN = Royal Australian Navy
RN = British Royal Navy
RNN = Royal Netherlands Navy
SNLF = Special Naval Landing Force (Japanese Marines)
SQD = Squadron
TO&E = Table of organization and equipment

SYMBOLS

II = company	III = regiment
X = brigade	XX = division
XXX = corps	XXXX = army

Note that the Japanese referred to various pieces of equipment, including planes, tanks, artillery, and even rifles by the last two digits of the year it was adopted into service. For example, the Zero fighter (00) as this was the 2600 year in the Japanese calendar (AD 1941). Thus the Type 96 Nell bomber was from the last two digits of 2596, according to the Japanese calendar, or our AD 1936. The term Nell was applied by the Allies to this plane—fighters were masculine (thus the Zero was called the Zeke) and other air units were given feminine names.

Ship displacements are based on normal loads, not full, whenever possible. Plane ranges are normal and not extended ranges.

Preface

The Mediterranean is the ocean of the past, the Atlantic, the ocean of the present, and the Pacific, the ocean of the future.
—John Hay, Secretary of State

*T*he war in the Pacific during World War II was one of the most fascinating struggles in the history of the world. The distances involved were immense: the Indian Ocean and two Atlantic Oceans could fit into the Pacific Ocean; the distance from Singapore to Manila is 1,345 miles; and from Darwin, Australia, to Singapore, 1,900 miles. In comparison, the basic limits of Hitler's Germany, from Amsterdam to Moscow, is only 1,575 miles. Many of the weapons used were virtually unique to the Pacific Theater of war, as well as relatively new. Naval air power came of age there and the war ended dramatically with the ushering in of the Atomic Age. Though in the European Theater strategic air power and submarine warfare failed to decide victory in favor of one side or the other, Japan was successfully brought to her knees by the garrote of American bombers and submarines. The amount of treasure, resources and lives expended during the great struggle was enormous. Five of the great powers were deeply involved in the war before it ended. America used fully one-third of her mobilized economic strength against the fifth strongest great power, Japan, and suffered one-third of her dead in the Pacific Theater.

Many Americans born after the war have been fascinated by the massive aircraft carrier operations, midget submarines, gung ho Marines, as well as knowing that if the invasion of Japan had taken place, the men in their families would have gone ashore against people whose motto in the closing days was "Let 100 million die."

The Midway Campaign would be the decisive battle for the Pacific. It would be at Midway that the Japanese Samurai sword of naval air power would be blunted and dulled for the remainder of the struggle, and would never again surpass the skill of America.

In contrast to the war in Europe, the war in the Pacific was fought between different races. With racist sentiments rampant on both sides, it was not uncommon to hear Americans label their enemies as "monkey-men" and apes while the Japanese referred to their foes as beasts and demons. This hatred resulted in numerous atrocities committed by both sides. Stories of Japanese brutality during the war, particularly the Bataan Death March and the Rape of Nanking, have become infamous. Fully one-third of the Australian prisoners captured with the Australian 8th Division at Singapore did not survive the war. Two American airmen shot down at Midway, Frank O'Flaherty and Bruno Gaido, the latter a hero of a raid on the Marshalls in January of 1942, were picked up by the Japanese destroyer *Makigumo*. After a week of interrogation they had weights attached to their legs and were dropped overboard. However, Allied soldiers committed crimes of their own. One Marine admitted that he and a buddy captured a Japanese soldier in the late morning, exchanged photographs of families, then, after eating lunch, they executed their prisoner. Furthermore, the American fire bombing of civilian populations of Tokyo and Osaka, and the atomic bombing of Hiroshima and Nagasaki can not be considered anything less than high tech atrocities. Such acts only reinforce the words of Civil War General William Tecumseh Sherman: "War is Hell."

The war in the Pacific is not as well known as the one fought against Germany. Historians are more likely to make use of German sources than Japanese ones for an English speaking audience. A problem for the Western historian is the Japanese language—it is not as easily understood by Westerners as other European languages.

The goal of *The Midway Campaign* is to give the reader an overview of some of the events culminating in the decisive battle of Midway.

I would like to thank several people who have helped in various ways on The Midway Campaign, including Harry Rowland, Richard Pfost, Andrew Smith, Jeff Kingston, Ben Knight, Larry Hoffman, Alessandro Massignani, Akira Ishikawa and Makoto Sasaki who helped on order of battle material, my wife Beth Queman who did the maps, John Cannan who did much of the early editing of this edition, and all the stout lads and lassies at Combined Books who made all this possible. Of course, I am responsible for any errors that may lie within.

—Jack Greene
Baywood Park, California

Prelude to Pearl Harbor

December 7, 1941, a day of infamy....In Europe World War II continued to rage in bloody conflict. Nazi troops had just pulled back from their attempt to take Moscow after General Winter entered the fray. Operation Crusader was moving ahead in North Africa and General Rommel was about to begin his first withdrawal after the long siege of Tobruk. The Atlantic submarine war entered a period of calm as German U-boats were transferred into the Mediterranean. The Free French recovered the island of Reunion in the Indian Ocean from the Vichy French after a short engagement. However, despite these critical events, the pivotal incident of the war was about to occur halfway around the world at an island paradise called Hawaii.

Why did Japan attack Pearl Harbor on 7 December 1941? What were the motivations? It was the United States which defended the status quo in Asia and stood in the way Japan's dreams of empire. There is no denying that in the 1930s Japan was building an empire, primarily on Chinese territory. This Japanese desire for territorial expansion, fueled by the need to secure access to raw materials and markets, was predominately promoted by a fanatically nationalistic officer corps, a product of Japan's unique society. Japan invaded and took the Chinese province of Manchuria (renamed Manchukuo) in 1931-32. In 1937, the Japanese severely defeated Chiang Kai-shek's Nationalist Chinese forces and won control of the most economically valuable sections of China. By 1941, the unsated Japanese military was poised to invade Southeast Asia to seize the vital supplies of raw materials there and cut off the tenacious Chinese from outside support.

In 1941 Japan's economic position was stretched. An Allied embargo was in place after Japan's seizure of French Indochina in July. Although Japan was the fifth most powerful economy in the world, only 10% of her oil needs were met by home resources. The 4,500,000 tons of stockpiled oil were not sufficient to meet the demands of the Japanese nation. Japan's problems were not limited to economics.

Japan's military officers, especially her middle-echelon commanders, were involved to a large degree in national politics. It was expected that the Ministers of War and Navy would be serving generals or admirals. Thus the influence of the military was unusually strong. At the start of the war, General Hideki Tojo was Prime Minister, as well as Minister of War.

Several assassinations, attempted coups, and the unrest which racked Japan in the 1930s grew out of the nationalistic fanaticism and a form of Japanese Fascism that had its largest influence within the middle ranks of the military, primarily the army. One such officer was Colonel Tsuji, allegedly involved in the Bataan Death March, who served with General Yamashita (the Tiger of Malaya) in the Malayan campaign, and later served in the Japanese Diet in the 1970s. His influence on generals was considerable and he affected the course of events to a degree far greater than his rank would normally warrant.

It should be understood that Japan's decision to attack the Allies was not an easy one, and many within Japan, including Emperor Hirohito, had grave reservations. Right up until 7 December, the advisability of this action was questioned. However, the War Party in Japan was in power. War to them appeared inevitable and the longer the delay, the stronger the Allies, especially the U.S.A., would become. Thus Japan slipped towards her first defeat in 2,600 years as a nation.

Japan's army saw the U.S.S.R. as the primary enemy while the navy viewed America in that role. The army saw the future for expansion in the north, while the navy saw it in the south. Ironically, the army led the cabinet that launched a largely naval war in which air power proved decisive.

CHAPTER I

The Japanese Situation

The most important branch of service in the war of the Pacific was the navy and Japan had the best trained force in the world. No other naval force surpassed the Japanese on a combat ship by combat ship basis. But Japan's problem lay in what Japan *had not* trained for adequately—anti-submarine and convoy operations—and the inability of Japan's economy to compete against her enemies in a lengthy war. In a short, quick and decisive war Japan could survive and triumph. The Japanese shipbuilding industry was not set up for mass-production of warships, much needed as escorts for convoys. Japan had a romantic view of war that really did not address the tedious need for convoy and anti-submarine work.

Admiral Toyoda Soemu remarked in 1937 to a British officer, "We lag behind in the material agencies of war; we therefore try to keep our personnel equal or superior to that of any other navy." In the pursuit of this excellence, Japan regularly sent her ships on training missions to the far north. Tougher conditions prevailed there, and for the most part the Japanese practiced out of sight of other nations. Men usually received only three days off a month, thus giving rise to the saw that a typical work week was "Monday, Monday, Tuesday, Wednesday, Thursday, Friday, Friday!" It was not unusual to have men, and sometimes ships, lost in these practices. The Japanese trained hard!

At the start of the war, Japan's fleet had ten aircraft carriers, of which six were large fleet carriers. Carriers were efficient and carried a large number of aircraft (70-90 per ship), but like the

On the Allied side in World War I, both Japan and Italy felt short-changed in the peace settlement by the Western powers.

Americans, the Japanese had not adopted the British practice of armoring decks, and was thus vulnerable to damage from the air. With a speed of 30 or more knots, they were the most powerful single weapon at the start of World War II in the Pacific.

In terms of battleships at the start of the war, Japan had ten that dated from World War I. Heavily reconstructed after the war they were faster than America's battle line (the *Nagato* and *Mutsu* could reach 26 knots), but individually they were not the superior of America's ships. The most noteworthy of the ten were the four *Kongo* class battleships, originally built as battle-cruisers. At 30 knots, they could steam with the carriers, and armed with eight 14-inch guns each, they were clearly superior to any American heavy cruiser.

Under construction at the start of the war were several *Yamato* class superbattleships armed with nine 18-inch guns, weighing 64,000 tons and capable of a speed of 27 knots. The *Yamato* ship took 49 months to build and they were bigger than any American ships which were limited in size by the Panama Canal. They could fire at such long ranges that they could sink enemy ships

18

by firing over the horizon while planes spotted the accuracy of the shots.

Japanese strategic and tactical doctrine for its ships called for the whittling down of the enemy's numbers at long range before decisive ranges were obtained. The long range shooting of the *Yamato* reflected this philosophy perfectly. When this tactical doctrine was formulated in the late 1930s, it required air superiority to work and remained unaware of the future impact of radar.

All of the major navies built up 10,000-ton heavy cruisers between the wars. To compare Japanese heavy cruiser capacity, here are statistics from each major nation:

	ATAGO	HOUSTON	HMAS CANBERRA
	12781 tons	9050 tons	9870 tons
Primary Armament	10 8-inch	9 8-inch	8 8-inch
Secondary Armament	8 5-inch DP*	8 5-inch/25 AA**	4 4-inch AA**
Torpedoes	16 24-inch (with reloads)	—	8 21-inch
	35.5 knots	32.5 knots	31.5 knots
	4 to 5-inch belt armor	3 to 3.75-inch belt armor	narrow 4-inch armor belt
	6-inch turret armor	2.5-inch turret face armor	1-inch turret armor

*dual purpose, anti-aircraft as used as surface combat capable
**anti-aircraft

It should be noted that the Japanese knowingly violated the weight restrictions of various pre-war naval treaties, as did Germany and Italy. Of the Western democracies, only France exceeded the treaty restrictions on some ship types, though the U.S.A. did go over on the *Lexington* class carrier.

Japan had a large force of older light cruisers built in the early 1920s. Smaller than most Allied light cruisers, they were fast, and one was usually assigned as a flagship to a destroyer squadron. A few were built during the war, but were largely unexceptional vessels.

Japan began experimenting with aircraft carriers in the early 1920s, even when available airplanes were still primitive.

Japan's destroyer force, (given meteorological names) totaled 175 ships, and a maximum of 130 destroyers existed at any one point in the war. A total of 129 were sunk during the war. Japan's destroyers excelled in ship-to-ship combat, usually being larger and more heavily gunned (2,000 tons with six 5-inch guns) than the Allied ships (1,500-1,800 tons with four or five 4.7 or 5-inch guns), and with the secret long lance 24-inch torpedo, which was issued to the Japanese fleet in 1935 (to the post-*Fubuki* class destroyers and larger heavy cruisers). The long lance carried a larger warhead than most Allied torpedoes (1,080 pounds versus the British 21-inch MkIX with its 810 pound warhead and the American 21-inch Mk15 with a 825 pound warhead). It also had a longer range and speed; the long lance could cover 21,900 yards at 48-50 knots, the British torpedo 11,000 yards at 41 knots, and the U.S. torpedo 6,000 yards at 36-38 knots. It should be noted that torpedoes could have longer ranges if set for slower speeds; thus the long lance could conceivably travel 43,700 yards if set for a speed of 36-48 knots! As it ran on oxygen, it did

This unusual Japanese photograph illustrates clearly the improvised nature of early aircraft carriers.

not leave a wake and could not easily be spotted. Ironically, this torpedo was developed with the unknowing assistance of the British in the 1920s. Japanese officers were visiting a British warship when they noted oxygen equipment aboard the vessel and automatically assumed the Royal Navy possessed oxygen driven torpedoes. This was an error, for the British had by that time abandoned plans to build such a weapon. The Japanese, however, poured time and money into developing an oxygen propelled torpedo and, to the regret of many an Allied sailor, were successful. When first used during the battle of the Java Sea, the loss of the R.N.N. *Kortenaer* was erroneously attributed to a mine. Not until after the war was the long range of this weapon fully understood by the allies.

Japan's naval forces excelled in night combat, the form of fighting used to advantage during the Russo-Japanese War. All of Japan's surface ships, including heavy cruisers and battleships, were combat ready for night actions. Japan had also reconstructed two older cruisers and armed them with 40 long lance torpedoes each. Named the *Oi* and *Kitakami* (5,500 tons, four 5-inch guns, 36 knots), they were given unit combat roles, to find from right on the edge of or even beyond the horizon. These ships could cause severe disruption to an approaching fleet of older and slower battleships. In night actions they were to follow heavy and light cruisers pushing towards the heart of the enemy fleet. Once there, they would undertake a massive launching of their deadly torpedoes.

Japan's destroyers were adequate for anti-aircraft work, but they lacked the mass of weapons that characterized Allied warships. In anti-submarine duties, Japanese ships were only of a marginal ability due to their lack of the new electronic and sonar equipment needed to detect threats from below the surface.

The Japanese had three types of submarines, a long range cruiser (seven were built), the standard I-type (or *Kadai*) for cooperation with the main fleet and the RO type for coastal work. Several carried midget submarines (46 tons, 19 knots submerged, and armed with two 18-inch torpedoes) which were first introduced in 1938. Several were used at Pearl Harbor with negligible results. The I-boat was the most important, given a long range, high speed, heavy gun armament and good seakeeping qualities. A typical one, the I-61, weighed 1,635 tons surfaced, had a surface speed of 20 knots (8.5 submerged) and was armed with one 4.7-inch gun, and carried a total of 14 torpedoes. The most advanced types carried a float plane, a 5-inch and two 25mm guns, had a range of 14,000 miles at 16 knots, and weighed 2,589 tons surfaced.

There were several problems with Japanese subs. They were employed with the fleet instead of being used for sinking transports—a major failure in doctrine. They had slow diving times due to their size; they were poor at maneuvering when submerged, making them easy prey for attacks with depth charges. When surfaced, the large conning tower of a Japanese submarine could easily be picked up by radar, a problem that led to the sinking of many such vessels later in the war. Furthermore, the living conditions of a sub crew were poor and long range missions took their toll on sailors.

All in all, the Japanese navy was tough, but lacked the ability to absorb losses over an extended war. Compounded with the failure to protect her merchant shipping, this would limit her ability to replace her losses and keep her war machine humming. Professor Saburo Toyama has stated

The Japanese Navy's neglect of merchant marine protection is astonishing. It had few plans for this vital mission, and even after its importance was recognized, the navy supplied too little, too late. At the start of the war, the navy had no ships assigned exclusively to escort duties.

The seeds for Japan's eventual defeat were present from the start of the war.

The Japanese army was a formidable force, though it was over-extended, poorly organized and lacked proper weaponry and equipment. It consisted of 51 divisions. Of these, 21 infantry divisions and an army air brigade were tied down in a long war in China which had dragged on since 1937. Facing Mongolia were another two divisions, and in Manchuria there was an army air division with 13 infantry divisions. While Japan and Russia had signed a nonaggression pact, Japan had not withdrawn one unit from Manchuria's Kwangtung Army, because her leaders had learned to fear Soviet military power. In 1939, Japan had suffered a terrible defeat at Nomanhan at the hands of Soviet forces under future Soviet Marshal Zhukov during a dispute over Manchurian/Mongolian territory. The Imperial Japanese Army suffered the virtual destruction of the 23rd Infantry Division as a result of the encounter. Japan's Korean and Home Island garrisons took another 5 divisions as well as an army air division. Thus, the land forces for the thrust south were limited. However, Japanese strategists had devised a shuttle method. After one Allied position was occupied or neutralized, the next one in the chain would be softened up and prepared for an invasion by the same forces that had just secured the previous objective.

The army itself was not rigidly organized (see appendixes). The infantry divisions had primarily a triangular organization of three regiments, but several enjoyed the older four-regiment organization and some of the lesser units, such as garrison units, consisted of stripped down units lacking engineering, artillery, etc. Thus, when confronting the Japanese army in combat, an Allied unit would be unsure of its unique order of battle. This was in contrast to the more standard and universal organizations of the Allied, especially American, units.

American submariners on the prowl after the outbreak of war. The Japanese failed to foresee the impact of submarines on merchant shipping.

Often the Japanese advanced in two columns. One column held the enemy by a frontal assault while the second column turned a flank, thus enveloping the enemy. In Malaya the second column often moved amphibiously along the coast to turn the Allied flank and thus force a defeat and retreat. Leading the way for these columns was a reconnaissance regiment of about battalion strength which included armored cars, sometimes tanks, and sometimes cavalry. The reconnaissance unit pushed forward until stopped, and then deployed to identify the enemy front and units involved.

Japanese tactical doctrine called for a battalion front of 1,600 yards. A regiment covered about three times this front, and often on the attack two battalions advanced on a front with the third battalion as a reserve unit. Infiltration tactics, learned largely from the 1918 campaign in France, were heavily relied upon. The individual soldier, supported by close artillery and air support, was key to further advances.

Tank units were independent regiments for the most part. Sometimes crews abandoned vehicles and joined assaults on foot if confronted with an obstacle. While one can admire such élan, well-trained crews were often lost during such attacks. Finally, tanks were held in reserve until the enemy front was clearly viewed, and then used in a breakthrough maneuver.

Japan had many and varied types of artillery. The Imperial military possessed heavy artillery types, due to its experience during the siege of Port Arthur in the Russo-Japanese War of 1904-05. However, Japan lacked large numbers of such guns comparable to the big 155mm batteries common in the artillery-heavy American army. The use of light mortars was extensive in the Japanese army and offered the opportunity for close-in support of infantry units.

Relying heavily on men, the Japanese army did not have enough or the right kinds of equipment. Their tanks were inferior, and artillery and ammunition were not sufficient. Japanese motorized divisions, usually with at least one regiment on foot, lacked adequate transportation by Allied standards throughout the war.The Japanese soldier himself was daring in the attack and on the defensive, often choosing to die when others would surrender. He was often willing to sacrifice his life for his nation and the entire military was infected with the constant desire to advance. The Japanese army was primarily an offensive weapon and with this element of spirit could follow up a victory quickly. At the same time such tactics could have detrimental effects. If attacking a well prepared position, the Japanese could, and did, suffer tremendous losses. Once the

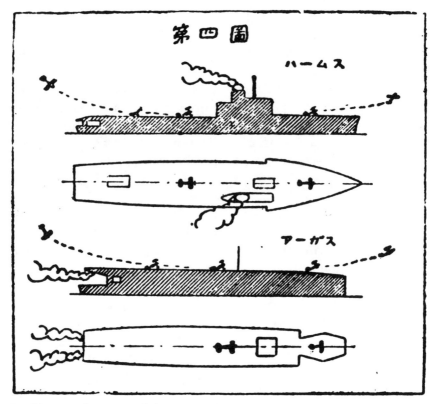

第四圖

ハームス

アーガス

In this rare drawing of the 1920s, the Japanese public was shown how aircraft would land and take off from aircraft carriers.

Japanese doctrine was understood, the Allies prepared for surprise attacks, especially night ones, and inflicted heavy casualties during enemy offensives.

While not an independent branch, the air force should be considered a separate entity. Both the Imperial Japanese Navy and the Imperial Japanese Army maintained their own air forces that, at the start of the war, were on par with the best of any of the great powers. The Allied view that Japan's aircraft were poor copies of obsolete Western designs proved to be a major advantage for the Japanese. The first six months of the war showed just how wrong the Allies were. However, as the war continued, two major flaws appeared. One problem was that while the Japanese aircraft industry produced a great many planes (52,242 combat aircraft were produced in the 1941-45 period), it was not flexible enough to adopt new aircraft designs. This was in part due to the fact that many skilled workmen were drafted by the armed services. A second flaw was that while many aircraft were fast and adequately armed, they were also inadequately armored. Thus, many Japanese planes were lost with their crews in cases where an Allied plane with armor and self-sealing fuel tanks only suffered damage.

1942 Aircraft Production Figures

U.S.A. - 49,445 aircraft

U.S.S.R. — 25,430 aircraft

Britain — 23,671 aircraft

Germany — 15,556 aircraft

Japan — 8,861 aircraft

Italy — 2,818 aircraft

The Japanese army air force entered the war with approximately 1,500 aircraft. Of this total, 650 were committed to action against Malaya (3rd Hikoshidan or Air Division) and the Philippines (5th Air Division). This concentration against Malaya was due to the Japanese naval air commitment against the Philippines, as the Japanese naval air was better trained for operations across the seas and had long range aircraft.

The Japanese naval air force numbered 3,000 airplanes of which 1,400 were frontline combat aircraft. Some 503 were assigned to the 11th Koku Kantai (11th Air Fleet), which consisted of land-based aircraft. At the start of the war, the 11th consisted of three air flotillas, the 21st, 22nd, and 23rd. The rest served on board ships, including the elite 1st Air Fleet which was the best trained air force unit in the world. It was the 1st Air Fleet that attacked Pearl Harbor.

The Japanese army air had been assigned the role of guarding the seas surrounding the Japanese Empire after World War I. Later this force was used extensively in the war against China, so in the early part of the war in the Pacific, American planes did not encounter Japanese army aircraft extensively until late 1942 in battles in the South Pacific.

The ultimate failure of the Japanese aircraft industry lay in its inability to produce more advanced aircraft quickly as the war progressed. This was combined with poor defensive characteristics of the aircraft. Finally, Japan usually kept units on the front lines too long and thus attrition took its toll on trained pilots. The Allies withdrew toughened cadre from time to time to rebuild units and send veteran pilots back home to help train new ones. As the war went on, the Allies produced better trained pilots and Japan's initial pilot edge eventually was lost.

Nakajama Ki27, or Nate, mainstay of the Japanese Army Air

CHAPTER II

The American Situation

O n 7 December 1941, the United States did not occupy a
dominant position in the Pacific, but nonetheless it appeared to
be a formidable power. The main prop of American military
strength in the region was the U.S. Navy.

At the start of the war the U.S.A. had a battleship-oriented
fleet which was undergoing an immense naval buildup, Con-
gressman Carl Vinson's two-ocean navy rearmament program.
During the 1920s and much of the 30s, American leaders had
neglected the navy and had even failed to build it up to the
limits allowed under the Washington and London treaties. This
was due primarily to finances, as well as pacifist tendencies that
swept the country (and other Western democracies) after the
dreadful losses of World War I.

Also affecting the growth of the navy was the impact of
General Billy Mitchell. A radical advocate of air power and a
man who made a strong impression on Admiral Yamamoto
when the Japanese officer was assigned to Washington D.C. in
the 20s, Billy Mitchell had an effect on American military
thinking far beyond that of any other general. Mitchell passion-
ately argued for the primacy of the American air arm over the
army and navy, warning, "If a naval war were attempted against
Japan,...the Japanese submarines and aircraft would sink the
enemy fleet long before it came anywhere near their coast," and
"Air power has completely superseded sea power and land
power as our first line of defense." While his assertions are

possibly true in today's world, Mitchell was far ahead of his times.

Mitchell's impact on the Navy was to slow the construction of battleships. His experiments in sinking warships, his most famous target being the former German battleship *Ostfriesland*, not only showed the need for improved deck armor, but also unsettled the public's faith in the almighty battleship. Despite such tests, the Navy still considered the battleship as the primary weapon in any future war. They pointed out that the *Ostfriesland* experiment was conducted against a stationary target with no crew conducting either anti-aircraft fire to break up the attack nor damage control to man the pumps (but then the *Ostfriesland* did not have high pressure steam in her boilers or ammunition in her magazines to cause secondary explosions). Later experiments against the hulk of the new battleship *Washington* (launched but not completed due to the Washington Treaty) showed that even 2,000 pound bombs could not penetrate the thicker armor of a modern 1920s battleship. In that experiment, which even included torpedo hits, *Washington* survived, rode out a gale and later had to be sunk by gunfire from the battleship *Texas*.

The upshot of these demonstrations, along with treaty limitations, was that the airplane was developed throughout the 1920's and 30's while the evolution of the American battleship was artificially halted.

Fortunately, in spite of reduced appropriations, pacifists, Billy Mitchell, and the scrapping of many battleships, the navy remained strong and filled with enterprise. Still the conservative mind frame of the battleship admirals hampered necessary innovations. Before the war, the navy was dominated by the "gun school." It was normal to have the two top positions in the U.S. Navy held by a battleship admiral. The thinking of naval leaders was demonstrated in the fact that during the three years prior to Pearl Harbor, the *United States Naval Institute Proceedings* (the oracle of the navy) did not publish one article suggesting that the aircraft carrier would supersede the battleship as the backbone of the navy. Furthermore, when the building of the new two-ocean fleet began in 1936, battleship construction was way ahead of aircraft carriers, though considering the age of

The Japanese recognized the danger to naval vessels from aircraft at an early date, as these primitive anti-aircraft guns show.

most of the existing battleships, this was not surprising. The newest battleship in 1936 had been completed in the mid-20s!

In 1941 the battleship was still the key and all other ships (carriers, cruisers and destroyers) were auxiliaries to them. In terms of materiel at the start of the war, the U.S. Navy had a powerful battleship force made up of older battleships capable of 21 knots. While slower than the Japanese battleline, they were more heavily armored than the Japanese and were very accurate in their gunnery practice. Secondary roles for the battleships were only partially explored, with shore bombardment envisioned as a possible role, but high explosive shells necessary for such operations were lacking except for a small supply left over from World War I. Separate task forces for specific operations were being used, but only in a limited fashion. With the arrival of the first fast (27 knots) battleships laid down in 1937, the U.S. Navy was able to construct the powerful task force concept which evolved into the dominating power in the Pacific War.

Pre-war U.S. aircraft carrier, showing evolution from conventional naval vessel.

The new U.S. fast battleships lacked adequate internal hull subdivision and their armor was too thin, but they had excellent 16-inch guns, and the armor plate was modeled on the German "Wotan hart" (samples of which were "found" in a U.S. Steel subsidiary in the 1930s, apparently through industrial espionage).

The conservative navy brass eventually came to recognize that airpower would affect battleships, and as early as 1939 they saw a need for additional anti-aircraft gun protection for their capital ships. When the war in Europe broke out, it quickly became apparent that the British anti-aircraft cruisers (converted World War I light cruisers of the C class-4,290 tons, eight 4-inch guns, 27.5 knots) were worth their weight in gold. From this would come the U.S. Navy's *Atlanta* class anti-aircraft cruiser (6,718 tons, sixteen 5-inch guns, eight 21-inch torpedoes, 32.5 knots—also viewed as offering a lot of fire power in a night surface action due to the rapid fire of the 5-inch gun) as well as a steady addition of antiaircraft guns on the capital ships. Even by the time of Midway, the navy's large ships were being covered with extra anti-aircraft gun positions.

Though dominated by the battleship school, the aircraft carrier did receive a great deal of attention in the interwar period. At the start of the war America had six large fleet carriers, and a smaller aircraft carrier, the *Ranger*, that stayed in the Atlantic for the duration. As the war approached, the building of 26 *Essex* class carriers commenced. Since these ships would not come on stream until 1943 and 1944 it was realized that an interim carrier would be needed. Initially carrier escorts (conversions from merchant ship hulls) were seen as part of the answer, but eventually President Roosevelt intervened and pushed for the conversion of the *Cleveland* class CL hull to light carriers. Nine such conversions occurred, and all were in service by 1943. As with so much of America's war effort, large numbers using similar designs were the keynote of her building program.

Cruisers were the largest surface warships built during the interwar period. They had long range for fighting in the Pacific, were armed with either 8-inch (heavy cruisers) or 6-inch guns (light cruisers) and weighed in at 9,000 to 10,000 tons. Probably the biggest deficiency in the cruisers built was the lack of torpedo armament. The gun school so dominated the navy that torpedoes were limited to destroyers. However, on a 10,000-ton treaty limit, the navy built some excellent gunnery platforms. The rapid-fire (6 to 10 rounds per minute per gun) 6-inch gun carried on the light cruisers of the *Brooklyn* class (9,767 tons, fifteen 6-inch guns, eight 5-inch guns, 32 knots) gave a tremendous broadside punch, especially in a close range night action. Such a ship, at night, was superior to a heavy cruiser armed with eight to ten 8-inch guns firing three to five rounds a minute. The heavy cruiser had an advantage in daylight action due to its longer range and accurate shells with heavier weight for better armor penetration at long ranges.

America's destroyers were sturdy vessels, but were inferior on a one to one basis to Japan's. Averaging about 1,600 tons, armed with four or five 5-inch guns, eight to sixteen 21-inch torpedoes, and steaming at about 35 knots, they had only one advantage: there were lots of them. America's destroyers suffered from faulty torpedoes well into 1943, but were quite good for anti-aircraft duties and anti-submarine warfare. Not until the *Fletcher* class came into service did the navy have a destroyer that could match Japan's best.

America's submarine arm was strong, though like the destroyers it too was armed with a flawed torpedo, which would

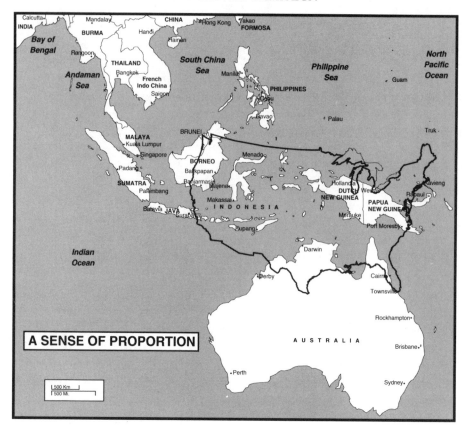

A SENSE OF PROPORTION

keep the Japanese losses from submarines dramatically low in the first part of the war. Interwar submarine designs were based on the German U-boats of World War I, specifically the U-135. They had a long cruising radius which allowed for deep penetration into the vast Pacific Ocean. A typical submarine was the *Perch*, launched in 1936. She displaced 1,330 tons (1,997 when submerged), had six 21-inch tubes, one 3-inch deck gun, and could steam at 18.8 knots on the surface and 8 knots when submerged. Range at 10 knots was 11,000 nautical miles. By the end of the war, the effect of the navy's submarines on knocking out Japan's merchant fleet and transports was decisive.

The United States Navy seldom trained crews of ships larger than destroyers in night tactics since it was believed that capital ships should not engage in such battles. Admiral James O. Richardson, who preceded Admiral Kimmel in command at

Pearl Harbor of the Pacific Fleet, attempted to remedy this in 1940. This night combat training was due in part to the lessons learned by the British against the Italian and German navies early in the war. One such lesson was the battle of Cape Matapan fought off southern Greece in March of 1941. There three British battleships firing at 5,000 yards at night were instrumental in sinking three heavy cruisers of the Italian navy. When Richardson held a night time naval maneuver, it resulted in "a confused night battle between the two fleets, with some near collisions, undesired illuminations, and missed gunnery and torpedo opportunities."

While the navy had its strengths and weaknesses, the U.S. Army and Army Air Corps were almost wholly unprepared to fight a major war in the Pacific. The American army was not the best fighting force in World War II due in part to the anti-military traditions of the American republic dating back to the Revolution. In the interwar period there was a strong wave of anti-militarism which affected the army. Fundamentally, the army was dominated by conservative officers who pushed the artillery arm and maintained a nonflexible infantry force. Somewhat like the British army in these respects, the American army was capable of changing and growing, and thus becoming by the end of the war a decisive force for victory.

The United States Marines were a much more aggressive force than the army and had studied the problems created by a war in the Pacific. Amphibious operations were required in the region and the U.S.M.C. had the plans and prototype equipment ready for such operations. One of the early architects of Marine planning was Lietenant Colonel Earl "Pete" Ellis. In 1921 he had completed his brilliant Operations Plan 712-H: Advance Base Operations in Micronesia. This plan assumed that Japan would start the war and that the Marines would be key to holding bases in the Pacific and then leading the way back. The Ellis plan was the starting point for a war in the Central Pacific in World War II and the Marines would be the offensive land arm of America in that fight.

The main army decision after Pearl Harbor was to reinforce the various outposts in the Pacific—from the Panama Canal to Alaska—and halt the Japanese advance. Though the main effort

U.S. ambassador Joseph Clark Grew met with Japanese foreign minister Togo in November, 1941. It was too late for diplomacy.

was against the Axis powers in Europe, the process of stemming the Japanese advance required more resources than first realized. In the course of early 1942, four second rate National Guard divisions were assigned to the Pacific Theater, the 41st and 32nd divisions to Australia, in part to allow Australian troops to remain in other theaters, and the 37th to Fiji in support of New Zealand. In March, the 27th Division (with four instead of the usual three regiments) joined the 24th Hawaiian Division, the only complete regular division in the Pacific, in Hawaii. The 1st Marine was preparing to go to New Zealand, and later to Guadalcanal.

The garrison in the Philippines consisted of one incomplete regular division: the Philippine Division. Two reserve divisions and ten national divisions made up of Filipinos rounded out the garrison. Unfortunately, none of the Filipino divisions were properly trained or equipped.

An American infantry division totaled 15,245 men in 1941, consisting of three regiments, three light artillery battalions and one medium artillery battalion. A full strength division had

1,834 vehicles, twelve 155mm guns, thirty-six 105mm howitzers, eight 75mm guns, sixty 37mm anti-tank guns, thirty-six 81mm and eighty-one 60mm mortars. Each of the three battalions in a regiment had a headquarters company, a heavy weapons company, and three rifle companies.

The Army Air Corps was understrength and many of the planes it fielded were dated compared to those used by other air forces. By May of 1940 the Army Air Corps was authorized to expand to 54 air groups totaling 4,000 tactical aircraft and over 200,000 men. By the autumn of 1941, 84 groups were contemplated. By 7 December 1941, the Army Air Corps broke down as follows:

ARMY AIR CORPS	
	GROUPS
Heavy Bombardment Groups	14
Medium Bombardment Groups	9
Light Bombardment Groups	5
Fighter Groups	25
Observation Groups	11
Transport Groups	6
TOTAL	**70**

As can be seen, the goal of 84 air groups was still a paper figure and the 70 air groups here listed were understrength and still contained obsolete aircraft.

President Roosevelt, in May of 1940, called for 50,000 planes a year annually from America's manufacturing sector. Programs were established to produce 50,000 pilots a year. This effort eventually overwhelmed the Axis. It must also be remembered that throughout the early part of the war America was busy preparing new designs for airplanes, primarily in response to the incredible weapons produced by Nazi Germany. But by looking to the future, America assured the Allies that new and better aircraft, like the Mustang or B-29, would be developed as the war progressed.

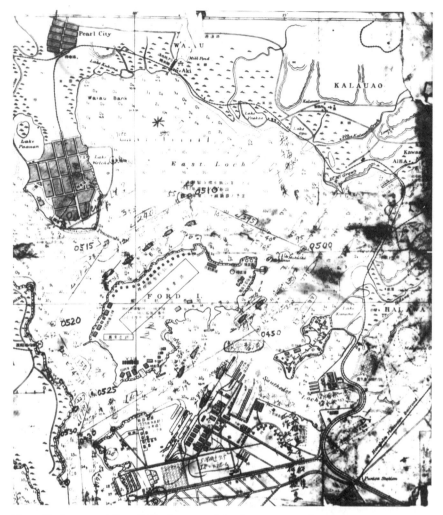

Detailed map of Pearl Harbor used by Japanese submarine crew in December, 1941.

As with so much of America's war effort in 1941 and 1942, the navy, army and air corps was not prepared in equipment or training—the U.S.A. was simply not ready for war.

CHAPTER III

The Commonwealth Situation

*H*istorian H.P. Wilmott said of Great Britain's policy on the eve of war with Japan, "In the place of a deliberately conceived strategy reigned confusion, unreality, and weakness, shrouded by wishful thinking." Frankly, the military might of Great Britain, as well as the Commonwealth, was thinly stretched, and Winston Churchill's attention was firmly riveted on the war in Europe. Further, the seeds for unrest lay ready in Britain's Asian colonial possessions, especially India where a well established independence movement was already growing.

Looking to the Far East, the British Empire had positions scattered throughout: Hong Kong, Malaya, Burma, the Commonwealths of Australia and New Zealand, the Solomons and Gilbert Islands (as well as other island outposts stretching across the Pacific), and the jewel of India, second most populated region of the world. The Royal Navy was already heavily committed against the Axis in Europe and losses had been heavy. Little could be spared to protect British possessions in Asia from a full-scale military attack.

What did Britain have to face Imperial Japan? For the most part, the Royal Navy believed in ships of moderate dimensions. Her battleships of the *Prince of Wales* type were probably the weakest modern battleships built after World War I. The British Government believed that the naval treaties of the 1920s would continue to exert a deadening hand on world naval construction. Thus, this new class of modern battleship was armed with the smallest gun (14-inch) of all modern battleships. It weighed in at 35,000 tons and could steam at 29 knots. Still, this class was a powerful addition to the British navy.

Britain's carriers were well built ships. Their armored decks allowed them to suffer damaging dive-bomber hits which knocked out their American or Japanese counterparts. However, British carriers usually carried about one-half the number of planes as the Japanese and American ships.

Royal Navy cruisers and destroyers were ships of moderate dimensions, but, as with Commonwealth ships, were well crewed.

Britain had heavily developed night combat tactics as a direct outgrowth of experience against Germany in World War I. The British, along with the Germans and Japanese, were the best experts at surface night combat at the start of World War II, especially when employing capital ships in that role.

Britain's biggest advantage was that her crews were well trained and filled with veterans of two years of a war that had seen numerous operations at sea. The major disadvantages the British faced were an unwise underestimation of the Japanese navy and the fact that the Royal Navy was stretched very thin.

Ironically the British assistant Naval Attache George Ross, later Rear Admiral, while serving in 1933-36 in Tokyo, reported on the 24" oxygen powered Long Lance torpedo, but his report was "dismissed in the Admiralty as unlikely."

Ross would later go on and secure the rights to the excellent Swiss designed 20mm Oerlikon anti-aircraft gun. This came about at a dance party Ross sponsored in Tokyo in 1935. During the party he asked an attractive blonde lady, Lola Gazda, to dance, and discovered that she was the wife of the repre-sentative of the Oerlikon Machine Tool Company who was in Tokyo to try to sell to the Japanese this new gun. Lola Gazda's husband Antoine and George Ross became friends and in 1937 they tried to sell to the resistant Admiralty this new weapon, which was far superior to the Vickers 0.5 machine gun. The Oerlikon, an advanced weapon that required only one man to fire it and was more accurate than the Vickers, was not accepted by the Admiralty even after 238 meetings. Finally, in 1939, with the help of Lord Louis Mountbatten and certain key gunnery officers such as Captain Stephen Roskill (who would go on to write the British Official Naval History of the war), the 20mm anti-aircraft gun was accepted into service where it gave an excellent account of itself.

Great Britain primarily relied on the military strength of Australia and India to protect her Asian possessions. The Australians had several militia divisions training throughout Australia by early 1942, which were considered to be about half the value of one of the regular Australian divisions. It should be noted that a full strength Australian division had seventy-two 25-pounders, much heavier gunning than a comparable U.S. division. There is no question that at this point in the war the Australian regular divisions were better trained for combat than any American or British unit, with the possible exception of the U.S. Marines. Dudley McCarthy, the official Australian historian, said of the Americans that there was "...some lack of realism in the outlook of the newly arrived formations. Staff work seemed defective and training methods somewhat unpractical."

India, too, made a valuable contribution to the war effort. While her best units, the 4th and 5th Indian, served in the Middle East and Africa, and proved equal and sometimes superior to comparable European troops, India now had to face a new enemy that was increasingly threatening her eastern border. India also had to deal with a domestic independence movement and some pro-Japanese sentiment throughout the war. Though India virtually lacked its own navy, she did manage to put to sea various sloops for convoy duty in the course of the war. India also made important economic contributions to the Allied cause during the war as well. However its army, which had quadrupled the number of troops between 1939 and 1942, was of the greatest importance to the Allies. Unfortunately, the forces in India were under-equipped. In 1941 the Indian army did not have one modern armored car or tank and anti-tank training was deficient. It was also lacking in support and technical units of all sorts (especially artillery) and officers. Worse still, it also had to be concerned with the

Northwest frontier and the Afghan border, as well as internal security.

In terms of airpower, the situation was even worse as virtually no modern aircraft existed in the Far East, a weakness which was compounded with the underestimation of Japanese airpower. Airfields in India and support roads were totally lacking on the frontier with Burma. Finally, the manufacturing ability in India and Australia was extremely limited. In a word, the Far East was a vulnerable part of the British Empire.

The Dutch contribution to the war in the Pacific cannot be glossed over. While small, the Netherlands' competent navy was a threat and her submarines inflicted substantial losses on the Japanese. Their supreme commander Vice Admiral Conrad Helfrich got the nickname "ship-a-day Helfrich" largely due to the success of the Dutch subs. After the first two months of the war, Helfrich obtained supreme command of naval forces in the Netherlands East Indies at British as well as Dutch urging. This was due in part to his aggressive nature, and the feeling that the American Admiral Thomas C. Hart, originally in command of the forces, was not of a sufficiently offensive mindset.

Helfrich was instrumental before the war in getting the Dutch "1940 Fleet Plan" passed. This called for the building of three battle cruisers, a tanker, 12 submarines and six minelaying subs. While not realized, especially after the fall of the Netherlands homeland to German invasion in 1940, the Dutch later updated the plan calling in February of 1941 for a navy to consist of three battlecruisers, two carriers, five light cruisers, 24 destroyers and 21 submarines. These battle cruisers were envisioned as a force of raiders against the Japanese navy, capable of sinking any of the enemy's heavy cruisers and running from anything bigger. This plan was modeled on the German pocket battleship concept. It was assumed this threat would help protect the Dutch East Indies. It should be noted that this strategy was the same that the *Prince of Wales* and the *Repulse* were to fulfill when originally sent out by Churchill in 1941. The realities of 1941 made it impossible for this plan to be implemented.

Unfortunately the Dutch colonial army was made up largely of Indonesians, many of whom resented Dutch rule. The white settlers were enrolled in local militias, but were not only few in number, but hurt the economy when mobilization required their absence. The Dutch air force in the Dutch East Indies consisted of about 34 P-40s, 31 Brewster Buffaloes, 36 Glenn Martin bombers (A-10s), and about 22 older fighters. All of these planes were too few and too old.

All in all, the Allied forces were ill-prepared to meet the massive onslaught by the might of Imperial Japan in December of 1941.

CHAPTER IV

Air Raid, Pearl Harbor

7 December 1941

*T*he attack on Pearl Harbor was masterminded by the Japanese Admiral Isoroku Yamamoto. A strong advocate of air power, he had been instrumental in equipping the Japanese naval air force with powerful and long range aircraft, as well as helping to facilitate the construction of the world's largest aircraft carrier fleet—ten carriers at the start of the war. Yamamoto spent time in Washington, D.C., in the 1920s, where he gained the reputation as an excellent poker player—the bluff was a trademark of his strategy.

As late as 1937 the fleet doctrine for Japanese aircraft carriers for Japan was similar to the American policy: providing an air umbrella for the surface fleet as it advanced towards the enemy. The concept of employing carriers to project firepower deep into the enemy territory became official Japanese doctrine in 1938. Chief of the Naval General Staff Admiral Osami Nagano, who studied English at Harvard (as had Yamamoto), indicated after the war that this idea was learned from the Americans. With this doctrine change, Yamamoto was given the weapon to achieve his policy goals.

Yamamoto's goal was to hurt the American fleet enough so that it would be incapable of influencing the Japanese strike south into Southern Asia. If key capital ships, especially American aircraft carriers, were damaged or sunk, then the American fleet would not intervene while Japan secured the key resources

The enigmatic Admiral Isoroku Yamamoto, architect of the Pearl Harbor attack. He was told by Tokyo that war had already officially been declared.

needed to fuel the Japanese war economy. A successful attack on Pearl Harbor would achieve this. A precedent for this type of attack had been set in 1940 when the British bombed the main Italian fleet at Taranto and scored a marked success by surprising the Italians in harbor and sinking several battleships. This success was scored with only one carrier. Why not six?

There were several critical problems that needed to be addressed in this attack. Of primary importance was how to get the Pearl Harbor attack force to the Hawaiian Islands. The Japanese tanker fleet could accomplish this although the carriers could only have a small escorting fleet. Further, to achieve sure success, surprise was the key. Tactical surprise was an element to be gained at the time of the actual raid.

While Yamamoto devised the idea, Commander Minoru Genda prepared the overall plan, and Genda's friend Commander Mitsuo Fuchida worked out the details. It was Genda who wanted to employ high level planes to drop modified 16-inch shells from the *Nagato* class battleship against the American ships at Pearl Harbor. Fuchida planned for these planes to attack at 3,000 meters (9,843 feet), instead of the usual

5,000 meters (16,404 feet). The latter altitude would be above anti-aircraft fire, while the former would allow the bombs to just penetrate the armored decks of the American battleships.

Fuchida also disapproved of the conventional nine plane formation and adopted a five-plane formation:

The advantage of this formation was that it gave Fuchida more attack units, and he could vary their concentrations. Additionally the numbers worked out evenly with a total of 50 horizontal bomber planes on board the attacking Japanese carriers.

The overall Japanese plan called for the fighters to sweep in, and if command of the air was achieved, to attack and strafe the air installations. Then torpedo planes would attack the aircraft carriers present with torpedoes with special fins allowing them to operate in the shallow waters of Pearl Harbor. Dive bombers would then roar in to destroy the carriers so that they could not possibly be salvaged, as the Italian battleships at Taranto had been. If carriers were not present, then the planes would attack the battleships.

The second wave would not contain torpedo bombers as their losses would be too high with a then fully aroused American enemy firing from anti-aircraft gun positions. The second wave would work over the island defenses instead. The Japanese goal was to sink all carriers and at least four battleships. American land based air power was to be smashed.

The commander of the attack force was Vice Admiral Chuichi Nagumo, who was not the best choice for this role. An admiral of average abilities, he was uncomfortable with carrier airpower. He was a battleship admiral and had no previous practical experience with carriers before being given that command. A perfectionist, he also had a tendency to take counsel with his

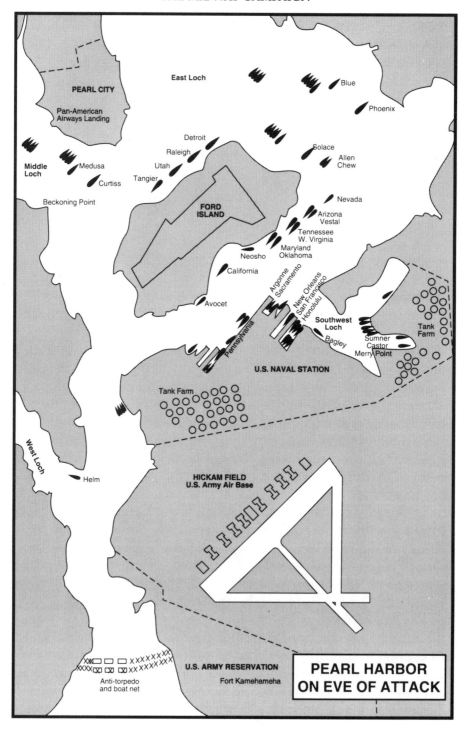

PEARL HARBOR
ON EVE OF ATTACK

fears. Genda always blamed the Japanese Personnel Department for assigning Nagumo to this position, which he had received largely through seniority.

As the Japanese attack force moved across the Pacific there were two threats to the surprise factor. One was a Russian freighter which was sighted early in December during the approach to the Hawaiian Islands. To this day, the English speaking public does not know what the Russian freighter radioed to the Soviet Union that evening when she checked in with Vladivostok. Also, there was the American Ultra (or Magic in the Pacific) operation. This was the U.S. intelligence service operation in which Japanese codes were broken and sensitive Japanese communications were read. Also a Dutch searchplane sighted Japanese transports proceeding south towards Malaya on 6 December (Far East Time) giving additional warning of the approach to war.

Ultra revealed that Japan was about to launch an attack against the Netherlands East Indies, British possessions, and the U.S.A. However, in Washington, it was never perceived that Pearl Harbor would be attacked. U.S. strategy was based on what its leaders expected the Japanese to do, not on what the Japanese were capable of doing. This was fueled by the perception that the Japanese were not formidable adversaries, a cardinal error as events were to prove. What was expected by America's leaders was an attack against America's possessions in the Far East, principally the Philippines and Guam. Sabotage by the 157,907 people of Japanese blood living at Pearl Harbor was viewed as the main concern of local Hawaiian commanders. Thus, General Short, the army commander, ordered that all planes be massed close together at the various island airfields to easily guard against sabotage. Instead of protecting the planes, the move made them easy targets for attacking Japanese aircraft.

The entire question of what was known through ULTRA and the other espionage services on the eve of war is still clouded in mystery. The Australian naval Captain Eric Nave, who was "a remarkable cryptanalyst," and his colleagues (which included the capable Dutch Intelligence service) apparently, while serving at Singapore's Government Code and Cypher School (GC&CS), obtained information that led him to conclude that an attack on Pearl Harbor was likely. At the time of the actual Pearl Harbor attack, Nave had returned to Australia to work with the Australian equivalent of the GC&CS, the Central Bureau. Yet what was done with this information is still unclear. Part of this is due to the continued closing of British archives to historians on this topic as of this writing.

However, at least one piece of information was sent by the British Intelligence Service. One of their agents, Dusko Popov, learned that the Japanese were making inquiries to Germany about Pearl Harbor. Information requested involved not just ammunition dumps, airfields and naval installations, but even very tactical information like torpedo nets, used by ships to protect themselves from torpedoes while at anchor at Pearl Harbor. The information was sent, unfortunately, to the FBI, and J. Edgar Hoover, who distrusted Popov as a possible German double agent, and so nothing was done.

The Japanese also maintained an intelligence service with a very few agents in the Hawaiian Islands and on the Continental United States, a five man radio team in Mexico listening in on naval radio traffic, and they maintained a huge signal intercept site in the Marshall Islands at Jaluit. Additionally, it may be that they were receiving intelligence from the Soviet Union, including one December of 1940 report from the British Chief of Staff warning Winston Churchill that Hong Kong, Malaya, and the British and Dutch East Indies "were indefensible."

All this would culminate in the disaster at Pearl Harbor. There is no doubt that America had failed to properly prepare against an attack on Pearl Harbor. Until 1940 the American fleet was based on the West Coast. In that year, Washington decided to move the fleet to Pearl as a "message" to Japan. The Admiral commanding, James O. Richardson, was incensed over this decision and twice journeyed to Washington in attempts to have this decision changed. Instead, Richardson was relieved of his command and Admiral Husband B. Kimmel was appointed.

Worse still, Pearl Harbor lacked the proper equipment needed to detect an enemy attack. Admiral Richardson had seen this as a major problem. Though radar had just arrived on Oahu, it was still very new and not properly used. Radar was so new that when a set revealed approaching enemy aircraft on 7 December,

Captured Japanese photo of first bomb to fall at Pearl Harbor, on or just aft of Maryland *and* Oklahoma. *Banking plane shows low altitude at which much of the attack was carried out.*

the report was ignored. PBYs and other long range reconnaissance aircraft were too few and could not properly cover all approaches to Pearl Harbor. America had failed to go into war production soon enough, and most of the weapons and planes that were produced often went to the Philippines or to the Atlantic Theater, or to the Allies. Finally, there was a failure to anticipate an attack. Admiral King commented on the American attitude that an "unwarranted feeling of immunity from attack...seems to have pervaded all ranks at Pearl Harbor, both Army and Navy."

So across the Northern Pacific, outside normal shipping lines, steamed the approaching Japanese task force loaded with more than 350 aircraft on the way to strafe, bomb and torpedo. Unfortunately for the Japanese, all the American carriers were absent that morning from Pearl Harbor, although the *Enterprise* (19,875 tons, 18 fighters, 36 torpedo bombers—usually only 18 on board—37 dive bombers, and 5 utility aircraft, eight 5-inch guns, 32.5 knots) with Admiral Halsey on board was approaching harbor and was scheduled to tie up before the attack, but was delayed. The signal to attack on 8 December 1941 (Japanese time) was received on 2 December when 940 miles from Midway Island. The message was "Climb Mount Niitaka." Mount Niitaka is the highest mountain in Formosa, which was the highest point in the Japanese Empire in 1941.

The opening round began not with planes, but with midget submarines. While unsuccessful in this attack, and disappointing throughout the war, the Japanese launched five midget submarines early in the morning towards the harbor entrance. All were lost, one by the destroyer *Ward* on patrol off the harbor at about 0645 on 7 December 1941. The sub's conning tower was sighted by a PBY on air patrol. The reaction of the observer was "My God, a sub in distress." But it was in the defensive sea area in which all subs were to be attacked and sunk if submerged. The *Ward* closed, fired on it, depth charged it, and reported that it had sighted and sunk a submarine in the defense sea area. Some of the officers were concerned that they had attacked an American sub, while the ensign on the PBY, William Tanner, assumed his career would be forever maimed for following orders.

The first Japanese wave of the torpedo planes and horizontal bombers attacked the battleships at battleship row along Ford Island. The fighters, after securing control of the air which was abdicated by the Americans, strafed the various airfields to ensure enemy aircraft would not get off the ground. A flight of Val dive bombers were detailed to work over the naval aircraft at Ford Island. Hickam and Wheeler army airbases received attention too. The second wave would work over the airfields once again.

So the attack began.

The reaction to the Japanese attack on this "Day that will live in infamy" had its morbidly humorous moments. Initially some Americans thought the attack was a drill. Seaman Robert Osborne, based with a utility plane squadron on Ford Island, couldn't understand why American planes were bombing Hawaii. He remembered thinking that "Somebody is going to catch it for putting live bombs on those planes." One of the seamen on

Midget submarine used in the attack on Pearl Harbor. They were the only Japanese naval vessels lost in the engagement.

the doomed *Arizona* saw the approaching enemy planes and remarked, "This is the best goddamn drill the Army Air Force has ever put on!" The message went from the fireroom of the battleship *California* to the head on the *Nevada*, "This is a hell of a time to hold general drills." Commander Herald Stout of the destroyer minelayer *Breese* had standing orders that no general quarter drills would be held before 0800 on Sunday. When the alarm sounded he left his breakfast to chew out the officer of the watch. On board the battleship *Oklahoma* the PA system announced, "Real planes, real bombs; this is no drill!"

Watertender Samuel Cucek looked into the head on the destroyer tender *Dobbin*, called to Fireman Charles Leahey, "You better cut that short, Charlie, the Japs are here."

On the light cruiser *Phoenix*, Ensign Ted Hechler, Jr. recalled running onto the deck with the General Quarters klaxon horn sounding in his ears. There he saw,

Lieutenant William K. Parsons, attired in immaculate whites, standing there waving his arms at us. He held a batch of papers in his hand, (he had evidently been on duty) and was shouting, "Come on, come on. It's war, it's war. ". . .I was propelled on my journey by the sight of a torpedo plane that flew past the Phoenix at deck level. It carried a big red ball on the side. As I reached my station, our battery was already training out. The awnings which were still up from the admiral's inspection had to be taken down so the guns could train out. Locks were chopped off the ammunition boxes. . . . We fired numerous rounds at the aircraft, but much to my dismay, I did not see any flack bursts from our shells. We later replaced the ammunition, but I never learned the cause for the failures.

Chief Petty Officer Albert Molter, gardening at his Ford Island residence, thought a drill was in progress, until his wife Esther called to him, "Al, there's a battleship tipping over."

Colonel William Farthing was in the control tower of Hickam Field, the main Army Air Corps base near Pearl, when he saw a line of planes approaching and begin diving. Farthing assumed they were Marine planes from Ewa Airbase. He remarked to Colonel Bertholf, "Very realistic maneuvers. I wonder what the Marines are doing to the navy so early Sunday?"

Rear Admiral William R. Furlong, on board the ammunition ship *Oglala*, paid little attention to the planes until he saw a bomb drop from one of them. Furlong thought, "What a stupid, careless pilot, not to have secured his releasing gear." As the plane turned and the red meatballs on the wings were seen he shouted, "Japanese! Man your stations." His next order flashed to all ships in the harbor was "All ships in harbor sortie!"

The first ten minutes of the attack brought virtually no resistance from the American fleet. It allowed the Japanese to

The lightly damaged **Maryland** *fights fires on the capsized* **Oklahoma**.

deliver their most grievous blows against the anchored battle-ships off Ford Island.

The *Oklahoma* (29,067 tons, ten 14-inch guns, twenty 5-inch guns, 20.5 knots) took three torpedo hits and began to list to port. After one more torpedo slammed into her, the *Oklahoma* continued her heavy list and then capsized eight minutes after the attack had begun. A horrible fate awaited many of her crew over the next few days who died locked in the dark bowels after the ship turned upside down and oxygen slowly ran out.

The *West Virginia*'s officer of the deck, Ensign Roman L. Brooks, thought that the *California* had suffered an accidental

Although technically "sunk," the **West Virginia** *and many other ships at Pearl Harbor were repaired to fight again.*

internal explosion after it was struck by one of the first bombs to hit the ships off Ford Island. Brooks ordered, "Away fire and rescue party!" thus bringing hundreds of men up on deck and avoiding certain death when the first torpedoes hit the *West Virginia*. The ship took six torpedo hits and two bomb hits before it was sunk.

Captain Mervyn Bennion remarked at the start of the Japanese attack to his Marine orderly "This is certainly in keeping with their history of surprise attacks." Bennion suffered a stomach

Pearl Harbor's most famous victim, the Arizona *sinks after a bomb struck its main ammunition magazine.*

wound and died during the attack, although he was conscious to the end. He was one of the 103 lost and 52 wounded on board the *West Virginia* that day. Lieutenant Claude Ricketts and Boatswain's Mate Billingsley saved the ship from the fate of the *Oklahoma* by working the knobs and levers that counterflooded against the flooding caused by the torpedo hits. These two men saved the lives of hundreds of their crewmates.

When the *Arizona* (sister ship to the *Oklahoma*) blew up at Pearl Harbor, it was due to a bomb that hit the forecastle alongside the second main turret. It pierced the deck and exploded the main magazine. As Walter Lord described it, "...a huge ball of fire and smoke mushroomed 500 feet into the air. There wasn't so much noise—most of the men say it was more a 'whoom' than a 'bang'—but the concussion was terrific. It stalled the motor of Aviation Ordinanceman Harand Quisdorf's pickup truck as he drove along Ford Island. It hurled Chief Albert Molter against the pipe banister of his basement stairs. It knocked everyone flat on Fireman Stanley H. Rabe's water barge. It blew gunner Carey Garnett and dozens of other men off the *Nevada* and Ensign Vance Fowler off of the *West Virginia*. Far above, Commander Fuchida's bomber "trembled like a leaf."

On the *Arizona*, Rear Admiral Isaac C. Kidd was killed, along with Captain Franklin van Valkenburg, just after the quartermaster had reported to the captain a bomb hit. A moment later "the ship was shaking like an earthquake had struck it, and the bridge was in flames." Firefighting continued until 1032 when she was finally abandoned. Casualties on the *Arizona* were the most of any ship lost that day, a total of 1,103 killed and 44 wounded out of 1,511 on board on 1 December. She had taken one torpedo hit and eight bomb hits.

Captain Cassin Young, winner of the Medal of Honor, was on the repair ship *Vestal*, afire from two bomb hits earlier, which was anchored next to the *Arizona* when she blew up. Over 100 of the 466 men on board were literally blown overboard from the resulting explosion! The same explosion also put most of the burning fires out. Orders to abandon ship were issued, but countermanded as an oil-covered Cassin Young came up to the officer of the deck and inquired, "Where the hell do you think

California begins to sink. Although lightly hit, her watertight compartments had been opened up for inspection prior to the attack.

you're going?" The reply of "We're abandoning ship" brought a "Get back aboard ship! You don't abandon ship on me!"

The *Tennessee*, protected from torpedoes because she was inboard of the *West Virginia*, received just two bomb hits, although the debris from the explosion of the *Arizona* hurt her. The *Tennessee* lost only five men and 21 wounded. The battleship *Maryland* suffered even less, being hit by two bombs and losing only four men and 14 wounded.

The *California* (34,858 tons, twelve 14-inch guns, twenty 5-inch guns, and 20.5 knots, sister ship of *Tennessee*) was badly damaged. While hit by only two torpedoes and two bombs, she was prepared for inspection on Monday—most of her watertight compartments had been opened up or the doors had been loosened. Thus, in an "unbuttoned" state, the *California* flooded easily, and slowly sunk so that by 10 December she finally settled on the mud of the bay bottom. She also suffered from severe oil fires and lost a total of 98 men killed and 61 wounded.

The *Nevada* was one of the more fortunate of battleships that day, actually getting underway and attempting to sortie to sea. In the initial few minutes of the attack she suffered one torpedo hit forward and two bomb hits. Ensign Joseph K. Taussig, Jr., used the anti-aircraft guns on the *Nevada* so well that little other damage was done initially, though he was wounded in the leg. By 0850 the *Nevada* cast off and began to proceed towards the harbor entrance. The Japanese, seeing the *Nevada* underway, tried to sink her in the harbor entrance, thus bottling the American fleet up, but, though hitting her five times with bombs, the *Nevada* beached herself in a safe position. Fifty died on her, with 109 wounded.

The only other battleship present was the *Pennsylvania*, which was slightly damaged, in drydock with two destroyers, both severely damaged in the attack.

Chaplain Howell M. Forgy served on the *New Orleans* (10,131 tons, nine 8-inch guns, eight 5-inch guns, 32.5 knots) at Pearl Harbor. He remembers:

> the clang-clang-clang continued stubbornly, and the shrill scream of the bosun's pipe beeped through the speaker. "All hands to battle stations! This is no drill! This is no drill!"
>
> But I wasn't buffaloed....This must be some admiral's clever idea of how to make an off-hour general quarters drill for the fleet realistic....I ran to the well deck, where I could get a clear view of the harbor. Off to our starboard quarter, about five hundred yards, the mighty *Arizona* was sending a mass of black, oily smoke thousands of feet into the air. The water around her was dotted with debris and a mass of bobbing, oil covered heads. I could see hundreds of men splashing and trying to swim.
>
> Others were motionless.
>
> Flashes of orange-red flames snapped out of the anti-aircraft guns, bright against the jet clouds ascending all along battleship row. The cage-like foremast of the *Arizona* poked through the smoke at a crazy, drunken angle. The *Weavie*—that's what we called the *West Virginia*—looked as though her back had been broken. She was sagging amidships, and her bow and stern angled upward.
>
> Forward of the *Weavie* the *Oklahoma's* main deck was disappearing beneath the water. She was rolling on her side, and her big bottom was coming up. I could see hundreds of her crew jumping into the water. Dozens of others were crawling along her exposed side and bottom, trying to keep up with the giant treadmill.
>
> I wondered if the devil himself could have immuned these planes against our shells. What was this new, horrible, evil power that

The destroyer **Shaw** *goes up in a spectacular explosion.*

turned Pearl Harbor into a bay of terrible explosions, smoking ships, flames, and death?...A long ribbon of black crepe trailed out behind it as a plane disappeared. It crashed in the backyard of (the) Naval Hospital. We got one! They could be hit!

I felt better...I guess I shouted and screamed as loudly as any one. Mike Jacobs, master at arms, was standing near me. He grinned at the string of smoke in the sky and drawled, "I guess chaplains can cuss like bosun's mates when they have to."

On the light cruiser *Detroit*, sister ship to the *Marblehead* and *Raleigh*, the 3-inch anti-aircraft guns had protector caps on the shells. The men manning the anti-aircraft guns had to bang the shells against the gun shield to knock the protector caps off.

Among the Pacific war's first victims, U.S. sailor washes ashore after Pearl Harbor attack.

The Marine barracks emptied and for hours they fought with machine guns and rifles as well as patrolling the base. In the process, it was noted that food had not been sent out to the troops, and that the cooks and messmen had grabbed rifles and were in the field. Some enterprising Marine opened the brig and the prisoners became prisoners-at-large and cooks.

The army had two divisions, the 24th and the 25th, on the island of Oahu. Many of the troops joined in the defense that day, and some died. Unfortunately their anti-aircraft batteries had only training ammunition available, and men of the 27th Infantry Regiment remembered one sergeant refusing to issue guns, because he could not release guns without orders from the adjutant.

The *Christian Science Monitor* had a correspondent, Joseph Harsch, in Honolulu on the 7th. Harsch woke up his wife that morning and told her, "Darling, you often have asked me what

The Japanese did not escape unscathed. In fact, U.S. forces returned a fair amount of anti-aircraft fire.

an air raid sounds like. Listen to this—it's a good imitation." They fell back to sleep a bit later! It was the same Harsch who had interviewed Kimmel the day before. When Harsch had asked if Japan would attack America in the Far East, Kimmel responded, "No, young man, I don't think they'd be such damned fools."

As the *Enterprise* and her task force entered Pearl that night, Admiral Halsey surveyed the damage done. Finally he growled, "Before we're through with 'em, the Japanese language will be spoken only in hell!"

Total losses in life for the Americans that day were 2,403 killed, and 1,178 wounded. All eight battleships were sunk or damaged, along with three light cruisers, three destroyers, and four auxiliary craft. The Japanese lost six fighters and 14 dive bombers. Part of the failure to shoot down more planes was due to poor high altitude anti-aircraft fire. Much of that fire ex-

Conning tower of midget submarine destroyed at Pearl Harbor. The Japanese continued to use submarines with conventional naval forces and ignore their possibilities for anti-shipping strikes.

ploded behind the planes due in part to the American prewar methods—training calling for towing a target sleeve at speeds no greater than 127 m.p.h. The fire control director could only follow a target moving at 150 m.p.h. No Japanese aircraft in the attack that morning flew that slowly.

Two questions arose among Japanese commanders from the action that day: was a second attack by the Japanese air units feasible and were the targets hit the correct ones? Genda suggested another attack to Nagumo after the second wave of planes return to the carriers. Genda wanted the primary targets of a second attack to be dockyards and fuel tanks. An "occasional ship" would be an extra. Interestingly enough the proposal was not for another attack that day, but the following day. This was because the Japanese did not know where the American carriers were, but they did know that some land planes

Although not deliberately targeted, there were also civilian casualties at Pearl Harbor.

remained for a possible counterattack. Genda wanted time for further intelligence to come in before another onslaught was launched. Secondly, the Japanese planes had been rearmed with weapons against ships and changing weapons in the afternoon would mean too long a delay during short daylight hours of December. Another attack was feasible, but Nagumo, pleased that he had accomplished his orders, decided to returned home, complacent in the fact that he had few losses for such a tremendous victory. Preserving Japan's strongest weapon was important to him.

Never again would the Japanese be in such an advantageous position. Had Nagumo allowed a second attack, the war might have turned out differently. It was not unlike winning a great victory in a battle but not following up with a firm pursuit to destroy the remaining enemy forces. Admiral Nimitz said of the

*Belatedly on guard, these American troops at Pearl Harbor display
the antiquated uniforms and equipment with which U.S. forces began
the war.*

failure of Japan to follow up the first attack, "The fact that the
Japanese did not return to Pearl Harbor and complete the job
was the greatest help to us, for they left their principal enemy
with the time to catch his breath, restore his morale, and rebuild
his forces."

As far as targets go, most authorities agree that the fuel tanks
should have been a priority. The destruction of the fuel
(4,500,000 barrels of oil were present) at Pearl Harbor would

Despite decades of tension, the outbreak of war found both sides curiously unprepared for a prolonged modern conflict.

have effectively moved the American fleet back to the West Coast and affected American submarine operations adversely. The submarine arm was left untouched, a grave error, as they could immediately go over to the attack. Ensign Taussig always wondered why the ammunition at West Loch was not bombed. The *Nevada* alone had one thousand four hundred and forty 14-inch shells stored there with two thousand eight hundred and eighty 70-pound bags of smokeless powder (she was being furnished new projectiles).

The final error by Japan in choice of targets was Pearl Harbor, itself. This surprise attack unified the United States and overnight ended all talk of isolationism. It did not leave America divided or dismayed, but unified the country in a way that no other overt move could have done. Rear Admiral Chuichi Hara, commander of the 5th Carrier Division, remarked that Roosevelt should have given the Japanese a medal for the attack! Vice Admiral Matome Ugaki, Chief of Staff to the Combined Fleet, wrote in his diary on 16 December, 1941, "But a blow to Hawaii must have stung them (The U.S.A.) to the quick. So we must bear in mind, on reflection, that they have an enormously predominant air strength - planes and carriers - and we cannot forecast what game they will play to revenge this mishap. Of this future threat we cannot be too careful." The bombing ensured that America would fight the war to the bitter end. The only way Japan could have justified the attack would have been if at least one or more American carriers had been present on 7 December at Pearl.

Pearl Harbor was a disaster, though it could have been much worse than it was. That it was a failure of American command, of this there is no doubt. Admiral Kimmel and General Short could have received clearer instructions from Washington, but Washington was unsure of what to do and what was about to happen.

Admiral Kimmel and General Short were required to cooperate closely to defend Pearl Harbor, but they did work closely together. Radar was present on the island after an extraordinary effort, and yet the effort to make it operational 24 hours a day was not given. The later Secretary of the Navy James Forrestal determined that Admirals Stark (Chief of Naval Operations at the time of Pearl Harbor) and Kimmel, ". . . particularly during the period from November 27 to December 7, 1941, failed to demonstrate the superior judgement for exercising command commensurate with their rank and assigned duties." General Short later acknowledged in his testimony on Pearl Harbor that he failed in his command.

There were many tragedies yet to be enacted after the air raid. Internment camps for Japanese nationals and even U.S. citizens followed. Colonel Cornelius C. Smith (U.S.M.C.) told of a Filipino-American coming by his headquarters on 10 December. The Filipino wanted to see the general. The then Sergeant Smith said that the general was busy and that the Filipino should talk to him instead. With a grin on his face, the Filipino related how he had, "Got four Japs in the truck, no good man, I kill them." They were there, in the truck. The Filipino then said that he "Got six more under house," and he did. The Japanese had been his neighbors on Oahu.

CHAPTER V

The Fall of the Philippines

8 December 1941 - 6 May 1942

*T*he Japanese viewed the Philippines as an important enemy bastion lying on the flank of their advance against South Asia. The possible threat of the islands to Japan's vital shipping lanes could not be ignored. So, even though the Philippines was not that rich in resources, Japanese planners felt the they must be attacked and seized. This action would contain strategic benefits as well. Once in control of the Philippines, Japan could then use the southern islands of the vast archipelago to launch air attacks against the Dutch East Indies.

The situation in the Philippines was unique and fascinating at the beginning of the war. The main battle was fought on Luzon, the largest island, where the capital, Manila, is located. Originally under the U.S. military's Rainbow warplans, the garrison in the Philippines was to fall back to Bataan Peninsula at Manila Harbor, and turn it into a fortress to be held for six months. The American fleet was supposed to appear from the east to save the situation. In reality, most thoughtful leaders looked at the garrison in the Philippines as a forlorn hope.

In April of 1941 General Douglas MacArthur retired from American service to take command of the Philippine army. MacArthur felt that with large reinforcements, especially in the long range and overrated B-17 bombers and P-40E fighters, he could hold Luzon, the main island, and cause havoc to the Japanese with the new B-17s. Another advantage to holding the

71

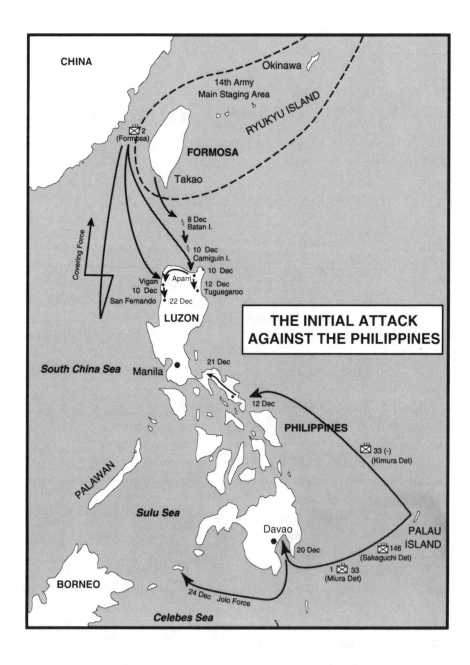

THE INITIAL ATTACK AGAINST THE PHILIPPINES

Philippines was that there the army could be expanded without limits, unlike America's home armies still under pre-war congressional restraint. When MacArthur advocated that older World War I equipment be sent to help this rearmament effort, it was implemented.

MacArthur was recalled to the U.S. Army on 26 July 1941, as a Major General and quickly promoted to Lieutenant General. At the same time, the Philippine Army and U.S. Army forces in the Far East were placed under his command.

MacArthur had the support of the American Asiatic Fleet made up of Admiral Thomas C. Hart's flagship the heavy cruiser *Houston*, one old light cruiser, and 13 World War I four-piper destroyers (so named for their distinctive smokestacks). These forces headed south so they would not be overwhelmed by Japanese air and sea power. Also present were various small craft, including PT boats and 17 submarines. The submarines could have been a decisive weapon, especially against slow Japanese transports, if their torpedoes worked. American torpedoes ran too deep and, since their detonators were too fragile, would not explode when impact was directly at 90 degrees on the target; they had to hit only at acute angles. What made the situation worse was that it was not recognized as an ordnance problem and was blamed on the submarine commanders due to their tactics and lack of ability!

On 7 December there were 35 B-17s (with 13 due to arrive shortly), 107 P-40Es (700 mile range, 6 machine guns, 354 m.p.h.), and a few more than 70 older fighters (mostly P-35As) in the Philippines. The biggest advantage with having the P-40Es, or so the Americans thought, was that there were no Japanese fighters that had the range to escort Japanese bombers from Formosa. Thus, the Japanese would be forced to establish airbases on Luzon before adequate fighter protection could be given to their bombers. This was an incorrect assumption, as the Japanese Zero, with the naval air forces based in Formosa, could fly to strategic American airfields at Clark and range over most of the north-central portion of Luzon. All the Zeros not on carriers were based on Formosa. This meant that Japan did not need carriers for operations against Luzon, but could employ them all against Pearl Harbor. The ability of the Zero to operate

Part of MacArthur's hastily militarized Philippine scouts, dwarfed by their Springfields and with headgear more suited to their former role as Philippine Constabulary.

for 15 minutes over the Philippine battle zone at a radius of 550 miles from their bases in Formosa was the result of intensive pre-war training as well as modifications to the plane.

The army situation still looked promising for MacArthur. He had the 4th Regiment of Marines, though MacArthur never used it except for garrison work. He had a division of regulars in the form of the Philippine Scouts (primarily long service and very loyal Filipinos, about 10,233 officers and men) and a second reserve division of retired constabulary and scouts. There also existed ten Philippine divisions, each of 7,500 men. These, however, were newly mobilized with the third regiment of each division having only been called up a few days before the war started. They were also poorly equipped, especially in artillery and machine guns. Their rifles, old Springfields, were overly large for the diminutive stature of the average Filipino soldier. Additionally, MacArthur had the 192nd and 194th Tank Battalion (each consisting of Company A, B, and D) of 54 Stuarts each (12.23 tons, one 37mm gun, two MGs, 51mm armor, 36 m.p.h. crew of 4). Douglas MacArthur could field a fair amount of artillery, including 155mm field guns. Also formed were two provisional self-propelled units made up of 75mm guns mounted on trucks. Finally, he had a fortress at Corregidor which, as long as it held out, made Manila Harbor a bottle with the fort the cork. The Japanese could not use Manila until Corregidor was captured.

Most of the American force was based on Luzon, although three Filipino divisions and minor units were based on other islands in the Philippine archipelago. A small but interesting battle for Mindanao transpired between Japan and the Filipino-American army in April and May of 1942. Facing the Filipino-American forces there was the Kawamura detachment and Kawaguchi detachment.

The Philippines maintained an intelligence service at the outbreak of war, being deployed to Corregidor by Christmas of 1941. It made use of several FBI trained *nisei*, or second generation Japanese-Americans, to help in understanding the Japanese language. This intelligence group was ordered evacuated on 4 February, 1942, and was completely off Corregidor by April of 1942, except for six enlisted men. Ordered to Melbourne, Australia, it joined there with with the Central Bureau of Australia and a contingent from the Singapore station Government Code and Cypher School, to form the basis of MacArthur's intelligence team. Named the "Fleet Radio Unit, Melbourne," it became known as FRUMEL.

The Japanese navy totally dominated this area of the Pacific, and with the loss of the British battleships *Prince of Wales* and *Repulse* on 10 December, had no fears of losing it even temporarily.

In the air the Japanese army fielded the 5th Air Division and the navy based the 21st and 23rd Air Flotillas. Also present at

Elite Japanese naval landing troops go ashore at Lingayen Gulf. In contrast to their American opponents, Japanese forces displayed a high level of initiative and ingenuity in the campaign.

Kagi Airfield in Formosa was the 1001st Air Transport Unit and the 1st and 3rd Yokosuka Special Naval Landing Force. Numbering 849 men each, with 750 of them being combat troops, they were Imperial Japanese Navy paratroops. These units were saved for use in the Dutch East Indies.

The Japanese army attacking MacArthur's army was actually inferior in numbers by a factor of 2 to 1, yet the Japanese army was a veteran force with a clear objective solidly planned for. It also ended up dominating the air and sea, sapping the morale of the Filipino-American force.

The Japanese planned to open the war against the Philippines with an air raid against various airbases on Luzon, but as it was night there when Pearl Harbor was bombed, the Japanese were concerned that they would not gain a surprise against the American air force. But luck and fate took a strange turn.

It was fogged in on the morning of the 8th over Formosa, so the Japanese could not leave for the attack. With nervous apprehension the Japanese feared that by the time they would be able to leave for the raid, the Philippines would certainly be aware of the attack on Pearl and would be alert for an air attack...yet the Japanese caught many planes on the ground and inflicted terrible losses on the American Army Air Corps that morning, destroying 53 P-40s, 18 B-17s, and about 30 other aircraft. Tactical surprise had been complete with bombing attacks at Clark followed up with an hour of strafing by 84 Zeros. The Japanese lost seven planes. The American army was equipped with anti-aircraft guns that had ammunition dating to 1932—much of the ammunition were duds, and "most of the fuses were badly corroded," according to Colonel Sage, commanding the 200th Coast Artillery.

The truth of this air disaster will never be completely revealed, and there never was a complete inquiry, unlike over Pearl Harbor, as to why it had occurred. Part of the problem lay with the relationship between MacArthur and President Manuel Quezon of the Philippines. MacArthur had been raised by his father Arthur MacArthur, an American Civil War hero and governor-general of the Philippines, in these islands at the turn of the century and loved that nation. Quezon hoped briefly that he could declare neutrality for the Philippines, thus sparing that country from the ravages of war. MacArthur, aware of this, possibly wanted to see Filipino neutrality become a reality, and ordered his forces not to do anything until "...Japan commit(s) the first overt act."

So, when word of the air raid on Pearl Harbor arrived, MacArthur could still say that no overt act of war had occurred, yet, *against the Philippines*. Thus MacArthur and his staff refused Army Air commander Major General Lewis H. Brereton's request to attack Formosa immediately with his B-17 bombers.

Later that morning the Japanese launched an air attack against some minor targets in the extreme north of Luzon which caused some fighters in central Luzon to rise. They had to land to refuel, which is when the then no longer fog-bound bombers and fighters from Formosa arrived over central Luzon to find sitting ducks, thus the disaster occured.

Over the next few days the Japanese gained total control of the air and sea in preparation for making landings. The Japanese faced a major problem in that they lacked sufficient ships to land troops in the more vital invasion of Malaya and conduct major

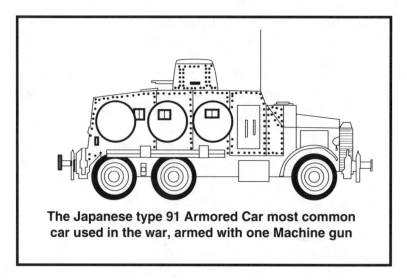

The Japanese type 91 Armored Car most common car used in the war, armed with one Machine gun

landings on Luzon. So, the initial move was to land small detachments on the northern portion of Luzon, in sparsely populated, mountainous terrain, with few and poor roads, left virtually undefended by MacArthur. In the first two weeks of the war, the Japanese were able to consolidate these early gains and bring primarily short ranged army air units onto Luzon.

With the invasion of Malaya accomplished, ships were moved northward to pick up the bulk of the 48th and the 16th divisions as well as two tank regiments, under the command of Lieutenant General Masaharu Homma. The 48th landed between the 22nd and 24th of December at Lingayen Gulf, north of Manila, while the 16th came ashore at Lamon Bay on the 24th, to the south of Manila. The Japanese plan called for an advance towards Manila and a battle of encirclement, a favorite strategy learned from von Moltke in the 19th century and employed in the Russo-Japanese War of 1904-05. The decision to seize Manila, as opposed to seeking the destruction of the American and Philippine forces, was one that general Homma queried. Tokyo insisted on Manila, probably for the prestige its capture offered. MacArthur had deployed his troops, the I and II Corps, at various landing points along the coast.

The landing on the north side of Lingayen Gulf, involving 85 transports with supporting warships including two battleships witnessed almost the entire 48th Division coming ashore with

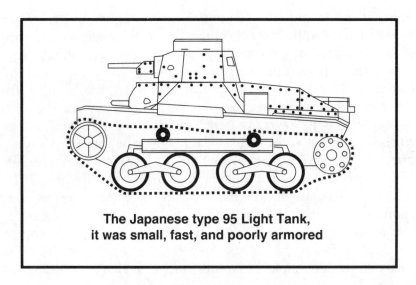

**The Japanese type 95 Light Tank,
it was small, fast, and poorly armored**

both tank regiments. Approaching overland from the north was the Tanaka Detachment made up of infantry which had landed earlier in the month and had now advanced to a point just north of Lingayen Gulf. The Tanaka Detachment hit the American flank at the same time as the landing to provide distraction as the Japanese came ashore. Four Filipino divisions and an understrength Philippine Scout cavalry regiment, the 26th, a collection of mounted men along with some light armored scout cars, faced the Japanese landing forces.

What is interesting about this landing is that it came as no surprise, other than that it came on 22 December instead of in January. It was a logical landing point and maneuvers had been conducted in that area many times. Homer Lea in his prophetic *The Valour of Ignorance*, written in 1909, mapped the exact spot for invasion by the Japanese. Yet the official historian of the campaign, Dr. Louis Morton, wrote later, "Despite the warning, the Americans seem to have been ill prepared to drive off the invaders."

The main problem was that the Filipino troops were simply not capable of engaging in combat in a mobile environment. For example, the 71st Division advanced with a battery of self-propelled 75mm guns against the Japanese. They did not execute their maneuver rapidly, and instead were attacked by the 4th

Tank Regiment and 48th Reconnaissance Regiment. The tanks were a threat that the 71st had little defense against, and so they fell back and Baguio, the Philippines' summer capital, fell.

Next the Japanese moved to consolidate their invasion and pushed southward. They accomplished this quite easily, with only the 26th Cavalry offering any serious resistance. The 26th covered the withdrawal of the Filipino divisions, and in the words of General Wainwright, "Here was true cavalry delaying action, fit to make a man's heart sing. Pierce (the commander) that day upheld the best traditions of the cavalry service." The 26th also lost half of its strength due to combat losses. The Japanese used the 4th Tank Regiment as a point unit, and the Filipino-American Army had virtually no weapons to stop it. The continuous retreat, lack of proper weapons to stop the enemy and slim hopes for relief had a devastating effect on morale.

To the south on Luzon at Lamon Bay, the 20th Regiment of the 16th Division in 24 transports landed on 23rd of December. Some air support came from the Japanese seaplane carrier the *Mizuho* (12,150 tons, six 5-inch guns, 24 floatplanes, 22 knots). Also offering support was the Japanese force that had landed at Legaspi. It had covered the 150 miles from that port city and appeared on the flank of the Filipino 51st Division. The 51st resisted, but was forced to fall back primarily due to the pressure of the 16th Reconnaissance Regiment. Total Japanese losses were 268 killed and wounded, but 7,000 men of the 16th Division were ashore.

What is vital to note here is that the Japanese advances were being spearheaded by relatively speaking "elite" units. The 16th Reconnaissance Regiment in the south, and the two tank regiments and the 48th Reconnaissance Regiment in the north led the advances. They had the best equipment, were the most motorized, as well as best trained to lead the advance. Facing them were units which had inferior equipment, and lacked the proper training to deal with the forces which confronted them. This would be a common occurrence in all theaters of the war, that the side with the edge in equipment, and with the troops to use it, would win out, until the next new edge came along. This theory of the elite unit winning the battles of World War II seems

Although taken by surprise, the Filipino-American resistance was more stubborn than the Japanese had anticipated.

borne out by these early battles in the Pacific leading to the destruction of Japan's key edge at the start of the war, her carrier strike force, at Midway.

The rapid advance of the Japanese and intelligence information that 80,000 to 100,000 Japanese troops had landed, convinced MacArthur that he could not defeat the enemy on the

U.S. and Philippine soldiers on the Bataan Death March improvise stretchers for comrades who had fallen by the wayside.

beaches as he had hoped. Therefore an order to retire to Bataan was issued. Insufficient stores were rushed there, something that could have been accomplished earlier in the campaign. Manila was declared an "open city," and the Japanese entered the Philippine capital before the end of December. Yet before the withdrawal was complete, several short sharp actions were fought as the Filipino-American army fell back to one river after another on the island of Luzon. The Japanese advanced down Luzon's central valley north of Manila, with another prong racing down on the western side of the valley.

Corregidor falls, the largest surrender of American forces ever.

In the south the Filipino 51st steadily fell back suffering losses the entire way. It had to hold long enough to allow Manila to be emptied of supplies, but it also had to be able to retreat fast enough when called upon to race through the city and slip into Bataan on the north side of Manila Bay. Manila acted as a bottleneck. Considering the green troops and lack of equipment, this operation was successfully carried out and no major units were cut off in the withdrawal into Bataan. This was due in part to the Japanese belief that with the fall of Manila the war in the Philippines would be over.

Thus, the Japanese did not expect much resistance from the Filipino-American army after Manila fell. They were then surprised by a series of sharp bloody actions before Bataan by an enemy that was no longer retreating.

The fight began as Malaya quickly fell, and General Homma's Japanese 14th Army was now mired in a slow siege of the peninsula which incurred high losses to both sides. A student of the campaign, H.P Wilmott, said General Homma had "the three most successful generals in history....Their names were Hunger, Disease, and Despair."

The "battling bastards of Bataan" kept the smaller, but better trained and supplied, Japanese army checked, defeating their attacks from both frontal and flanking amphibious operations. Eventually, the 4th Division was sent as a reinforcement to the 14th Army. The lack of food, medicine, ammunition, and supplies took their toll on the Filipino-American forces. Bataan had to surrender, leaving Corregidor holding out, but for how long?

By that time there had been a command change. MacArthur, along with President Quezon, was ordered out to Australia. At first MacArthur wanted to "share the fate of the garrison" when the issue of evacuating him out of the Philippines was raised. A direct order from Roosevelt and the knowledge that he would be able to fight the Japanese from Australia persuaded MacArthur. The actual journey began on 12 March 1942, the famous ride on a PT-boat (54 tons, four 21-inch torpedoes, 39 knots) to the southern islands and eventual flight to Australia. Once there, MacArthur symbolized the commitment America had made to the defense of an ally feeling terribly threatened by an advancing and victorious enemy, a defense that Great Britain had failed to provide. General Douglas MacArthur's reception by Australia was both strong and positive. MacArthur's determination to fulfill his "I shall return" promise stood largely on the base that Australia would give him.

Bataan had fallen on April 9th, and 78,000 men became prisoners. Thousands died in the Bataan Death March to prisoner of war camps. Many Japanese acted in callous and barbaric

Corregidor's garrison marches past wreckage from Japanese bombardment. They received somewhat better treatment than those who had surrendered earlier at Bataan.

fashion towards the half starved prisoners; many who fell by the wayside were shot. Food and water was scanty, but some prisoners did escape into the bush to fight on.

For Corregidor, with thousands living on short rations in tunnels, under frightful bombardment, the end was inevitable. In May of 1942 Japanese troops and three tanks landed on the island. On the 6th General Wainwright, commanding since MacArthur's departure, surrendered the entire archipelago, including Filipino-American troops fighting elsewhere in the Philippines.

There are two key points about the fighting in the Philippines. First, General Douglas MacArthur, although he received the Medal of Honor for this campaign, conducted it very poorly. His planes were caught on the ground, his fortress redoubt was inadequately prepared, his strategy in allowing Japanese forces to consolidate their position in the north combined with his inability to deal with a smaller enemy army do not give him high marks. But, as a "Great Captain" of war, he learned from his errors, and in the next few years established beyond a doubt that he was one of the most brilliant generals that America has ever produced.

Secondly, the Filipino-American army had been unable to stop the Japanese, an enemy that for much of the campaign was never greater than nine battalions in strength. The Japanese timetable was not affected greatly and although General Homma's career in the Japanese army was finished, Japan had used little in the way of resources to capture these islands. Still, the fact that resistance lasted into May of 1942 told the world that the Japanese juggernaut could be fought and brought to a standstill.

CHAPTER VI

The Malayan Campaign

8 December 1941 - 15 February 1942

Winston Churchill noted that the fall of Malaya, and the surrender at Singapore, "was the worst disaster and largest capitulation in British history." Though the British outnumbered the Japanese forces in overall numbers, the Japanese were facing second rate units that were poorly equipped and trained for static warfare. The British forces also suffered from inept leadership, lack of air and sea support, and were supported by an almost feudal society with a civil administration unable to properly aid the military. Field Marshal Wavell wrote in a dispatch two days after Singapore fell, "The trouble goes a long way back; climate, the atmosphere of the country (the whole of Malaya has been asleep for at least 200 years), lack of vigor in our peacetime training, the cumbrousness of our tactics and equipment, and the real difficulty of finding an answer to the very skillful and bold tactics of the Japanese in this jungle fighting."

Malaya itself was an obstacle. The climate, high humidity, heat, and rain is such that it takes a minimum of two months for troops to get used to it. The heavy rains on this peninsula create swamp-like conditions in vegetation-choked rivers and streams. Mountains peaking at 7,000 feet run down the center of the peninsula, inhibiting movement. The west coast of Malaya had most of the population and ports, but both coasts had important ports that needed to be protected from Japanese landings. Allied strength was also dispersed by the need to garrison various airfields near areas of potential civil unrest with an inadequate number of planes of obsolete types (built often in spots designated by the RAF, but not where the British army, which had to defend them, wanted them located).

The sought-after jewel of Malaya was the naval base and seaport of Singapore. Sitting on the Straits of Malacca, it was a base into which Britain had poured resources for 20 years, so that the British fleet would have a naval base which it could operate if engaged in a war with Japan. Lord Jellicoe, the former commander of the British fleet at the battle of Jutland, and key point man in getting the base of Singapore started, concluded in 1919 that, "the safety of the bases of Colombo and Singapore is vital to Australia and New Zealand; and the safety of Sydney and other naval bases in the South Pacific is of the greatest importance to India." Jellicoe had earlier stated that "Japan is as much a bogey to India as it is to Australia." As for Australia, Jellicoe rightly concluded that "*it must be recognized that Australia is powerless against a strong naval and military power without the assistance of the British Fleet*(Jellicoe's italics)." So the construction of a base at Singapore was recommended to protect both colonial India and the underpopulated and immense Australian continent from invasion by Japan. Its loss would expose Australia to raids or invasion and would open the Indian Ocean to attack. Malaya was also economically crucial to the Allies as it contained 38% of the world's rubber and 58% of the world's tin.

Vice Admiral Ugaki, the chief of staff to Admiral Yamamoto, drew a list in December of 1941 of what Japanese forces in Southern Asia hoped to achieve. Those goals were:

1) The destruction of the enemy fleet.

2) The destruction of enemy bases and the securing of Japanese bases.

3) The encouragement of anti-British movements in India.

4) An East-West link-up between the Axis powers.

It is important to look at number four above very closely. Admiral Raeder in Germany was calling for a link-up of Germany and Italy with Japan in the Indian Ocean as well, and briefly had Hitler's ear. His plan called for Rommel and the Italo-German army to push right through Egypt into the Middle

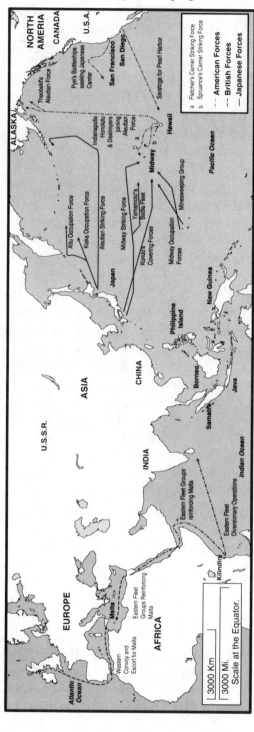

As the Axis air and Italian fleet was defeating the British Mediterranean Harpoon and Vigorous Operation, the Midway Operations unfolded in the Pacific.

East while the Panzer armies in Southern Russia marched east, then south, through the Caucasus mountains with both thrusts linking up in Persia or Iraq. This strategy if successfully implemented would have most likely been the one to bring about success for Axis arms. The fall of India would have followed and with it Churchill's position as head of the British government would have been threatened. However, the paths of the Axis powers would turn away from this key to victory. The Italian path would end with El Alamein, the Germans would fall on the steppes of Stalingrad, while the Japanese would see their first coffin nail at Midway.

It should be noted that Japan at this time envisioned an independent Arabia and India liberated by Axis forces. The capture of Singapore was a key step in this objective. Only the halting of the Japanese army on the Burma-India border and the defeat of the Japanese navy at Midway could halt the implementation of these goals. A vital impediment to the success of this scheme was the unwillingness of the Japanese army to supply troops for future operations. The Japanese army did not want the navy to know that troops were available, thinking they might want them for other operations in the Pacific. This would be a key factor for the Japanese not invading Ceylon (Sri Lanka) and would vitally affect Japanese planning in 1942.

The first step in the seizure of Malaya was the occupation of French Indochina, more important than the Burma Road in supplying the Nationalist Chinese forces at this stage of the war. So when France fell to Nazi Germany in 1940, the Japanese took that opportunity to seize Indochina in a bloodless move, a move completed by July of 1941. It was this seizure that brought about the trade embargo by the Allies against Japan which was the final straw forcing her to attack Pearl Harbor.

To conduct the attack against Malaya, Lieutenant General Tomoyuki Yamashita was chosen to command the 25th Army. Yamashita graduated fifth in his class at the Military Academy at Hiroshima in 1908. Probably the most brilliant Japanese general of the war, his campaign and victory in Malaya was one of the most outstanding campaigns of World War II. Thus he earned the title of "Tiger of Malaya." Yamashita finished the war in command of the main Japanese army on Luzon in the

Philippines, beaten by MacArthur, but he was not conquered by him. He surrendered with the end of the war only to be sentenced to death at the war crimes trials for atrocities committed in Malaya by troops under his command.

Four divisions were assigned to the 25th Army, but Yamashita, because of the problems entailed with supplying four divisions, asked only for three. Yamashita was assigned the excellent 5th (motorized by Japanese standards and having four instead of the usual three regiments), the 18th and the Imperial Guard divisions. It should be noted that the Guard Division was actually a newly trained formation without recent combat experience and was not highly regarded. Further, its commander, Takuma Nishimura represented a different faction within the Japanese army than the one of Yamashita. To complicate matters further, Prime Minister General Tojo, who resented Yamashita's army-wide popularity, assigned Colonel Tsuji directly to Yamashita's staff to keep an eye on the general. This was done after Tsuji had completed his vital assignment of preparing the plans for the campaign.

Colonel Tsuji had 30 officers on Hainan Island in China and Formosa (Taiwan today) planning the campaign against Malaya. The environment in South China prepared these officers for the Malayan climate and the conditions they would have to fight in. Various units in the campaign were preparing on Hainan and Formosa as early as April of 1941. After the Japanese victory in Malaya, due in part from this planning, Colonel Tsuji remarked, "For the first time in history, an army carried out a blitzkrieg on bicycles!" For intelligence, the Japanese used over 180 officers who in turn recruited locals to prepare for the invasion of Malaya. The German Abwehr (Secret Service) commented that this level of preparation was even more thorough than Nazi Germany's plans for the invasion of Norway in 1940, which was a very difficult feat in itself.

Yamashita had the 3rd Tank Regiment, three engineer regiments (needed to repair the numerous destroyed bridges of Malaya), and two additional regiments of heavy artillery to assist in the campaign. The 3rd Air Division of the army gave its support, and the Japanese navy also gave aid beyond transporting the initial invasion force.

Hideki Tojo, Japanese prime minister and a leader of the nation's informal "war party."

Facing the invading Japanese army was the more numerous, but inferior in combat effectiveness, Commonwealth army under the intelligent but uninspiring Lieutenant General Arthur E. Percival. The overall commander of the Far East was Air Marshal Sir Robert Brooke-Popham, headquartered at Singapore. Defending Singapore were the 1st and 2nd Malaya Infantry Brigades. Primarily fortress troops, they were insurance against a coup de main against the city itself and operated the powerful coast defense batteries. One of these brigades was roughly the equivalent of a Japanese regiment. The 8th Australian Division, made up of two instead of the usual three brigades and which had been "milked" for some of its cadres to support operations in North Africa, along with the 12th Indian Brigade guarded the mainland areas near Singapore. North of Malaya in prepared and fortified positions along the border of Thailand and at various northern coastal ports were the 11th and 9th divisions of the III Indian Corps commanded by General Heath. The corps consisted of four brigades, with a fifth additional brigade as a reserve unit. It was the III Corps that first felt the brunt of the Japanese attack. None of the troops were properly trained, due to Malaya being a backwater for the first part of the war.

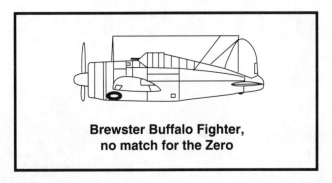

**Brewster Buffalo Fighter,
no match for the Zero**

Before the war the British command requested 100 tanks, but they were not forthcoming. During this campaign, Britain was unable to send any tanks to Malaya, in part due to Churchill's feeling that this would be a dispersal of strength. It also was evidence of a general attitude towards the potential of the Japanese enemy. One battalion commander in Malaya remarked to Brooke-Popham while reviewing his battalion, "Don't you think they are worthy of some better enemy than the Japanese?" Brigadier Stewart, who commanded the 12th Indian Brigade, also commented to Brooke-Popham that, "I do hope, Sir, we are not getting too strong in Malaya, because if so the Japanese may never attempt a landing." Less than a year later, Stewart's brigade, lacking air support and under constant attack, was chased by the Japanese 4th Guards Regiment and eight tanks for a fortnight before escaping.

The saddest situation for the British was in the air. Pre-war studies stated that it was desirable to have 582 planes based in Malaya—336 would be the bare minimum required to defend Malaya—but on 7 December 1941, Britain fielded 246 airplanes there. Of these, 88 were disabled, and of the remaining 158 planes, the most modern fighter was the overweight Buffalo. The 36 torpedo planes were obsolete bi-plane Vildebeestes with a maximum speed of 137 m.p.h.! The Vildebeestes were "archaic and rickety bi-planes with fixed landing gear, masses of rigging wires and braces, and open cockpits." One pilot was quoted as saying that, "It was noted among the British crewmen after the war began that some Japanese casualties might have been caused when Japanese pilots caught sight of the Vildebeestes and laughed themselves to death." In the course of the campaign

The **Prince of Wales,** *just after arrival in Singapore.*

some Hurricane fighters (970 miles, twelve MGs or four 20mm cannon, 342 m.p.h.) arrived, but it was a matter of too little too late. It could be argued that the lend-lease shipment of Hurricanes to Soviet Russia fighting for her life against the savage German invasion of 1941 sealed the doom of Singapore and the garrison stationed there.

The British were not totally blind to the threat of Japan, although they certainly underestimated it. Churchill said in September of 1940 that "The Naval Intelligence Division are very much inclined to exaggerate Japanese strength and efficiency." However, one of the inadequate actions taken by Churchill in 1941 was to reinforce the British navy in the Far East. Force Z was created, made up of the new fast battleship *Prince of Wales* (36,727 tons, ten 14-inch guns, sixteen 5.25-inch guns, 28 knots), and the fast older reconstructed battlecruiser *Repulse* (32,000 tons, six 15-inch guns, nine 4-inch anti-ship

The ill-fated Admiral Tom Phillips on his arrival in Singapore.

guns, and six 4-inch anti-aircraft guns, 28 knots). The fleet carrier *Indomitable* (23,000 tons, 12 Fulmar fighters, nine Sea Hurricane fighters, 24 Albacore torpedo planes, 30 knots) was due to go with them but had run aground in a fog in Kingston, Jamaica, and no other suitable carrier was available. So Force Z was forced to rely on land based air, mostly belonging to the Royal Air Force and not the naval air arm. This was a key to the destruction of Force Z by the Japanese. In addition to Force Z, the British navy at Singapore fielded three old D class light cruisers (4,850 tons, six 6-inch guns, 12 21-inch guns, 27 knots) and six destroyers. Sadly for the British Empire, only one submarine was present in the Far East and that one was under refit. The omission of such a valuable weapon was a terrible blow to the defense of this region, especially since British submarines were reasonably capable craft, unlike the American submarines at that stage of the war.

The strategy behind the sending of this force was twofold. If the Japanese invaded Malaya, Force Z could be used with proper land based air cover to attack the enemy invasion convoy. Churchill actually felt that the Japanese were unable to invade Malaya and that Force Z would be of value in destroying the Japanese battlecruisers which the prime minister feared would be unleashed against British Far East trade routes. As

Churchill stated, "I cannot feel that Japan will face the combination now forming against her of the United States, Great Britain, and Russia, while already preoccupied in China....Nothing would increase her hesitation more than the appearance of the force mentioned....This might indeed be a decisive deterrent." The employment of Force Z was to be "that kind of vague menace which capital ships of the highest quality, whose whereabouts are unknown, can impose upon all hostile naval calculations." Churchill felt that Force Z could lose itself among the islands of Southern Asia and with its high speed could run from a strong enemy or "catch and kill anything" weaker. Churchill was taking a leaf from the employment of the German Kriegsmarine in which the battleship *Bismarck* or *Tirpitz* tied down many Allied warships in the Atlantic. This tying down by Force Z, coupled with the threat of the American fleet at Pearl Harbor, would be a combination of forces that Japan could not defeat, or so Churchill thought.

The Dutch had reported on December 2 that a large Japanese convoy was heading south. The Japanese tried to give the impression that the convoy was on its way to Thailand, but at a certain point it was obvious that it was proceeding towards the coast of Northern Malaya and the extreme southern coastal tail, or Kra Peninsula, of Thailand. It was at this point that the Japanese Vice Admiral, Jisaburo Ozawa, ordered a shadowing British Catalina flying boat to be shot down. This was on 7 December—on that side of the International Date Line it was almost a full 24 hours before the attack on Pearl Harbor—it was the first hostile act of the war about to begin in the Pacific.

Direct air support was limited as this was some distance from Japanese airbases in Indochina, near Saigon. The 5th Division was put ashore at the Malayan coastal town of Kota Bharu and engaged the 9th Indian Brigade. The invasion fleet came close to being humiliated when it was almost forced to withdraw by air attacks by the dated RAF Vildebeestes! The lack of proper air cover for the Japanese invasion fleet, and the loss of one transport, give an indication of what might have occurred if the British air units had been up to minimum strength of modern aircraft. Losses amounted to about 500 men for the 5th Division, virtually all these occurring at Kota Bharu, but the entire division was ashore within 24 hours either in Northern Malaya, or heading towards the Thai-Malaya border. The British never planned for such a quick landing of hostile forces in Malaya. Thai resistance to the Japanese invasion, which also involved the seizure of the capital of Bangkok, lasted about 24 hours.

British reaction to the invasion was to dispatch Force Z, made up of the *Prince of Wales* and *Repulse* with four destroyers, to engage the enemy transports. If Force Z had been delayed even just two days, it would have had strong additional reinforcements including the Dutch light cruiser *Java*, the heavy cruiser *Exeter*, and others. The hard driving Admiral Tom Phillips, the new admiral in charge of the fleet in the Far East, who sailed with and commanded Force Z, was under the impression that in terms of air opposition, he would meet only Japanese army air units supporting the enemy invasion. Phillips thought these planes were armed with the incorrect type of weapons, i.e., ground attack weapons and not armor-piercing bombs and torpedoes, so he moved quickly in the hopes of disrupting the invasion of Malaya.

Phillips was terribly ill-suited for the command of Force Z. For most of the war, he had seen action only at a desk job and lacked modern combat experience. Worst of all, he maintained faulty and old fashioned notions about the ability of ships to withstand air attack without proper fighter protection. He was noted in the British navy for arguing that a battleship with room to maneuver and given an adequate anti-aircraft armament could survive the onslaughts of enemy planes. Just before the war, Phillips believed that the torpedo hitting percentage from torpedo planes in combat would be less than 15%. It proved to be 22% against his two capital ships!

Another factor debilitating Phillips' mission was the erroneous estimate of Japanese naval strength his force would eventually face. British intelligence intimated that the Japanese forces were made up of the rebuilt fast battleship *Kongo*, three heavy cruisers, two light cruisers and 20 destroyers. In actuality Phillips was faced with two *Kongo* class battleships, seven heavy and three light cruisers, and 24 destroyers. The overall Japanese naval command was under Vice Admiral Nobutake Kondo. A gunnery specialist, he was a cautious man of few brilliant qualities. The immediate convoy escort force was under, in the words of Professor Marder, the "first-class fighting admiral, and the Navy's foremost tactician," Vice Admiral Ozawa.

In London on 9 December, Admiralty officials were discussing sending Force Z to the American West Coast to join with the remnants of the American battleship fleet, or to "vanish among the innumerable islands, exercising a vague menace as rogue elephants." By then it was too late; Force Z had gone to sea. Phillips hoped to surprise the Japanese, get in among the enemy convoys in the Gulf of Siam off Northern Malaya, or possibly engage the lone *Kongo*, then retire before hastily organized long range bombers could attack his ships. The British Admiral was convinced that no torpedo plane could operate very effectively beyond a radius of 200 miles, as that was the British experience. In actuality, the Japanese did operate at a radius of 1,000 miles with the requisite skill required. Finally, Phillips sailed hoping that he would receive fighter protection. Force Z was not promised this support, and indeed the flotilla did not receive it as air losses during the first two days of war in the Pacific were substantial and there was a lack of communication with proper air authorities on Phillips' part. Wishful thinking by Phillips would bring about the loss of Force Z.

The Japanese knew by early December that the *Prince of Wales*, and possibly her sister ship *King George V*, was present at Singapore. Yamamoto had decided on the basis of this information to move a unit of the highly trained and skilled Kanoya Air Corps from Formosa to the Saigon area. The Genzan and Mihoro Air Corps were also stationed in Indochina. These were good units, but lacked the training against ship targets that the Kanoya Air Corps had undergone over the years. The Kanoya Air Corps was especially skilled at torpedo drops in shallow water, which was a common characteristic of the waters around Singapore.

Kondo knew that Force Z possessed radar, and he was intimidated by the modern *Prince of Wales* with its aura of an unsinkable battleship. Kondo proposed that the British enemy be attacked with bombs and torpedoes by day and by a destroyer attack at night.

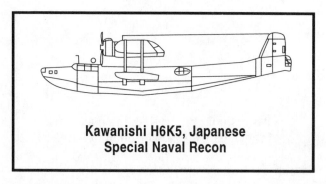

**Kawanishi H6K5, Japanese
Special Naval Recon**

When Force Z proceeded to sea on 9 December, it moved north as originally planned, but was sighted both by Japanese air as well as submarine forces. With surprise thus lost, Phillips turned back towards Singapore when a false report arrived telling of an invasion at Kuantan in central-south Malaya. The admiral did not inform Singapore of this change in plans and though a force of Buffalo fighters was standing by to give escort, it was not sent until the fate of Force Z was sealed. Even had Phillips relied on these planes to protect his ships, the obsolete Buffalo probably would have proven ineffective against Nell and Betty naval medium bombers.

Meanwhile the Japanese organized a strike of 18 planes from the Kanoya, 17 planes from the Genzan, and 18 planes from the Mihoro Air Groups. Weather conditions on the 9th of December were so bad that all the planes had to return, although not before three of them had sighted an enemy force at night and dropped flares over it—this turned out to be Ozawa's flagship the heavy cruiser *Chokai*. Vice Admiral Jisaburo Ozawa was present with his five heavy cruisers (*Chokai, Kumano, Mikuma, Mogami,* and *Suzuya*), with two light cruisers (*Kinu* and *Yura*), and four destroyers nearby in separate squadrons. Ozawa did not expect airpower alone to sink these enemy capital ships so he intended to attack at night with his force. At 2030 Ozawa was 50 miles from Force Z. By 2120 this range fell to between eight and 22 miles. A night action between the *Prince of Wales* and the *Repulse* against five Japanese heavy cruisers probably would have been strictly decided on a basis of who saw whom first, although Admiral Phillips tactical ability was inferior to that of Admiral Ozawa.

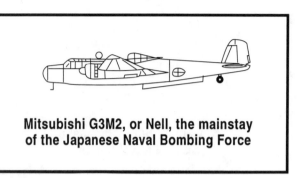

Mitsubishi G3M2, or Nell, the mainstay of the Japanese Naval Bombing Force

Kondo ordered Ozawa to fall back for several reasons. First, the Japanese force had not trained together and was hastily compiled, and second, the destroyers were low on fuel. Third, weather conditions were not good and the Japanese feared the new weapon called radar rumored to be on the British ships. Finally, Ozawa realized that the British force was now no longer heading for northern Malaya, but towards the south central Malaya area. Ozawa could not account for the reason the enemy was heading in that direction and was therefore understandably suspicious. Kondo decided to order the withdrawal of Ozawa, and instead of running the risk of defeat in detail to the British, he ordered a concentration of all key surface combat units. Kondo's decision to concentrate the entire fleet, led by the battleships *Kongo* and *Haruna*, gave him the possibility of engaging the enemy in the morning. They concentrated that night and headed south at 24 knots. Early in the morning Force Z was sighted by air reconnaissance and orders were issued for an immediate air attack.

The first wave was of 16 Nells armed with torpedoes and nine Nells from the Genzan Air Corps armed with one 1,102-pound bomb each. The second wave was of eight Nells armed with torpedoes, eight Nells armed with two 551-pound bombs each, and 17 Nells armed with one 1,102-pound bomb each of the Mihoro Air Corps. The final wave, from the Kanoya Air Group, was composed of 26 Bettys armed with the most modern torpedo available to the Japanese. All planes departed for the attack on Force Z between 0625 and 0800.

Japanese air tactics called for a simultaneous attack by both horizontal bombers and torpedo planes. It was recognized that the bombs in question were too small to penetrate the decks of the British battleships, but the resulting "confusion in the target ship through the damage caused by hits" made it easier for the attacking torpedo planes. At this point the Japanese knew that larger bombs were needed for harming battleships, and used such weapons at Pearl Harbor by converting 16-inch shells to bombs. But that weapon was available only in limited numbers and none were available in this Southern Theater of the war.

Torpedoes cause more damage when set for a deeper depth. The ideal position to hit a battleship is as deep as possible, but to set a torpedo too deep will allow it to possibly go under a target ship and thus miss altogether. In the approaching action, the Kanoya Air Corps, which scored the most torpedo hits, set their torpedoes for an in-between setting of four meters (about 13 feet), which was ideal for cruisers, but not the ideal six meters for battleships. So, if the setting had been for battleships instead of for cruiser targets, it could be assumed that the resulting damage would have been greater than it was.

The Japanese expected losses to be about one-third of the planes involved in the attack. They lost just three planes in the battle against Force Z, although several more were damaged. When compared to the losses of the Bettys against the *Lexington*'s Task Force in the February 1942 battle off Rabaul, one can gain a sense of what the lack of good fighter cover meant.

The first attack took place from the nine bombing Nells of the Genzan Air Corps in which the bombers mistook the little destroyer *Tenedos* (1,090 tons, three 4-inch guns, four 21-inch torpedoes, 36 knots—built during World War I) for a battleship and wasted their attack. All bombs missed with none falling closer than 100 yards from the destroyer. Mistakes like this occurred throughout the war on both sides.

The air units were despairing of finding Force Z when a reconnaissance plane located the force and made the proper signals. By 1100 the first attacking planes arrived over Force Z and began launching their runs. Ideally the Japanese planes would have concentrated and launched an attack as a complete unit, but having been in the air for hours, they were concerned about their fuel and so went in as they arrived on the scene.

Most of the crew of the **Prince of Wales** *were rescued as the ship was sinking.*

The first attack began at 1113 with unbelievable noise created by 5.25-inch dual-purpose guns, Oerlikons, Bofors, and the "chattering, ear-splitting rhythm of the multiple pom-poms." The main attacks were against the *Prince of Wales* and the *Repulse*, while some damaged planes dropped bombs on the destroyers. The bombers came in at about 9,750 feet to 13,000 feet. Torpedo planes launched their torpedoes at 325 to 1,300 feet from the target ship.

The first attack by the Mihoro Air Corps scored one bomb hit on the plane hanger of the *Repulse*. A small fire resulted which was quickly extinguished. The second attack included the *Prince of Wales*. Torpedo planes of the Genzan group came in low and the torpedo officer of the *Prince of Wales* remarked to Admiral Phillips, "I think they're going to do a torpedo attack," to which Admiral Phillips replied, "No they're not. There are no torpedo aircraft about." The attack scored two torpedo hits on the port side of the *Prince of Wales* which damaged the boiler rooms and slowed her to 15 knots speed. Flooding was severe and counter-flooding (to correct the list of the ship) placed the ship low in the water. The steering control was damaged and all the 5.25-inch dual purpose guns were placed out of combat from electrical failures and flooding damage.

The third attack from units of the Mihoro group missed their target, the *Repulse*. Captain William Tennant of the *Repulse*, with help from the navigating officer, H.B.C. Gill, avoided this attack by "steaming at 25 knots....I maintained a steady course until the aircraft appeared to be committed to the attack when the (ship's) wheel was put over and the attacks providentially combed." Calm orders for 30 degree turns first to one side then 30 degree turns to the other side was the standard procedure that kept the *Repulse* free of torpedo hits, until the Kanoya Air Corps arrived.

The fourth attack at 1220 was deadly. Six of the incoming 26 Bettys attacked the crippled *Prince of Wales* and scored four hits on the starboard side, correcting the list from the first attack, but dooming the vessel. Her speed dropped to about nine knots. The *Repulse* was simply overwhelmed. Tennant in describing this attack said, "I found dodging the torpedoes quite interesting and entertaining until in the end they started to come in from all directions and they were too much for me." The first hit slowed her to 15 knots and jammed her rudder, thus letting the next four hits rip her side open. Orders for abandoning ships were forthcoming at 1225. In five minutes both ships were on their last legs. By 1233 the *Repulse* had capsized and then, as described by Lieutenant John Hayes, "She reared into the vertical as the stern disappeared. Just the bow, half gray, half reddish bottom color, hung for a moment in a last defiant gesture to the sky; then that too slid back into a cauldron of bubbles while the water blackened from oil in convulsive eddies, and the *Repulse* was gone."

Two additional attacks scored only one bomb hit on the *Prince of Wales*, but that bomb hit knocked out additional boiler rooms. There were 18,000 tons of water on board the *Prince of Wales*, speed was reduced to 6 knots, and losses were heavy. At 1315 the ship was ordered to be abandoned. One sailor was heard to remark to a friend, "Come on, chum, all them explosions 'll have frightened the blinkin sharks away." They then jumped into the water. Phillips, and Captain Leach who had fought the German battleship *Bismarck* with the *Hood* in May of 1941, both went down with the *Prince of Wales*. Some 513 men from the *Repulse* and 327 men from the *Prince of Wales* died in the attack.

As for Vice-Admiral Phillips' decision to remain on board and die with his flagship, one senior officer stated later, "Tom Phillips would have had great difficulty in facing the situation if he had survived, and for that reason many officers would sympathize with his decision not to leave the ship." The problem with this decision is that it was a personal decision that overlooked the context of the situation. Phillips commanded the Far Eastern naval forces, and not just Force Z. Had Phillips survived, his hard driving nature might have helped in saving the situation in Malaya and he possibly could have learned lessons quickly enough to make up for ignorance displayed at this point in the war.

The loss of the *Prince of Wales* and *Repulse*, coupled with the Pearl Harbor raid, caused the status of surface ships and especially battleships within the American and British navies to be viewed by many as useless except for convoy duty. Coupled with a steel shortage, the construction of battleships in America was severely curtailed, while in Britain the *Lion* class battleship was delayed and later canceled because of cost and questions of its effectiveness. However, later surface naval battles redeemed the value of the battleship and gave it new roles as a powerful anti-aircraft platform and for shore bombardment duties.

Admiral Sir Dudley Pound said in 1943 of the destruction of Force Z, that "we all under-rated the efficiency of the Japanese air forces, and certainly did not realize the long ranges at which they would work." The *British Daily Mail* wrote, "There has been a tendency to underrate their machines and airmen. We should hear no more of that." Vice-Admiral Ugaki noted that, "Nothing more brilliant than this remarkable success...by destroying the *Prince of Wales* it may be said that we have avenged the *Bismarck* in the Far East, on the opposite side of the earth." Ugaki went on to say, "I cannot but recognize the remarkable power of airplanes, seeing the results since last night. These battleships . . . proved to be poorly equipped for a defensive battle . . . ." The upshot of all of this was that Japan's confidence in victory in Malaya was enhanced, while there was a corresponding loss of morale for the troops in Malaya. There no longer existed a strong

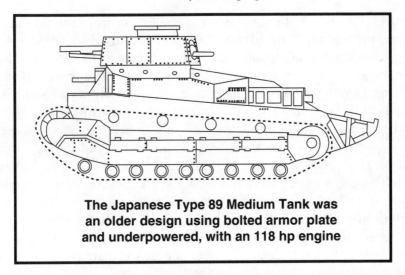

**The Japanese Type 89 Medium Tank was
an older design using bolted armor plate
and underpowered, with an 118 hp engine**

naval force to contest the command of the sea at Singapore.
Singapore was now a beleaguered fortress.

The Japanese were ashore and consolidating their position in
Thailand in just three days from the start of the war. A reinforced
regiment of the 5th Division was pushing down the eastern coast
of Malaya towards Singapore. This force captured Kuantan on
30 December from elements of the Indian 9th Division. But it
was on the west coast where the real fighting occurred.

There were several problems facing the rest of the III Indian
Corps. It only had three brigades to defend northern Malaya and
the prize of Penang, a small island city and seaport. Originally
it was intended for the 11th Indian Division to enter Thailand
and seize strategic defensive positions, including the ports
invaded by Japan. This plan, Operation Matador, did not occur
except for a small abortive advance contested by Thai troops. So
the Indian troops, primed for an offensive, suddenly found
themselves on the defensive. Waterlogged from recent rains they
were deployed at Jitra in defensive positions which covered
several important airfields, and were supposed to offer resistance for up to three months.

The two other regiments of the 5th Division advanced towards Jitra and began an immediate night attack on the 11th.
The 5th Reconnaissance Regiment (about 300 men), supported
by ten medium tanks, pushed in, capturing an unmanned

anti-tank battery—the troops were sheltering from the rain and were not warned. The advance was halted, largely from attacks by famed Indian Gurkha and British infantry battalions. The Japanese responded by moving units around the enemy flank and employing their artillery with good effect. By the evening of the 12th the Commonwealth troops were retreating. Over 3,000 Indian troops surrendered (the 15th Indian Brigade was reduced to a quarter of its strength), and in the ensuing blunders, over 300 trucks and armored cars, 50 field guns, and 50 heavy machine guns were lost to the Japanese. A position meant to last for weeks had fallen in 36 hours of fighting to two Japanese battalions and a company of tanks. The III Indian Corps under General Heath fell back steadily, holding at various positions and managing to conduct a reasonable retreat, though with attendant heavy losses and decline in morale.

The effect of this defeat so early in the campaign, coupled with the destruction of Force Z, cannot be underestimated. The momentum had clearly shifted to the Japanese side. Further, after the fall of the nearby airfields with runways in good repair, the Japanese Army Air's short range aircraft could now be properly employed. Yamashita had written in his diary on 10 November, "If Indian troops are included in the British forces defending Malaya, the job should be easy." The poor performance of the Indian troops was in part due to the lack of adequate equipment and training, but it was also due to the fact that these commands had been "milked" over the first two years of the war for other units stationed mostly in the Middle East. This practice was now being paid for in full.

Part of the reason the defense at Jitra failed was that at many times the front was too long. One British brigade covered a front of six to seven miles. The British probably should have used small forces to tripwire the Japanese advances, fortifying key river crossings to slow up advances, and then strongly counter-attacking against the isolated Japanese spearheads. For their part, the Japanese typically practiced what they learned to call the "Fishbone Attack." A tank force advanced up the road, then turned its turret to one side and fired at enemy positions in adjacent plantations. Meanwhile, the artillery opened on those same positions so that there was incoming fire from two sepa-

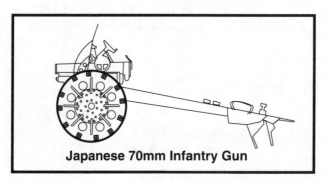

Japanese 70mm Infantry Gun

rate directions. The Allies had only a few weapons capable of dealing with the tanks, and usually they were sited in the wrong spots! The name was derived from the tanks being like the ribs on a fish's backbone, steadily moving down a road, with the Japanese artillery being the backbone.

The Imperial Guard now came up and it, together with the 5th Division, pushed south. The 18th Division still had not arrived and was marching up from ports in Thailand. Penang was captured on the 19th, along with a tremendous amount of shipping. This allowed the Japanese to employ a new weapon against the retreating British forces—amphibious operations. Incredible as it sounds and lacking any supporting warships on that side of Malaya, the Japanese constantly outflanked British positions as they drove south from the seaward flank. Japanese airpower was also employed and though it did not inflict many casualties or significant damage, the effect on morale was disastrous.

As the Japanese continued to advance, they received tremendous amounts of important supplies from the British Army itself. Dubbed "Churchill rations," they came from two key sources. One was the British Army which in its retreat often failed or did not have time to destroy accumulated supplies. Secondly, a scorched earth policy, such as the one used in Soviet Russia at the time of the German invasion, was not implemented in Malaya or in most of Southern Asia during the Japanese offensive since the Allies thought they would shortly be retaking the captured areas. There was also a feeling that the Asian colonial population could not survive if this were implemented. Finally the British Official History points out another reason. In

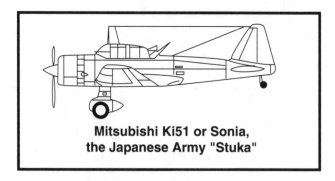

**Mitsubishi Ki51 or Sonia,
the Japanese Army "Stuka"**

describing the work of the "denial teams" busy in the final days destroying goods of value to the enemy, it notes that these teams were hindered.

> [denial teams] were...greatly handicapped, when they began the denial of plant and machinery, by the fact that some persons with vested interests did their utmost to delay the destruction of their property by lodging appeals with local authorities. Some firms, whose head offices were in Britain, Australia, or India, even appealed to their home Governments. Some went so far as to obstruct the work of the denial teams.

Ruthless determination needed to deprive the Japanese of vital supplies was lacking in the British Army. The end result was that Japan received help during the campaign from "Churchill rations" as well as immense amounts of other war booty and huge stockpiles of resources such as tin, coal, rubber, manufacturing and refining units left intact by the retreating British.

By early January the Japanese had captured Kuala Lumpur, today the capital of Malaysia. The 11th Indian Division was virtually destroyed at this point, but Commonwealth reinforcements were on their way (the 45th Indian Brigade of the 17th Indian Division arrived on 3 January, and later the British 18th Division), and the Australian 8th Division was about to make its stand. The commander of the theater, Brooke-Popham, was relieved of his command by a younger general, Lieutenant-General Sir Henry Pownall who had seen action during the fall of France in 1940. Percival had decided to cut his losses by withdrawing to the southern tip of Malaya (the state of Johore) and let his untested Australians have their chance, only to bungle the plan. He split the 8th Australian into two parts, reinforcing each with inferior British and Indian troops, and ignored the fact that the Australians were very flexible troops. Lieutenant-General Gordon Bennett, the commander of the 8th Australian, wanted to try some more aggressive tactics. Bennett felt that what was needed was less reliance on static defensive positions, and more aggressive counterattacks once Japanese forces were committed. Bennett was not allowed a real opportunity to implement his concept, and when the 8th was surrendered he escaped to Australia, only to find his reputation destroyed for leaving his troops. Yamashita noted that both the Indian and Australian troops in the campaign were second rate, a correct assumption since the best of both were serving in the Middle East.

One success the Australian 8th Division had was when they set up a classic ambush with one company at a bridge between Kuala Lumpur and Singapore. The Japanese had faced no opposition for about a hundred miles and were literally riding bikes six abreast with no scouts and ignoring rudimentary precautions. About 300 were allowed through to be disposed of by the troops behind the ambush. The bridge was then blown. As the Australian official history reported it, "the charge hurled timber, bicycles, and bodies skyward in a deadly blast. Almost simultaneously, Duffy's three platoons hurled grenades among the enemy and swept them with fire from Bren guns, Tommy guns, and rifles." The Australians fell back to a river position on the Muar and were prepared to fight there to hold the southern tip of Malaya.

However, the Japanese recovered, and pushing south with their two divisions on a broad front, managed to establish themselves on the opposite bank of the river. The Australians also faced the newly arrived 18th Division and were again outflanked by an amphibious operation. The entire time, even with 52 new Hurricanes present, the Japanese commanded the air, which meant that movement of Allied troops was largely limited to night marches. With this final position turned, the British were forced to retreat into Singapore itself. In the process the commander of the 9th Indian Division was killed in an ambush. Worse still, the entire 22nd and 45th Indian brigades were destroyed through aggressive Japanese advances before the only causeway connecting Singapore to the mainland was blown up on 31 January.

Singapore normally held 550,000 people in 1941, but by February of 1942, due to refugees the population had swelled to over 1,000,000 people. The island is 220 square miles, and has 70 miles of coastline. The distance from the island to the mainland varies from 600 yards to 5,000 yards, but troops had to be posted all around the island with the Japanese having mastery of the sea. Most of the heavy guns set up for coast defense between 1934 and 1941 were incapable of firing towards the mainland, and could only aid in defense against heavy warships at sea. The Japanese did not need such warships so the guns were of little value.

Present on the island were 21 Indian battalions, 13 British battalions, six Australian battalions, two Malayan battalions, and three volunteer units of Singapore volunteers. There were also two British and one Australian machine gun battalion and one reconnaissance battalion. These faced 27 battalions of the three Japanese divisions. Training and strength varied radically from unit to unit, especially among the allied units.

Over the next few days, artillery bombarded the Allied positions and the Japanese launched three air attacks against Singapore a day. Virtually all remaining Allied air units were withdrawn from Malaya. The befuddled Percival further exacerbated his doomed situation when he made the wrong guess as to where the main Japanese attack would come from. The Japanese set up a feint with the Guard to the east, while they attacked with the 18th and the 5th divisions in the west. The deception worked.

On the evening of 8 February, the Japanese, with 440 guns and 200 rounds per gun opened fire and using 100 motorboats and 200 collapsible launches invaded the island. Some 4,000 men were in the first wave and by the morning of the 9th most of the 5th and the 18th were on the island. The attack fell against the 8th Australian and weak 44th Indian Brigade and they simply were too few to stem the Japanese tide. The Japanese continued pushing and by the 14th had reopened the causeway and been joined by the Imperial Guard. The Japanese were starting to run low on artillery shells and the British resistance, especially their artillery, was taking its toll. One Japanese staff officer was concerned that it would be themselves and not the British who might have to surrender!

Percival met his lieutenants in a conference to discuss the ever darkening situation. The British commander wanted to continue the fight, but his subordinates, including Bennett, felt that the troops were worn out and surrender was the best course to be adopted. In the following exchange, Percival stated, "There are other things to consider. I have my honour to consider and there is also the question of what posterity will think of us if we surrender this large Army and valuable fortress."

General Heath retorted, "You need not bother about your honour. You lost that a long time ago up in the North (of Malaya)."

Still wanting to continue the fight, Percival gave orders to do so, but by the 15th recognized that the large civilian population was suffering, especially from lack of water. Food reserves were down to two days.

A cease fire was arranged for on 15 February. The British were to surrender unconditionally.

The total number of Commonwealth troops surrendered numbered around 138,708: about 67,700 Indians, 38,500 British, and 18,500 Australians were captured. The Japanese victory produced a tremendous amount of war booty including about 630 field artillery pieces, 54 fortress guns (some would be later used at Tarawa), 1,800 trucks, over 3,000 machine guns and much more. So not only did the Japanese get the help of "Churchill rations," but in the end they took most of the British equipment. The Japanese suffered 9,656 killed or wounded in the campaign in fighting that averaged about two engagements a day and advances that averaged about 14 miles a day, largely on foot and bicycle. The Japanese also repaired an average of five bridges a day during their advance.

For Britain, the fall of Singapore coincided with the famous "Channel Dash" in which two large Nazi warships with an escort successfully raced from ports in France up the English Channel to safety in Germany. Parliament was upset and there were calls for a shake-up in the war cabinet. Interestingly enough, considering that capitulation of Singapore was the greatest surrender of troops in the history of the British Empire, there never was a formal inquiry as to why this disaster occurred, in marked contrast to the congressional hearings on the Pearl Harbor defeat.

The Emperor of Japan, Hirohito, wrote of the victory,

> Our army and navy working in close cooperation in Malaya, have resolutely carried out difficult maritime escort tasks, transport duties and landing operations, and in the teeth of tropical diseases, and enduring intense heat, they have harried and hunted a strong enemy and broken through his defenses at every point, capturing Singapore with the speed of the gods, and destroying Great Britain's base in East Asia.
>
> We express our profound esteem for these deeds.

The Emperor thereupon renamed Singapore "Shonan" or "the radiant South." The first three days after the fall of Singapore Japanese Kempei Tai military police, with the aid of two battalions of infantry from the 5th Division, entered the city and large numbers of Chinese residents were taken, and many of them executed. Their alleged crime was supporting Nationalist China in its ongoing war with Japan. It is interesting to note that the numerous acts of brutality by the Japanese in this campaign, and later towards the prisoners, are virtually ignored in the Japanese Official History of the war. It is as if by not mentioning or addressing these immoral and illegal acts, they did not exist. Ironically, Japanese conduct towards Russian prisoners in the Russo-Japanese war of 1904-05 was quite good, but the war prior to that, the Sino-Japanese War of 1894-95 also witnessed numerous atrocities by the Japanese against the Chinese. What made World War II different? Was it because the enemy were morally inferior in Japanese eyes and thus it was acceptable to brutalize the enemy, even if they were helpless prisoners? Has it something to do with the psychological theory that a repressed people loosen their discipline once outside their own society? How does such behavior contrast with the American and British strategic bombing policy of annihilating entire cities, such as Hamburg, Osaka and Nagasaki?

There are many reasons for the British disaster at Singapore. First was the fact that the British underestimated their Japanese enemy. Furthermore, the troops defending Malaya were poorly trained, poorly equipped and poorly led. Secondly, proper fortifications were never built. Almost £40,000 of the funds allocated for the construction of defenses in 1939 were never spent, a fact not even known to Percival! The bridges should have been more adequately prepared for demolition and fortifications improved before 7 December 1941. One of the top British Engineer officers on the scene suggested this course of action, but it was never implemented properly. Thirdly, racism on the part of the British was obvious to the people of Malaya. Indian officers, even with the same rank as white officers, rode in different train cars by law. When Penang was lost only Europeans were actively evacuated; the local Indian, Malay, and Chinese populations were ignored and left to the invaders. This problem affected the labor troops as well. If properly exploited, the native population of Malaya could have been used for preparing fortifications, but wages were grossly low. Pay was allocated on a basis of race, (Tamil Indians were paid less than Chinese, etc.) thus laborers were difficult to find. It should be noted that 25,000 of the 67,000 captured Indian troops joined the Indian National Army, a Japanese puppet organization set up to fight the Allies on the Indian border with Burma later in World War II.

CHAPTER VII

The Fall of Guam, Rabaul, and Wake

7 December 1941 - 24 January 1942

*A*fter the bombing of Pearl Harbor, the Japanese unleashed a tremendous offensive against the woefully unprepared Allied possessions in the Pacific. The American possession of Guam fell easily to the Japanese. A physically large island, lacking an adequate garrison, virtually unfortified due to the provisions of the Washington Treaty of 1922, Guam was struck from the air on 7 December 1941. The Nankai or South Sea Detachment made up of the I, II, and III battalions of the 144th Regiment (detached from the 55th Division), reinforced with one battalion of mountain artillery, and a company each of cavalry, engineers, transport troops and field anti-aircraft, took the island on 10 December.

From Guam, this same Japanese force left for Rabaul, escorted by a minelayer division on 14 December. Distant cover was provided by four fleet carriers (*Akagi*, *Kaga*, *Shokaku*, and *Zuikaku*, escorted by two fast battleships, two cruisers, and seven destroyers) returning from the Pearl raid. The South Sea Detachment, commanded by the slight, balding Major General Tomitaro Horii, numbered 4,886 men and officers. At Rabaul, approximately 1,600 Australians, who knew they were unsupported, with meager coast defense and air defense at their disposal suffered air attacks while waiting for the Japanese invasion.

On the evening of 23 January 1942, the Japanese landed at Rabaul and all key points fell quickly. The garrison of the 2/22nd Battalion of the Australian 23rd Brigade, with a small number of men from the New Guinea Volunteer Rifles achieved one small check against a Japanese landing force. The enemy came ashore talking, laughing, striking matches, and at one point showing a flashlight and moved directly into a wired ambush complete with Vickers machine guns. But eventually this position was outflanked and overwhelming numbers took Rabaul. Kavieng, across from Rabaul on New Ireland, fell the following day to about half of the 2nd Maizuru Special Naval Landing Force (500 troops). This unit had been picked up at Truk earlier. The following day the rest of the Maizuru and all of the Kashima Special Naval Landing Force consolidated the position at Kavieng.

The Special Naval Landing Force (SNLF) were Japanese equivalent to U.S. Marines. Physically large and tall men were recruited for this service and they were trained for amphibious work. Their uniforms and equipment were essentially the same as the army and varied only in their insignia. They were a dependable source of troops to the Japanese Navy that always had to contend with a competitive Japanese Army. To the best of my knowledge no adequate study of these troops as been done in the English tongue.

Thus Rabaul, one of the most magnificent harbors in the South Pacific, passed into the hands of the Japanese Empire. From this fortress base enemy task forces went forth over the remainder of 1942 and into 1943. It was never retaken by the Allies as it was not needed in the Allied leapfrogging operations of the future months.

Japanese plans for moving against New Guinea now began. The one seed left that would keep the Allied struggle alive in these waters was the establishment of the Coast Watchers. Australia had planted two commando teams of 25 men each in New Guinea and the Solomons. Over the next two years these men, along with the regular troops that took to the bush instead of surrendering, as well as much of the local native and most of the European population, developed a communications network and rescue service that was extremely valuable in aiding the Allied cause.

It was only earlier at Wake Island that Japan received her first check and American troops distinguished themselves. Wake Island is really three small atolls separated by narrow channels around a lagoon, and is far from any other significant island in the north-central Pacific Ocean. On the island was a Pan American clipper refueling site and a small military base. The main garrison consisted of about 40% of the First Defense Battalion (447 men) and 60 navy men. Coast defense guns included six 5-inch guns, twelve 3-inch guns, and some .50 and .30 caliber machine guns. The coast defense battalion was new (established in 1939) and did not have a tight organization, but did offer some resistance to small raiding forces.

The approaching Japanese force consisted of Rear Admiral Sadamichi Kajioka on his flagship the light cruiser *Yubari* (3,141 tons, six 5.5-inch guns, four 24-inch torpedoes, 35 knots, the prototype for all Japanese heavy cruisers built in the 1920s and the 1930s), with six old destroyers covering patrol craft carrying 450 special naval landing forces of the 2nd Maizuru units. Additional fire support was given by the 18th Cruiser Squadron made up of the *Tenryu* and *Tatsuta* (3,948 tons, four 5.5-inch guns, six 21-inch torpedoes, 33 knots), two sister ships that were Japan's oldest cruisers in service; definitely a second string attack. Two Maru transports carried the garrison troops for the island after occupation.

Wake was first attacked by 36 twin engine Nell bombers, of the 24th Air Flotilla, on 8 December and air attacks continued through the 10th. They destroyed seven of the few Marine Wildcat (F4F-3) fighters on the island, as well as generally inflicting damage on everything else. The Japanese thought that they had softened up the island but they were about to come to understand the old naval adage about ships not liking to attack forts.

The Japanese force approached with three light cruisers (the *Yubari* was leading the two others) followed by six destroyers. Two "Maru" merchant ships and two patrol craft in two separate groups flanked the main column. The Japanese began firing on the island at 0522 at 6,000 yards range. The Marines did not return fire and allowed the Japanese column to approach. By the start of the third pass, oil tanks were afire and the residential area under bombardment, but the hidden guns hadn't been hit, and with the range being about 3,000 yards—the Marines opened fire.

The *Yubari* came under heavy fire, but was not hit. A smokescreen was ordered as well as an immediate retirement. One of the patrol craft carrying the assault troops was hit, the engine disabled, and the boat drifted ashore. As the retirement continued one of the Marus was hit and so Kajioka ordered three of his destroyers to attack the offending 5-inch gun battery (the six 5-inch guns were divided into three separate batteries). The *Hayate, Oite,* and *Mochizuki* (each 1,720 tons, four 4.7-inch guns; first two had six 21-inch torpedoes, the latter six 24-inch torpedoes with four reloads, 37 knots) screened the Marus by charging the offending battery and making more smoke. The *Hayate,* leading the attack, was hit squarely by about six successive 5-inch rounds and blew up with no survivors, killing 168 men. She thus became the first major fighting ship lost by Japan since the start of the war. The *Oite* and *Mochizuki* retired with the former suffering some damage and 19 casualties.

The attack continued without great results (only one Marine died that day) when four remaining Wildcat fighters came into view at 0724. The Wildcats strafed the Japanese ships, which forced the final retirement of the Japanese force. The Wildcats continued to attack, shuttling between Wake's airfield to get additional ammunition, and the Japanese force, when they scored their biggest success of the morning by hitting the destroyer *Kisaragi's* depth charges setting off a tremendous explosion and sinking her with all hands (150 men).

The Japanese thus retreated minus both troops and ships—the only instance in World War II when a sea invasion was turned back by the defenders.

The American garrison sent a coded message to Pearl of the repulse of the Japanese. As was the usual procedure they included filler to throw off the enemy code breakers which established one of the great myths of the war: "Send us more Japs!"

One major "might-have-been" in the Pacific War occurred at this time: what would have happened if the American Wake Island operation had not been canceled in mid-course?

America's soul was stirred when she read that valiant Wake Island had withstood the Japanese onslaught. Coming but a few days on the heels of Pearl Harbor and disasters throughout the Pacific rim, Wake Island caught America's attention and Admiral Kimmel thought he saw an opportunity for achieving a vital victory.

A relief force was sent escorted by a task force built around the fleet carrier *Saratoga*. The *"Sara"* carried 18 Marine Buffalo fighters to the island. With them was the supply ship *Tangier*, loaded with supplies for the island. Under the worst case scenario, the *Tangier* would be run aground at Wake, permitting some supplies to get through. To cover this force was Halsey and the *Enterprise*'s task force.

Finally the *Lexington*'s task force raided Japanese-held Jaluit Island as a diversion. Afterwards, this force headed towards Wake to support the *Sara*'s task force.

Meanwhile the Japanese advanced towards Wake Island with an overwhelming force, but a force unaware of any actual American relief expedition. The invasion force had her losses replaced and was slightly strengthened. The main air support came from Admiral Abe's *Hiryu* and the *Soryu*'s carrier division led by Rear Admiral Tamon Yamaguchi, one of Japan's best and most aggressive commanders. The carriers were escorted only by the heavy cruisers *Tone* and *Chikuma* (13,320 tons, eight 8-inch guns, twelve 24-inch torpedoes, 35 knots and five scout planes), and two destroyers. A surface force under Rear Admiral Goto commanding four of the oldest Japanese heavy cruisers and three destroyers covered the invasion force by steaming to the east of Wake Island.

Admiral Kimmel was relieved in the midst of the relief of Wake by a stodgy Vice Admiral Pye, the battleship division commander. Pye remained in command until Admiral Nimitz, then in Washington D.C., could arrive in Hawaii.

Vice Admiral Fletcher, in effective command of the relief force, was never a jack rabbit on the offensive, and was constantly refueling during the operation. Delay followed delay, and the relief force was still distant from Wake Island on 23 December, when the Japanese began their landing. Worse still, Pye recalled the American Naval forces even before the invasion began. At 0500, Wake Island radioed, "The enemy is on the island.The issue is in doubt."

The island fell that evening.

CHAPTER VIII

The Fall of the Indies

23 January - 3 March 1942

The Dutch, in many ways, were the most loyal and helpful ally in that part of the world because they depended on the larger powers to protect their last major bastion of strength. They lived up to their national reputation of being a stubborn and determined people; their ships fought to the end and their soldiers battled as best they could on land. Unfortunately for the Dutch rulers of Indonesia, the native populations were not the most willing of subjects. An independence movement was alive, led by future President Sukarno, but the Dutch were largely insensitive to it. Major guerrilla warfare against the Dutch had been prevalent at the turn of the century, and memories of that conflict had not faded.

The value of the vast and populous Dutch East Indies lay in the tremendous oil wealth of the islands, primarily Borneo, divided between Britain and the Netherlands. Strategically, these islands offered a barrier for any enemy approaching from the Indian Ocean or the Australian continent. To gather intelligence about the islands, the Japanese relied on visiting ships, business operations, as well as one unusual source—a brothel catering to upper class Javanese homosexuals who were high ranking officials within the Dutch administration.

The Japanese strategy entailed several southward thrusts from bases in Southern China, Indochina, the southern Philippine Islands, and Palau. One thrust aimed towards Malaya and

British-ruled Borneo; a second thrust, down through the center towards Dutch Borneo; and the third to Celebes, with an eventual aim towards the Spice Islands. This multi-front advance allowed for the possibility of periodic checks, although Japanese strength was too overwhelming to be halted for long.

The first check, and first Allied surface action victory of the war in the Pacific occurred on 23 January in the central area as Japanese ships advanced south towards Balikpapan. Only guarded by 200 Dutch soldiers, the Japanese 56th Regimental Combat Team captured this oilfield and port easily.

Attrition started when the invasion force arrived off the port, with B-17s damaging two transports. Then the Dutch submarine *K-XVIII* came in close and torpedoed the *Tsuruga Maru*. This submarine attack caused Rear Admiral Nishimura to deploy his flagship the *Naka* (5,595 tons, seven 5.5-inch guns, eight 24-inch torpedoes, 35 knots) and ten destroyers, (*Yudachi, Harusame, Samidare, Murasame, Suzukaze, Kawakaze, Umikaze* and *Yamakaze* (1,980 tons, five 5-inch guns, eight 24-inch torpedoes, 34 knots) and the *Natsuguma* and *Minegumo* (2,370 tons, six 5-inch guns, eight 24-inch torpedoes, and 35 knots; all these destroyers carried torpedo reloads) seaward to hunt for subs. Nishimura had no warning of an approaching enemy surface force since cloudy weather kept air reconnaissance to a minimum.

As soon as war had been declared, the U.S. Asiatic Fleet had been withdrawn to the Dutch East Indies. Shortly thereafter the remaining U.S. Army Air Corps bombers in the Philippines were evacuated to the Indies as well. Rear Admiral Glassford was dispatched with the light cruisers *Boise* and *Marblehead* with the old four-pipers *John D. Ford, Parrott, Paul Jones,* and *Pope* (1,190 tons, four 4-inch guns, twelve 21-inch torpedoes, 32 knots; in 1942 these destroyers were 20 years old). Unfortunately the *Boise* struck an uncharted rock and had to return to base while the *Marblehead* developed engine trouble and could not make better than 15 knots speed, so she was unable to participate in the night attack on the Japanese anchorage. If the cruisers had been employed in the attack, they most likely would have acted as gunnery support ships for the destroyers to fall back on after the destroyers launched a torpedo attack.

So, on 14 January 1942 Commander Paul Talbot took his ships in for the first surface engagement of the U.S Navy since 1898. His orders over voice telephone were simple and direct: "Torpedo attack; hold gunfire until the 'fish' are gone; use initiative and prosecute the strike to the utmost."

The Americans attacked boldly, steaming by Japanese destroyers which did not properly identify recognition lights of the attacking American ships. At 0316, the Americans fired their first twelve torpedoes at enemy transports outlined by burning fires of the oilfields, but missed the mark. The destroyers' second advance through the transports yielded better results: three Marus were sunk by torpedoes with an assist from some gunfire. The *Ford's* gunnery officer described this part of the action as "draw-shooting at its best. As targets loomed out of the dark at ranges of 500 to 1,500 yards, we trained on and let go a salvo or two, sights set at lower limits, using the illumination from burning ships."

The *Patrol Boat No. 37* (850 tons, two 4.7-inch guns, 18 knots with stern modified to land one Daihatsu landing craft), guarding the transports along with the *No. 36* and *No. 38*, was sunk by gunfire and torpedoes from the *Pope* and *Parrott* at the end of the action. Yet, after two passes through the enemy transports, the formation of four destroyers was getting scattered, so orders were issued to head home concluding the action at 0350. A short pursuit by the *Naka, Minegumo,* and *Natsugumo* failed to catch the retiring destroyers. In the battle, one hit was scored on the *Ford,* wounding four men. Glassford signaled the returning destroyers in the morning with a "well done"!

Palembang was a key airfield and oilfield in southern Sumatra. The island, larger in land area than Japan itself, was defended by seven Dutch battalions and a depleted fighter squadron of British Hurricanes. On 14 February, the day before Singapore surrendered, the Japanese attacked with part of the 1st Raiding Regiment, 380 parachute troops. These soldiers were armed with rifle and bayonet, 30 to 40 rounds of ammo, grenades, 2-inch knee mortars, pistol and hand grenades. As a fierce battle was fought at the airfield, the Japanese convoyed the 38th Division towards a landing on the island.

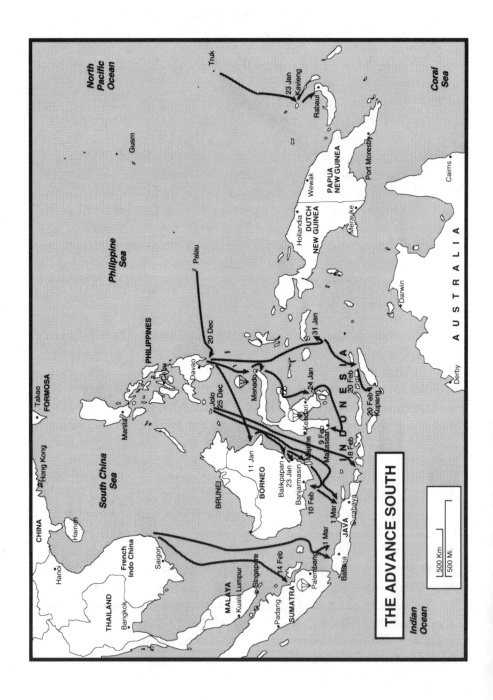

THE ADVANCE SOUTH

Vice Admiral Ozawa was covering the 38th, as well as threading his way through the vast exodus of Allied troops and civilians taking any boat possible to flee Singapore. Ozawa had the light carrier *Ryujo*, his flagship the heavy cruiser *Chokai*, the heavy cruisers *Mikuma*, *Mogami*, *Suzuya*, and *Kumano* (the latter four were sister ships, 12,400 tons, ten 8-inch guns, eight 5-inch dual purpose guns, twelve 24-inch torpedoes with reloads, and 34 knots), the old light cruiser *Yura*, and the destroyers *Shirakuma*, *Ayanami*, *Jsonami*, *Shikinami*, *Murakuma*, *Shirayuki*, and *Hatsuyuki*. Advancing towards him to engage in battle was Rear Admiral Karel Doorman, who spoke fluent English, with the light cruisers *De Ruyter*, *Java*, *Tromp*, the British heavy cruiser *Exeter* (8,390 tons, six 8-inch guns, four 4-inch anti-aircraft guns, six 21-inch torpedoes, and 32 knots), the Australian light cruiser *Hobart* (7,105 tons, eight 6-inch guns, four 4-inch anti-aircraft guns, eight 21-inch torpedoes, and 32 knots), Dutch destroyers *Banckert*, *Kortenaer*, *Van Nes*, *Van Ghent*, and the American destroyers *Bulmer*, *Barker*, *Parrott*, *Stewart*, *Pope*, and *John D. Ford* (all the American destroyers were four-pipers). After the *Van Ghent* struck an unmapped rock and sank, the *Banckert* was detached from the force to look for survivors. Faced with repeated air attacks from the *Ryujo*, with only four more hours of daylight, Doorman decided to retire and not risk a night action. While Doorman was facing a slightly superior enemy he did have the opportunity to attack and disperse an invasion convoy. Doorman himself is quoted as saying history would condemn his decision to retire. Thus an interesting "might-have-been" passes into history. Doorman lost the *Van Nes* to air attacks on the 17th of February while his force retired from action.

Meanwhile, the 38th Division completed the landing at Palembang after some delay. Southern Sumatra fell. Later, the Imperial Guard would capture northern Sumatra in a simple mopping up effort.

The Japanese began moving into high gear in the South Pacific during January with the victory at Pearl Harbor neutralizing the American threat, the campaign in Malaya going smoothly, and Imperial forces consolidating their position in the Philippines.

As a prelude to the capture of Java, the Japanese began moving south, capturing strategic positions in the outlying islands.

The eastern advance opened inauspiciously on 4 January when a surprise B-17 raid on the crowded harbor of Davao in Mindanao hit the second turret of the heavy cruiser *Myoko* with a 250-pound bomb and killed or wounded 64 men, sending her to Japan for repairs until 26 February.

During the first week in January of 1942 the Japanese began moving the 21st and 23rd Air Flotillas, both about 150 planes each, into the southern Philippine Islands. They gave proper air support for the move into Borneo and the capture of the key airfield at Menado on the north end of Celebes Island, the unusually shaped large island with the four arm-like projections in the north central section of the Dutch East Indies. The position was guarded by approximately 1,500 troops although fewer than 400 were regular troops.

The Japanese attack was in three dimensions. The invading force was covered by the 21st Air Flotilla and the Eastern Force. The attack consisted of a sea landing by the Sasebo Combined Special Naval Landing Force, which was the 1st and 2nd Sasebo. The strength of the invasion force was about 1,600 men organized into six infantry companies and two machine gun companies. The third dimension was supplied when the 1st Yokosuka was air-dropped. This paratroop unit, which started the war in Formosa, was flown in 25 Tinas (a modified Nell bomber, of which 25 were present in Formosa on 8 December 1941) in two waves. The first wave was of two companies numbering 334 men, and a second wave, re-using the same planes, of 185 men. The light machine gun company was not employed in this landing. Winds were strong and the drops were made from too high an altitude, but these Japanese Marine paratroops did siphon valuable Dutch troops away from the landing beaches.

The Allies launched a minor retaliation from the air, but the Japanese attack was simply overwhelming. By the 24th of January the airfield was being used by the 21st Air Flotilla, with two immediate effects: it cut off the Allied ability to fly air units to the Philippines and it moved the Japanese operational air radius south by 300 miles. The Japanese tactics used at Borneo

Nakajima B54 or "Kate," played a leading role at Pearl Harbor and in subsequent Japanese operations.

were repeated over the next month at Kendari on Celebes Island and at Ambon Island in the fabled Spice Islands.

The next move was a massive air raid by most of the force participating at Pearl Harbor. The target was the Australian port of Darwin in the desolate and underpopulated Northern Territories. Though Darwin had been a minor port, in early 1942 it was a vital base through which troops, planes, and supplies were funneled to the Dutch East Indies.

The Japanese decided to launch three attacks: an air raid against Darwin from four fleet carriers, the *Akagi*, *Kaga*, *Hiryu*, and *Soryu*, and supporting warships, along with two invasions, one to Timor and one to Bali, the closest large island to the west of Java, which contained an airfield for ferrying airplanes to that island.

Surprise was not secured on this attack. As the 71 Val dive bombers, 81 Kate torpedo planes armed with bombs, and 36 Zeros approached, they were sighted from a coast watcher base manned by aborigines. Still, the warning time was very limited. Unfortunately for the Australians, their only defensive aircraft were a handful of wretched Wirraways and a flight of 10 P-40s on the way through to Java. Some of the pilots had as little as 12 hours of flight time! They were "meat on the table" to the veteran Japanese Zero pilots and in the course of the raid all 10 P-40s in the flight were lost for one Zero and one Val destroyed,

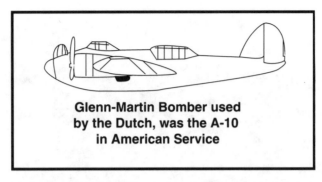

**Glenn-Martin Bomber used
by the Dutch, was the A-10
in American Service**

both to anti-aircraft fire. Captain T. Minto of the *Manunda*, a freighter at Darwin, recalls:

...the wharf was burning near its inner end; *Barossa* and *Neptuna* at the wharf both appeared to have been hit and *Neptuna* was on fire. *British Motorist*, off our bow, was sinking by the head. *Meigs* was on fire aft and sinking. *Mauna Loa* was down by the stern with her bow broken....[the] American destroyer [*Peary*] was on our port side, a solid mass of flame with burning oil all round her and what was left of the crew jumping into the burning oil. We manned our motor life-boat with four of a crew and went to their rescue and eventually picked up over thirty badly burnt and wounded men.

About 54 land based bombers roared in from Kendari and Ambon to add to the damage after the carrier planes hit Darwin. The old four-piper *Peary* was sunk, the harbor damaged, and about 250 men killed. Eight ships, including the *Peary*, were lost as well as valuable stores. The effect on morale was heavy, and even today the Australians remember this raid as the only major attack ever launched against their mainland. The Australian War Memorial at Canberra contains a special section devoted to it.

The attack against Bali was particularly aggravating as it was directly across from the eastern tip of Java. The Japanese were finding that their airbase on Celebes and Borneo suffered during the wet season, and they hoped, rightfully, that Bali would be drier so they could operate their land based aircraft close to Java and operate them more frequently. The Japanese sent in two transports carrying an infantry battalion from the 48th Division (the *Kanemura* Detachment) protected by the light cruiser *Nagara*, and the destroyers *Oshio, Asashio, Michishio, Arashio, Wak-*

aba, Hatsushimo, and *Nenohi.* The Allies, as was too often the case in this campaign, were out of position and undertaking several operations at one time. In retrospect, the Allies would have done better to have maintained a strong united naval force so that when a vulnerable Japanese convoy was sighted, their ships could proceed resolutely in an attack. As it was, Doorman had some ships on the east end of Java, some covering an aborted convoy to Timor, and a small force at Surabaya and Tjilatjap (a port on the south side of Java). He ordered the force at Surabaya (light cruisers *De Ruyter* and *Java,* the destroyers *Piet Hein, Ford,* and *Pope*) to go in first at night against the Japanese escort, followed by the Tjilatjap force of the light cruiser *Tromp* and destroyers *Stewart, Parrott, John D. Edwards,* and *Pillsbury.* Finally, a third group of eight Dutch PT-type boats went in, although they did not find any targets.

Thus came about the Battle of Badung Straits, easily one of the worst naval contests fought by the Allies in World War II. The Japanese had successfully completed their landing and were in the process of departing the waters by 19 February. Only the *Asashio* and *Oshio* (2,370 tons, six 5-inch guns, eight 24-inch torpedoes with reloads, 35 knots) were present with one Maru damaged from a bomb earlier in the day. The *De Ruyter* (6,450 tons, seven 5.9-inch guns, 32 knots) followed by the *Java* (6,670 tons, ten 5.9-inch guns arranged so only seven could fire on the broadside, 30 knots) went in first, trailed by the *Piet Hein* (1,310 tons, four 4.7-inch guns, six 21-inch torpedoes, 35 knots) a full 5,500 yards behind, and then the two American four-pipers about an equal distance behind. The Japanese destroyers opened fire, switched on searchlights, and threw starshells up for illumination. Beginning at 2300 on the 19th, both sides fired in earnest at a range of 2,200 yards with the Japanese destroyers virtually crossing the "T" of the Dutch, firing at the head of the column but lying slightly to the port of the two cruisers. The *Java* had her guns trained to port and returned fire, while the *de Ruyter* had her guns trained to starboard and did not return fire in the action. Only the *Java* received a minor hit at this point in the action. As the cruisers retired, the *Piet Hein* came into view and firing began again. At least one torpedo ripped open the *Piet Hein* at 2316 and she sank almost immediately (often incorrectly cited as due to gunfire). The *Pope* and *Ford* came up and exchanged torpedoes and gunfire with the two intrepid Japanese destroyers. Most of the fire missed, although the *Ford* suffered minor damage. The two Japanese destroyers, however, became confused and fired on each other for a few minutes before deciding that the enemy had departed.

The second phase of the battle witnessed the four American destroyers going in first with the Dutch light cruiser *Tromp* (3,350 tons, six 5.9-inch guns, six 21-inch torpedoes, 34 knots) at the rear of the line as the "heavy" to use her guns after the American destroyers fired their torpedoes. The four destroyers, steaming at 25 knots, launched 15 torpedoes at the enemy only to have all of them miss or malfunction. The two Japanese destroyers came out again to do battle. The *Stewart*, leading, saw the approaching Japanese destroyers at 0136, fired additional torpedoes and starshells, and opened gunnery fire at 0143. The *Stewart* received a direct hit on the bridge at 0146. When she swerved as a result, a near collision occurred between the *Pillsbury* and the *Parrott*. Enemy fire was so effective, and the formation now so confused, that the American destroyers did not charge the enemy transport as planned, but withdrew from the action. By now the Japanese destroyers were fully alert and proceeded to pound the *Tromp* which was using a bright blue searchlight making an easy target. The Japanese scored 11 hits on the *Tromp* while the Dutch vessel managed to hit the bridge of the *Oshio*, killing seven men. *Asashio* received minor damage in the action suffering 15 killed and wounded. But it was not over. Japanese destroyers *Michishio* and *Arashio* had returned from escort duty.

These two Japanese destroyers raced down the strait going in the opposite direction of the Allies and suddenly found themselves sandwiched between the *Edwards* and *Stewart* on one side, and the *Tromp* and *Pillsbury* on the other side. In a deadly action beginning at 0219 and lasting but a few moments, there "ensued a lightning exchange of shells, oaths, more shells, torpedoes." The *Michishio* was repeatedly hit, went dead in the water, suffering 96 killed and wounded.

Scoreboard: the island of Bali lost, *Piet Hein* lost, *Tromp* and *Stewart* going to the repair yards (the *Stewart* ended up being captured at Surabaya and served as Japanese Patrol Vessel #102 during the remainder of the war) for limited damage to the Japanese. The frustration over faulty American torpedoes continued.

Undersea warfare had drawn some blood, but not enough to stem the tide. By February the Dutch submarine force had been defanged. Of the original Dutch force of 15 submarines, only seven would survive after the Battle of the Java Sea, though they had cost the Japanese several Marus, many of them off of Malaya's east coast in December. Of America's submarine force, deployment had been difficult as the Surabaya base often did not have the right type of equipment or supplies for U.S. submarines and after 3 February, 1942 it was under regular air attack. While U.S. submarines sank one destroyer and 11 merchant ships through early March, it was at a cost of four submarines. Still, largely due to the sub force, by the end of these early operations, the Japanese had lost 220,000 tons of shipping, though only three Japanese destroyers were sunk. With a weak air force, it was now up to the surface navy to make a last stand.

The end was now near. The original plan was to move the veteran I Australian Corps, the 6th and 7th Australian Divisions, made famous in the desert fighting, to Java. The 7th would arrive first late in February and eventually be joined by the 6th. The 6th would fight in Sumatra while the 7th would deploy in Java, sandwiching the Dutch army of four regiments between them.

With a victorious Japan heading south and the fall of Singapore imminent, the Australian chief of staff, Lieutenant General Sir Vernon Sturdee, recommended to the Australian Labor Party prime minister John Curtin that I Australian Corps be returned to Australia. In addition, Curtin and Sturdee wanted the British 7th Armored Brigade, originally scheduled for Malaya and then for Java (it ended up in Burma in time for the retreat from Rangoon), and the Australian 9th Division to be returned to Australia as well. When this was cabled to Winston Churchill, a tempest ensued.

Eventually the 7th Australian was returned to Australia and assembled there in April while the 6th was detained in Ceylon for several months before going back home. The 9th remained in

Although their "best" troops were in North Africa, Australian reservists and volunteers dealt Japanese ground forces some of their first setbacks.

the Western Desert, and was replaced in Australia by the American 32nd Division.

It is interesting to speculate what might have occurred if the 7th Australian had deployed to Java. Arriving there in late February, it would have run the risk of being attacked by the superior Japanese air and naval forces. Also, the 7th was not shipped "combat loaded," that is with equipment and troops together in each ship, but in a hodge podge of various ships departing and arriving at different times. It most likely would have been destroyed on Java and would not have been present for the defense of Port Moresby later in 1942, where the Japanese received a decisive defeat in their struggle for New Guinea.

The Allies decided at some point that Java was not worth the fight. One has to feel compassion for the Dutch who fought loyally, and aided the fight in Malaya with planes and the use of bases well after that position should have been written off. In the final act, the remaining Allied ships fought the final battles in the defense of Java, first in the Battle of the Java Sea.

The Japanese plan called for two major convoys, one from the east and one from the west. As usual with Japanese strategic plans, there were several task forces at sea at the same time. Unfortunately, the Allies also split their limited naval strength. The Japanese western convoy carried the 2nd Division and 230th Infantry Regiment, while the Japanese eastern convoy carried the 48th Infantry Division (minus one battalion), and the 56th Regimental Group (the 146th Infantry Regiment, a company of armor, and the 1st battalion of the 56th Field Artillery Regiment).

Admiral Helfrich was overall commander in Java at this point. He first ordered the Western Striking Force, consisting of light cruisers *Hobart*, *Dragon*, *Danae*, and destroyers *Tenedos*, *Scout*, and *Evertsen*, formed on 21 February and operating out of Batavia (today the capital of Indonesia—Jakarta), to intercept the eastern prong of the Japanese advance. The force steamed out on the night of 26 February, and not finding the enemy it returned in the morning. The ships of the Western Striking Force were ordered out again on the 28th, to retire through Sunda Strait and fall back to Ceylon if no enemy was found. This was accomplished with the loss of the *Evertsen*. Admiral Helfrich later regretted not sending the Western Striking Force on to Rear Admiral Doorman on the morning of the 27th for if the Western Striking Force had joined up with Doorman's command for the Battle of the Java Sea, the Japanese western convoy carrying the 48th Division might have been turned back or even badly hurt. The only hope for the Allies at this point was to turn back at least one convoy to allow the Allied troops on Java to concentrate against the other Japanese beachhead.

Doorman sortied on the afternoon of 27 February. The *De Ruyter* led the column of cruisers, followed by the *Exeter*, the American heavy cruiser *Houston* (9,006 tons, nine 8-inch guns— the afterturret of three guns had been knocked out from an earlier bomb hit—four 5-inch guns, 32 knots), the Australian light cruiser *Perth*, sister ship to the *Hobart*, and the *Java*. The British destroyers *Electra*, *Encounter* (1,400 tons, four 4.7-inch guns, eight 21-inch torpedoes, 36 knots), and *Jupiter* (1,760 tons, six 4.7-inch guns, ten 21-inch torpedoes, 36 knots) screened the head of the column, while the American destroyers *John D. Edwards*, *Alden*, *John D. Ford*, and *Paul Jones* covered the rear, and the Dutch destroyers *Witte de With* and *Kortenaer* covered the flank.

The Japanese transport fleet consisting of 41 ships was disposed in two columns with 650 yards between ships and 2,000 yards between columns. It was sailing in a haphazard formation as was to be expected from merchant ship captains suddenly at war and in an organized convoy. Rear Admiral Takeo Takagi was slow in catching up to the convoy with his two heavy cruisers *Nachi* and *Haguro* (13,000 tons, ten 8-inch guns, eight 5-inch dual purpose guns, twelve 24-inch torpedoes with reloads, 33 knots), but he did launch scout planes from the heavy and light cruisers to keep the enemy in sight and to spot in the ensuing battle. Meanwhile, the escort moved to the front of the convoy and deployed for battle. Rear Admiral Raizo Tanaka, soon to become famous for the Tokyo Express off Guadalcanal, led with his flagship *Jintsu* (5,900 tons, seven 5.5-inch guns—six could bear on a broadside—eight 24-inch torpedoes, 35 knots), followed by *Yukikaze*, *Tokitsukaze*, *Amatsukaze*, and *Hatsukaze* (2,490 tons, six 5-inch guns, eight 24-inch torpedoes with reloads, 35 knots). The newer Japanese destroyers and most of the Japanese heavy cruisers were capable of reloading torpedo tubes, an operation usually lasting 20 to 25 minutes or less on the larger cruisers—a capability lacking in the Allied navies. Also, most of the Japanese light cruisers and the older destroyers carried older 24-inch torpedoes instead of the dreaded long lance. Tanaka has had his abilities rated as outstanding by American historians due to his conduct at Guadalcanal, but Japanese officers and historians rate him as only above average, feeling that outside of his specialty in destroyers, he did not show great ability.

The battle was spread over many hours and had six distinct phases. The first opened with a long range gunnery duel. Coming up in a separate column and opening fire at 1547 were the two heavy cruisers screened by the destroyers *Ushio* (leading) and *Sazanami*, *Yamakaze*, and *Kawakaze*. The scout planes launched earlier were used for spotting gunfire, but not with great effect. Finally, a third column, led by a sister ship to the *Jintsu*, came with the light cruiser *Naka* leading the *Asagumo*, *Minegumo*, *Murasame*, *Samidare*, *Harukaze*, and *Yudachi*. The destroyers in the two columns were older ones. Between 1547 and 1640 long range gunfire from the heavier ships did little damage. One 8-inch shell hit the *De Ruyter*, but failed to explode. At 1638 the *Exeter* was hit, severing a steam line, which reduced her speed to 11 knots and sent up a billowing cloud of white steam. During this time, the Japanese were busily firing torpedoes which the Allies did not know could travel great distances. The *Haguro* fired eight torpedoes at a range of 12.5 miles; the *Naka*'s column fired at ranges of 13,000 to 15,000 yards, and only gained one hit, but a critical one. The *Kortenaer* quickly sank at 1640 from the enemy torpedo—the Allies thought a mine was responsible since the Allies were not aware of the tremendous range of the long lance. The *Kortenaer*, as described by someone on *Perth* directly behind her, "capsized and dived under in a few seconds, then broke in halves." Doorman's goal of holding off the Japanese warships to allow his destroyers to get in among the enemy transports had failed. During this period of the battle the *Haguro* and *Nachi* fired 1,271 8-inch rounds, while the two Japanese light cruisers fired off 171 rounds of 5.5-inch ammunition. As was typical of daylight action in both the Pacific and Mediterranean in World War II, long range gunnery duels were almost never decisive; little damage could be done at such long ranges.

The second phase lasted about 30 minutes in which the confused Allied fleet, operating with two different languages and four nationalities, tried to get reorganized. Part of the confusion was caused by the *Exeter* which was not in complete control of her movements. The Allied fleet began to retire, pursued by the Japanese.

In the third phase the *Haguro* and *Nachi* fired at 19,000 yards on Doorman's cruisers at about 1720. It was a long range torpedo salvo which failed to score, and so the Japanese retired. Admiral Takagi had been less than exploitive of the Allied situation, and later at the Battle of the Coral Sea, he again showed a certain lack of aggressiveness. However, his 8-inch gunners had been trained to fire at ranges of over 22,000 yards, he did not want to risk a close-in action which might disable his heavy cruisers and expose his convoy to attack, and he had the secret long lance torpedoes which permitted attacks at extreme ranges.The *Jintsu* led a charge towards the smoke obscured Allied line, with the *Minegumo* and *Asagumo* closing to 6,500 yards before launching torpedoes. The smoke came from numerous Allied smokescreens and steam from the *Exeter*.

The *Encounter* and *Electra* moved to protect the *Exeter* by cutting their speed, throwing up a smokescreen and attacking the two closing Japanese destroyers. At 1730, the *Encounter* engaged the *Minegumo* in a ten minute fire fight at 3,000 yards, with virtually no damage occurring! The *Electra* hit the *Asagumo*, bringing her to a dead stop for a few minutes, but then took two direct hits, slowed, and finally sank at 1746.

Doorman did not give up and swung around one more time in hopes of damaging the nearby enemy convoy. The American four-pipers searched, but found nothing and at 1750 all enemy ships except the two Japanese destroyers *Minegumo* and *Asagumo* were out of sight.

The fourth phase opened with Doorman leading his force north, looking for the convoy. Meanwhile Takagi, knowing that Vice Admiral Takahashi with the heavy cruisers *Ashigara* and *Myoko* supported by two destroyers was near Surabaya, decided his main job was to protect the convoy and retired towards it. At 1830 both sides spotted the other again in the gathering gloom. Long range fire at 16,000 yards developed from the Japanese heavy cruisers, with the *Jintsu*'s column firing at 17,500 yards, the maximum range for her 5.5-inch guns. No damage was sustained, and the Allies turned away from the convoy.

The fifth phase opened with another northern thrust by Doorman—but with a reduced force; the Han *Jupiter* hit a Dutch mine and blew up at 2025; the four-pipers meanwhile had been ordered to return to Surabaya to refuel and pick up additional torpedoes. The *Encounter* had been detailed to pick up survivors from the *Kortenaer*, and the *Exeter* had retired from the action escorted by the *Witte de With*. So, the final advance was made by the *De Ruyter*, followed by the *Perth*, the *Houston* and the *Java*. At 2233, the *Jintsu* and its consorts steamed away from the Allies to protect the convoy leaving the *Haguro* (leading) and *Nachi* to deal with the Allies. The Japanese heavy cruisers reversed course to parallel the Allied column so that all were steaming in a northerly direction.

The cruisers exchanged fire for several minutes with neither side scoring hits. This duel was fought at 10,000 yards range. When range closed to about 8,000 feet, the *Haguro* launched four and the *Nachi* eight torpedoes. The *Java* was hit, "Instantly enveloped in hellish flames which leaped high above the bridge" and blew up. Moments later, the *De Ruyter* was hit as turned to comb the wake of the torpedoes. "Monstrous, crackling flames licked over her bridge and spread like wildfire over the ship's entire length...ammunition, detonated by the intense heat, sent white hot fragments flying into the night like demonic fireworks." Burning from end to end the *De Ruyter* would remain on fire for three hours. Admiral Doorman had the presence of mind to order the retirement of the remaining force and told them not to look for survivors. He went down with the ship. Captain Waller of the *Perth*, who now was the senior officer, withdrew. He later wrote of this decision:

I now had under my orders one undamaged 6-inch cruiser, and one 8-inch cruiser with very little ammunition and no guns aft. I had no destroyers. The force was subjected throughout the day and night operations to the most superbly organised air reconnaissance...[the Japanese] had ample destroyers to interpose between the convoy and my approach—well advertized as I knew it would be. I had therefore no hesitation in withdrawing what remained of the Striking Force.

Pursued by Takagi, Waller's force escaped in a squall.

The sixth phase took place on 1 March. The *Exeter*, after emergency repairs, the *Encounter*, and four-piper *Pope* sortied from Surabaya and fought a three hour and five minute daylight engagement with Takagi's heavy cruisers *Nachi*, *Haguro*, and Takahashi's *Ashigara*, and *Myoko*, with four destroyers. Trapped between the two groups of Japanese ships, the Allied ships were inevitably lost. The Japanese expended 35 torpedoes and 2,650 shells to sink the three Allied ships.

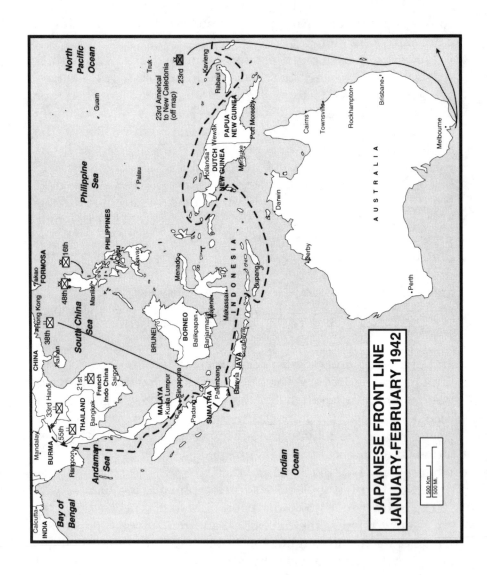

JAPANESE FRONT LINE
JANUARY-FEBRUARY 1942

The defeat of the Allies at the Battle of the Java Sea had several causes: lack of concentration and fatigue from constant operations, air attacks and enemy advances, as well as a failure to recognize the skill of the Japanese in night combat. Many of the Allied warships were older and, of course, lacked torpedoes comparable to the Japanese long lance. Lack of a common language and failure to use the navy codebook were also contributing factors. All in all, a sad day for the Allies, saved only by the bravery of the many sailors who died. It delayed the invasion for only 24 hours.

One aspect of the Battle of the Java Sea requiring discussion is the role of gunnery, for here was fought a long range gunnery duel that both sides had trained for in the inter-war period. The Japanese had the benefit of excellent spotting planes throughout most of the action (and good illumination later in the night action) and yet the number of hits at long range was minimal, and with only one major hit on the *Exeter*. *Exeter*'s own 8-inch guns suffered from a salvo spread of 500 yards at long range, and her range-finders were still poor. Nor was the *Houston* effective. In fact, it would not be until the introduction of radar that Allied long range gunnery improved. Comparing the results of ineffective Mediterranean naval actions, it would seem that, with the rare exception of a "lucky shot," long range naval gunnery failed to live up to pre-war expectations.

The four remaining four-pipers broke through Bali Straits and made it safely to Australia; the *Perth* and the *Houston*, however, decided to break through Sunda Straits, which were occupied by an entire invasion fleet numbering 56 *Marus*, two heavy cruisers, a light cruiser, and seven destroyers.

The *Perth*, with Waller aboard, led the *Houston* into Sunda Straits hoping to escape to Australia. The destroyer *Fubuki* first sighted the two Allied ships and alerted the immediate escort fleet. The problem was that the two Allied cruisers were directly opposite Bantam Bay, shaped like a bowl, with 56 Japanese transports sitting in it busily unloading. Only two destroyers, the *Hatukaze* and *Harukaze* were directly between the Allied cruisers that opened fire at any target, including the transports, that they could see. General Inamura's aide, on the Japanese aircraft transport *Akitsu Maru* (renamed *Ryujo Maru* for the operation as a ruse de guerre; 11,800 tons, twelve 75mm guns—two anti-aircraft—capable of launching, but not landing, 20 small planes like Nates, and carrying 20 Daihatsu landing craft—for this operation, it contained primarily tanks), commented on the start of the attack, "the tremendous sound of the guns...about 16 kilometers NNE of our anchorage there were two battleships continuously firing their large guns. To our left I could clearly see what appeared to be a destroyer (*Harukaze*) which was actively carrying on the fight." All the Japanese warships in the area hurried to the site of the battle while the *Perth* and *Houston* executed a wide loop, still firing at various enemy ships. As Professor Dull has written, "The *Houston* and *Perth* were now doomed to pay the price, as three Japanese cruisers and nine destroyers converged on them." The Japanese fired numerous torpedoes, as did the *Perth*, and sank four of their own transports, although three including the *Akitsu Maru* were later raised from the shallow bay and repaired.

The *Perth* was sunk trying to make her way through the straits. About midnight *Perth*'s Gunnery Officer, Lieutenant Hancox, told his captain that very little 6-inch ammunition remained, and Waller, deciding to try to force a passage through Sunda Strait ordered full speed and set course direct for Toppers Island. *Perth* had barely steadied on the course, when at five minutes past midnight, a torpedo struck on the starboard side. The report came:

Forward engine room out...speed reduced; and Waller said, "Very Good." A few minutes later Hancox told Waller that ammunition was almost expended, the turrets were firing practice shells and the 4-inch guns were reduced to star shells. Again Waller said "Very Good." A second torpedo hit under the bridge, "Christ! That's torn it...Abandon ship." Hancox asked: "Prepare to abandon ship?" "No! Abandon ship."

The 368 men who survived the sinking were treated well by the Japanese navy (as were virtually all Allied sailors in the battles around Java in 1942), although later the treatment in prison camps was different.

The *Houston* survived for an hour longer, after being hit repeatedly by shells and three torpedoes. Both her captain and second in command were lost. In all, 87 torpedoes were launched at the two ships. However, the Japanese had suffered losses as well. The aide on the *Akitsu Maru* noted that when shells came their way "the facial expression of the soldiers changed to anxiety." Later, when the *Akitsu Maru* went down the commander in chief of the 16th Army and staff had to swim to shore. Imamura's aide found him "sitting on a pile of bamboo about a hundred meters away. Dispiritedly I limped over to him and congratulated him on the successful landing. I looked around me. Everyone had a black face (with fuel oil) including the commander."

On 27 February, the old American aircraft carrier, the *Langely*, rebuilt from a collier in World War I, was heading for Tjilatjap with 32 P-40s. She was caught by land based bombers operated by the Japanese navy. Five hits were scored and she was lost.

Java would fall in a few days. There was little more that could be done. The Japanese came ashore at each end of the island and simply overwhelmed the Dutch army, stiffened by some small Allied units, including some American artillery units. One Dutch native regiment of infantry was marching on a road in the open in daylight, when it was strafed by Japanese planes, dispersing the entire unit and rendering it inoperative. The war was over in Java on 8 March.

CHAPTER IX

Burma and the Indian Ocean Raid

January - April 1942

Burma was viewed by the Japanese as a natural fortress which produced both rice and oil. It also contained the last main land route to Nationalist China, the Burma Road. Japan was determined to seize Burma, although the invasion of that isolated British colony would not be easy. The alignment of the mountain valleys and the thick jungle terrain made military movements difficult, as they ran the wrong way; general mountain ranges would have to be crossed successively.

The entire Southern Asia area was set up as a separate theater in which the Americans, British, Dutch, and Australians pooled their resources. General Wavell, who had fought against Rommel in 1941, was offered the post of Supreme Commander, and remarked upon accepting, "I have heard of men having to hold the baby, but this is twins!"

The initial forces defending Burma consisted of the 1st Burma Division made up of the 1st and 2nd Burma Brigades, and the 13th and 16th Indian Brigades. There was a lack of artillery and anti-aircraft equipment and the Indian units had been regularly "milked" of their best troops. Brigadier J.K. Jones, who commanded the 16th Indian Infantry Brigade, noted that in December, "Of the three battalions in the brigade none had been longer in it than six weeks. None of the battalions had carried out higher training of any sort during that year." The start of the

143

The Ledo Road to China in northern Burma, showing the difficult terrain encountered by both Allies and Japanese.

campaign saw 30 effective Allied planes stationed in Burma. The price of being unprepared was soon to be paid.

The Japanese invaded Burma with the 33rd Division consisting of three regiments, and the 55th Infantry Division consisting of two regiments. These two divisions shared one cavalry reconnaissance regiment (as usual with this designation, it was battalion strength) between them. The total strength of the invasion force was 35,440 men. The Burma Campaign got the leftovers from the main campaigns and really would not move

An unpredictable ally, Chiang Kai-shek nonetheless tied down large numbers of Japanese troops in China.

into high gear until January of 1942 when the 5th Air Division was transferred to the Burma front after Manila had fallen.

The Japanese began a series of night bombing attacks on the critical Allied port of Rangoon, which slowed up unloading of supplies by the local longshoremen who were scared to work under bombing attacks. Wavell directed the Burma forces to fight the Japanese as far east as possible and to retain Rangoon for as long as possible. A series of battles took place near the Sittang River in eastern Burma where the Allies suffered severe losses as the Japanese kept inflicting defeats by slipping around the Allied flanks.

At this point the Nationalist Chinese sent the 5th and 6th Chinese Armies (a Chinese army was equal to a British division in numbers). While they represented some of the better Chinese troops, including even motor transport, some of the Chinese troops were without proper equipment such as rifles. Additional reinforcements included two Indian brigades and the 7th Armored Brigade Group. The Japanese kept advancing and reinforcing their advantage in the air with the additional units available after the fall of the Dutch East Indies. During late March and early April most of the 18th and the 56th Infantry Divisions landed at Rangoon which had fallen on 8 March.

At this point it became an impossible situation for the Allies and a steady Japanese advance brought the fall of Mandalay on 30 April. By May, Japanese troops were on the border with India which now faced her most dangerous hour.

Also in early spring, the Japanese raided targets in the Bay of Bengal with two forces. The main strike force, under Vice Admiral Nagumo, consisted of the four fast battleships of the *Kongo* class protecting five fleet carriers. They were the *Akagi*, *Hiryu*, *Soryu*, *Shokaku*, and *Zuikaku* (the *Kaga* was in Japan). A smaller force made up of the light carrier *Ryujo*, six cruisers, and four destroyers raided the Bengal coast inflicting tremendous damage and even worse panic. Sea movement on this coast, in what today is Bangladesh, came to a standstill for many months leading indirectly to the starvation of hundreds of thousands in 1943.

Unfortunately, the Royal Navy lacked an adequate force to contend with this new Japanese onslaught. After the destruction of Force Z, the British were forced to fall back on a sea strategy they seldom used. They had to operate their Eastern Fleet as a "fleet-in-being," that is, they had to maintain some sort of reasonable strength in that theater that would appear to the Japanese as a threat. But that same fleet had to keep from engaging in combat except in the most favorable circumstances, for if it were lost, there would not be an adequate naval force to stop the continued Japanese advance. Going hand and hand with this was the conviction that Ceylon had to be defended to the utmost.

The new commander was Vice Admiral James Somerville, a flyer who regularly went up from the carriers previously based at Gibraltar, but was now stationed in the Indian Ocean. Having recently seen a well trained air crew on the fleet carrier *Ark Royal*, Somerville was disappointed in the newer *Formidable* and *Indomitable*. In his view, they were just not adequately maintained and their air crews were poorly trained. Fortunately, after Churchill's interference with the role of Force Z and its subsequent destruction, Somerville received only limited prodding from the prime minister, who was a forceful man who wanted his fleets to be constantly doing something, even when they should have been concentrating on training and staying alive.

Somerville could field the battleship *Warspite*, a modernized World War I vessel that had fought at Jutland. Armed with eight 15-inch guns, it could steam at about 24 knots. The other battleships of his force, *Resolution*, *Ramillies*, *Royal Sovereign*, and *Revenge*, were extremely poor World War I specimens that could only steam at 20 knots and were armed with eight 15-inch guns. The only way Somerville could hope to take the Japanese fleet was in a night action or by launching a surprise night air attack. The British admiral did have one ace up his sleeve in the form of a secret naval base at Addu Atoll in the extreme southern portion of the Maldive Islands which the Japanese never discovered. Due to the differences in speed between his units, Somerville divided his fleet into two separate units. One was his fast squadron containing the two fleet carriers and the *Warspite*, while the slower squadron contained the old battleships.

When intelligence sources alerted Somerville that the Japanese were coming, he deployed his forces to the sea on 2 April. Unfortunately, after two days of patrolling, he canceled the operation, thinking that Nagumo had abandoned his attack. Two heavy cruisers, the *Cornwall* and *Dorsetshire* (9,900 tons, eight 8-inch guns, four 4-inch anti-aircraft guns, eight 21-inch torpedoes, 32 knots) were ordered to Ceylon where the old light carrier *Hermes* and some minor craft were milling about Ceylon, when the Japanese struck.

The capital of Ceylon, the port city of Colombo, was hit at dawn on 5 April by 315 planes. Radar gave early warning of the attack and the Japanese planes that were concentrating on the port installations got into a real dogfight with 36 Hurricanes and 6 Fulmar fighters. Fifteen Hurricanes and four Fulmars were lost for the loss of one Zero, but six Val dive bombers were shot down as well. A flight of six Swordfish torpedo planes redeploying from Trimcomalee to Colombo came through during the air raid and all were destroyed. The destroyer *Tenedos* was finally sunk in Colombo harbor. However, Nagumo had failed to catch and destroy the British fleet.

Nagumo did find the two heavy cruisers, though, and they were attacked by 53 Val dive bombers. With no combat air patrol and caught on a clear day, the *Cornwall* and *Dorsetshire* were massacred. Diving from 12,000 feet to a 1,000 foot release point, the Vals scored eight hits on the *Cornwall* and put her under in eight minutes. The *Dorsetshire* was hit, but it was the numerous near misses which literally lifted the ship out of the water, destroyed the integrity of the hull and sank it by 1400. The main British force was just 84 miles away when this slaughter took place. Records state that 422 died in the attack and no Japanese planes were lost.

Nagumo took his force away for two days, still groping for the British fleet, then reversed course and sped in for a raid on Trimcomalee, on the other side of Ceylon from Colombo. An attack was launched on the port at dawn on 9 April 1942. It was made up of Kates and Zeros, as Nagumo wanted to hold back the Vals in case the British fleet was discovered. Twenty-two Hurricanes and Fulmars rose to shoot down three Zeros and one Kate. One pilot of a Fulmar commented later on the Zero, "the Fulmar was far too slow for these little bastards, who could turn on a sixpence, pull up into a stall, do a roll off the top, and cock ten thousand devils of a snook at you." Eight Hurricanes and three Fulmars were destroyed during the aerial battle. The damage rendered at Trimcomalee was quite deadly with one Kate blowing up the bomb storage dump while an additional Kate was lost. What was significant was that every raid cost the

Japanese planes, and more importantly, valuable air crews. Attrition was slowly taking a toll on the elite Japanese pilots.

After Nagumo's scout planes sighted the light carrier *Hermes* and destroyer *Vampire*, he attacked with 85 Vals. As a British naval officer commented on the attack, it "was carried out perfectly, relentlessly and quite fearlessly, and was exactly like a highly organized deck display. The aircraft peeled off in threes diving straight down on the ship out of the sun." The *Hermes* was hit 40 times by British count and sank within 20 minutes. The *Vampire* was also disposed of. The awesome ability of the Japanese pilots at this point was probably never surpassed in the course of the war.

Somerville had deployed his slow division back to covering convoys in the Indian Ocean and tried to ambush the Japanese, coming close (or possibly close to his own destruction), but failed to get a blow in after the action. The situation was bleak and Somerville did not know if the Japanese were going to return or not. He commented that he could;

> do nothing now to help Ceylon—they have practically no air force left so it looks to me as if the Japs can walk in any time they like. It really looks as if we might lose India just for the sake of a handful of aircraft and one or two decent ships.

But the Americans were busily bombing Tokyo with the Doolittle Raid and Yamamoto was planning for a decisive battle against the remnants of the U.S. Pacific fleet. India was saved although it faced a final shot from the Japanese in 1944 from their offensive against Imphal. Japan would get Burma, but nothing more. Some scholars believe that if the Japanese had mounted their major effort then in the Indian Ocean Basin that the British could have been knocked out of the war and the Axis powers of East and West could have linked up somewhere between the Middle East and India. Erich Raeder, the commander-in-chief of the German navy hoped for just such a course, but it was not to be.

CHAPTER X

The Early Carrier Raids

1 February - 17 April

By early 1942 the Pacific Fleet had seen the fall of Wake Island and the arrival of Admiral Nimitz, with Admiral Kimmel departing for a fate he did not fully deserve as the scapegoat for the Pearl Harbor disaster. The Southern Resource Area was still battling on against the Japanese onslaught, but the end in Southeast Asia seemed inevitable, given the strength of the Japanese and the weakness of the Allies in that theater. But the Americans did have a large surface navy, even minus the battleship line, and she still had her fleet carriers. Admiral King, commander of the entire navy, summed up the situation nicely in a letter to Secretary of the Navy Frank Knox, dated 8 February, "The 'defensive-offensive' may be paraphrased as 'hold what you've got and hit them when you can,' the hitting to be done, not only by seizing opportunities, but making them."

The first decision to hit the Japanese resulted from America'a commitment to protect Australia and New Zealand. It was impractical for Great Britain to shift enough forces to the South Pacific at that time, given her commitments to Europe, which entailed reinforcements from American land, air and sea forces to various strategic islands in the South Pacific. Such garrisoned bases would protect Australia and New Zealand from the Japanese and would provide a springboard from which the Allies could launch a counterattack later against Japan.

The most important contribution from the U.S. Navy at this early stage of the war was a carrier task force raid in the South Pacific. It was ordered by Admiral King and carried out by Admiral Nimitz. But before the arrival of this force in the South Pacific, the first successful American carrier raids in the Central Pacific were made.

Vice Admiral Wilson Brown and Vice Admiral William F. Halsey commanded the two carrier task forces that operated in the Pacific at this time. Ideally, both should have had two fleet carriers, but until the *Hornet* arrived from the Atlantic, Brown's task force had only one carrier. Brown tried to lead a raid against occupied Wake Island in January, but a Japanese sub sank a key oil tanker for the refuelling of his task force. So it fell to Halsey to carry out the first successful carrier raid.

The first raid was against the Marshalls on 1 February by Halsey's Task Force 8, which had been covering the *Yorktown* and a major convoy to Samoa loaded with troops and supplies to garrison that key post. Halsey was ordered, with the convoy safe, to raid the Japanese occupied islands in the Central Pacific. Rear Admiral Fletcher, with the *Yorktown*, would attack the Gilberts at the same time.

The Marshall Islands are a series of atolls in the Central Pacific about half way between the Hawaiian Islands and New Guinea. These atolls, or coral islands, usually have a lagoon and little elevation. Japan gained them from Imperial Germany in 1914 when she fought for the Allied cause. Vice Admiral Shigemi Inoue, who commanded the area from Rabaul, was one of the most air minded of Japanese admirals and was noted for saying, "who commands the air commands at sea." However, the admiral was more familiar with land based air and was about to receive some unique lessons in its use and application. The Japanese had nine Nell bombers and 33 Claude fighters (648 mile range, extended 250 miles by dump tanks, 2 MGs, 270 m.p.h.) of the Chitose Air Group and the Yokohama Air Group of the 24th Air Flotilla in the area for air defense. Additional reconnaissance planes operated in the area as well. This was a small force for such a large area, but Japan could spare little to a garrison as distant as the Marshalls.

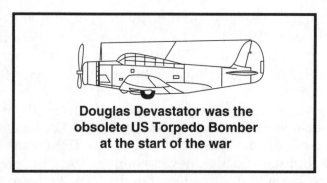

**Douglas Devastator was the
obsolete US Torpedo Bomber
at the start of the war**

As Halsey approached with the *Enterprise*, executive officer Commander Jeter, delivered a little ditty to the pilot waiting room which went:

> *An eye for an eye*
> *A tooth for a tooth*
> *This Sunday it's our turn to shoot.*
> *—Remember Pearl Harbor*

Not only would planes from the *Enterprise* get a crack at these Japanese controlled islands, but two shore bombardment groups were detached for gunnery practice. Rear Admiral Spruance had the heavy cruisers *Northampton* and *Salt Lake City* and one destroyer bombard Wotje, while the heavy cruiser *Chester*, accompanied by two destroyers, hit Taroa Island.

The *Enterprise* allocated 37 Dauntless dive bombers and nine Devastator torpedo planes (armed with bombs for horizontal bombing) with no fighter escort for Kwajalein Atoll. Wildcats armed with 100-pound bombs combined their attacks with shore bombardment groups by bombing and strafing the small islands Wotje and Taroa.

Surprise at dawn on Sunday 1 February was achieved in most of the attacks which found the harbor packed with small crafts and ships. Several Japanese ships were damaged at Kwajalein and Wotje, the principal one being the old light cruiser *Katori*. Spruance's cruisers engaged a small auxiliary gunboat (converted from a civilian craft) off Wotje in a spirited period of combat. The ship valiantly attacked the *Northampton* and *Salt Lake City* and was finally sunk in a 30 minute action with the escorting destroyer *Dunlop*. The navigator of the *Salt Lake City* remarked of the bravery and tenacity displayed by the crew of the enemy ship, "Well, if the Japs want to put up a monument to that little guy I'll contribute." It was the only Japanese ship sunk that day. American losses included four Dauntlesses lost in the Kwajalein attack.

Halsey stayed in the area most of the day, while the hornet's nest he had disturbed woke up more and more. The Japanese got an airstrike with the Nells going in on the *Chester* in the late morning, but the attack achieved nothing. The Japanese pilots wanted to rearm with torpedoes, but the torpedo depot was on Roi and the base there was too damaged. So, finally rearmed with bombs, five Nells under Lieutenant Nakai, went after the *Enterprise* about 1330.

As the Japanese Nells approached their target, they took advantage of cloud cover as well as an unconventional glide-bombing attack to get close to the *Enterprise*. The *Enterprise* had combat air patrol, the term for local fighter protection for the fleet below, with both fighters flying high and Dauntless dive bombers flying low to defend against attacking torpedo planes. Yet IFF (Identification-Friend or Foe) had not been installed yet, and with such a small strike mixed with returning friendly planes, it was difficult for the air patrol to achieve much against the incoming Japanese strike. Finally, to add to the confusion of Nakai's attack, several guns on the Wildcats jammed!

The Nells emerged from the overcast at 6,000 feet at about 285 m.p.h. Due to the lack of experience that Halsey's force had for real battle, their anti-aircraft fire was consistently behind instead of leading the attacking planes. These big lumbering twin engine bombers released their bombs at 3,000 feet, following through to 1,500 feet, but the *Enterprise*, moving at 30 knots speed, neatly maneuvered away from any hits. But then, as the Nells flew off in formation, one turned back toward the task force. It was Nakai's plane, apparently too damaged to return to base. He had decided to crash his plane into the *Enterprise* in a daring kamikaze attack. Closer and closer, Nakai chased the running American carrier which was firing with everything she had at the approaching plane which was becoming engulfed in flames. Finally, at the last moment, the *Enterprise* managed to turn as the Nell, now with both the pilot and co-pilot dead or disabled, flew straight on into the sea. John Lundstrom has written that the right wingtip of the doomed plane, "scraped the port edge of the flight deck opposite the island and tore off the tail of (a Dauntless) whose gun was manned (by the martyr of Midway, Bruno Gaido), parked forward. The wing ripped off at the fuselage and clattered onto the deck, spraying the area with gasoline from its ruptured fuel tank." The remainder of the plane fell into the sea. Bravery in this war was not a monopoly for either side.

At 1630 in the afternoon two more Nells made an attack on the *Enterprise*, a conventional attack at 14,000 feet moving at 160 m.p.h. The 5-inch anti-aircraft guns from the fleet opened up first, while the air patrol waited for the Nells to complete their attack and move away from the anti-aircraft fire. The Nells dropped their bombs, missing, and as they turned away the waiting air patrol moved in. Commander Wade McClusky, who commanded the fighters on the *Enterprise* and was later promoted to command of the ship's Dauntless dive bombers at Midway, was in charge of this flight. Lieutenant James G. Daniels III raced up behind one of the silver twin-tailed Nells and opened up on it. The Nell caught fire and as it plunged into the ocean Daniels yelled into his radio, "Bingo! Bingo! I got one!"

The *Yorktown* attacked the newly occupied Gilberts, location of Tarawa Atoll. The loss of six planes in this operation was primarily due to overcast stormy weather. There were few worthwhile targets in the island group, and the only real damage inflicted was the destruction of two Kawanishi H6K4 flying boats known as Mavis (2,981 mile range, 3 MGs and one 20mm cannon, 211 m.p.h.). These four-engine seaplanes had a tremendous range and were incredibly large, comparable to a Catalina or PBY. A third flying boat found the *Yorktown*. It was sighted and chased in view of the entire *Yorktown* Task Force. Two Wildcats, tiny compared to this monster craft, dived on it and steadily worked it over. Flame erupted along the fuselage, and as the plane headed for the sea engulfed in flames, the executive officer of the *Yorktown*, Captain J.J. Clark yelled into the microphone, "Burn, you son-of-a-bitch, burn!" One of the

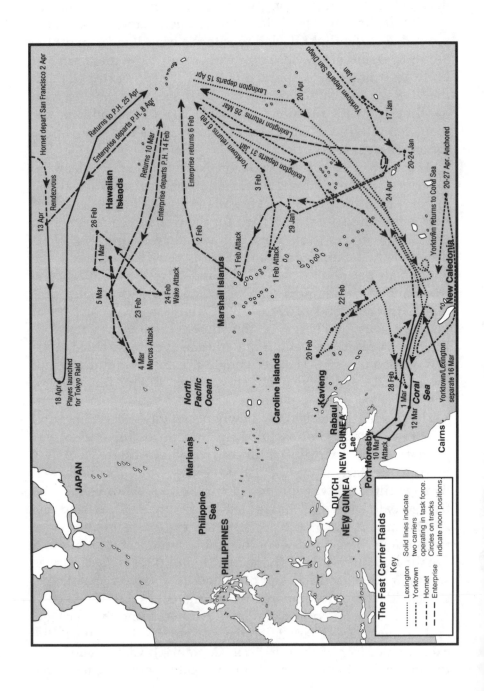

The Fast Carrier Raids

Key

.... Lexington   Solid lines indicate
----------- Yorktown   two carriers
– – – – – Hornet   operating in task force.
– — – — – Enterprise   Circles on tracks
                              indicate noon positions.

pilots who scored the victory chimed in by saying, "We just shot his ass off!"

So the first successful Allied counterattack in the Pacific had been made. The Japanese immediately responded by a sortie of four fleet carriers from Truk Lagoon, the main fleet base in the Central Pacific for the Japanese in the Caroline Islands. Fleet carriers *Shokaku* and *Zuikaku* were ordered to Japan in case of an attack there. A further 21 bombers were dispatched from Formosa to the South Pacific. Yamamoto's chief of staff Rear Admiral Matome Ugaki said of this attack, "The emphasis on our current Southern Operations (Malay, Philippines, Dutch East Indies) has left the Marshalls area with insufficient forces, so this was the enemy's opportunity and he seized it. He not only held our forces in check, but was able to obtain some significant results. This attack was 'Heaven's admonition for our shortcomings.'"

The next raid was against Rabaul by the fleet carrier *Lexington* (37,681 tons, 12 old 5-inch guns, 63 planes, 33 knots) under the command of Vice Admiral Brown. The *"Lady Lex"* and her sister ship, the *Saratoga*, were converted from battlecruiser designs that had been started but not completed in the early 1920s due to the Washington Treaty—a similar career to the Japanese carriers *Kaga* and *Akagi*. These giant vessels were quite popular in the navy, and the successful experience with them laid the foundation for the *Yorktown* class of fleet carriers. There were four heavy cruisers and ten destroyers with the *Lexington*. The plan called for an attack from the northeast of Rabaul and involved bombers from Australia hitting the island and a shore bombardment from cruisers.

The Japanese were alerted to this raid by heavy radio traffic from Pearl Harbor, which usually meant that a fleet carrier task force had departed that base. Flying boats spotted Brown's ships a full day before it was ready for an attack off Bougainville, the largest island in the Solomon chain and closest of those islands to Rabaul. Brown decided to cancel the "attack, but to fool the Japanese" so he proceeded on towards Rabaul the rest of the day and into the afternoon, but reversed course that night.

But the Japanese sent in new Betty bombers crewed by veterans who had attacked the *Prince of Wales* and *Repulse* just a few months earlier. Armed with bombs, 17 attacked the *Lady Lex* in two groups. The first group of nine went in at 11,500 feet at 195 m.p.h. The air patrol quickly knocked five down. Anti-aircraft fire was terrible, missing the Japanese by so much that it endangered the friendly air patrol. The four bombers missed with their bombs and then split up and dived for the "floor," but none from this group was to get home. Two Wildcats were lost in the encounter.

Lieutenant Commander John Thach made one kill when he realized that shooting up a Betty's fuselage killed or wounded the crew even if it did not bring the plane down. Later that day he got a second victory by firing at the fuel tanks. Thach's innovative influence on fighter tactics would prove vital in the coming months.

Meanwhile, a legend had been born. The second group of bombers came in for attack after all the Wildcats that had attacked and pursued the first group were low on ammo and fuel. Only two unused Wildcats were in position to defend the Task Force and one found that his guns were jammed. Butch O'Hare had the best aim of the fighter pilots on the *Lexington*, and his first dive into the Japanese formation nailed two. O'Hare dived low and then climbed back above the tight formation of Japanese bombers and came back down at them. He damaged a third craft which later ditched into the sea, and knocked down a fourth. Every Japanese gun in the formation was on his plane, while O'Hare's wingman with the jammed ammo belt was keeping his distance trying to get it to work again. By now the Japanese were at their bomb release point and anti-aircraft fire was exploding all around. O'Hare stayed in the thick of it. In the third pass he went for the lead plane to destroy the Japanese aim in the attack, as all planes in Japanese bomber forces released when the lead plane, which had the most skillful bombardier, dropped its bombs. O'Hare hit it, but the other four released their bombs well, but luckily missed their targets. O'Hare tried a fourth pass only to find he had run out of ammo. Still, he got three kills and damaged two planes that went down later. At the time he was credited with six kills which won him the distinction of becoming the first American Ace (five confirmed kills made one an Ace) in World War II. O'Hare became a hero later

Edward O'Hare, America's first Ace of World War II and the man for whom Chicago's airport was named.

to be immortalized when Chicago's airport was named after him.

The shock felt by the Japanese at the loss of all but two of their new planes (one was shot down on the way back by a Dauntless dive bomber on patrol) was substantial. Additional planes were ordered to move to Rabaul and the planned attack on Lae in New Guinea was delayed by almost a week, which allowed Admiral Brown to deliver his first, and only, successful port attack as a commander of a task force. It would be after Halsey's raids on Wake and Marcus Islands.

With the Japanese tied down in the Far East, the *Enterprise* raided Wake and Marcus Islands. Both are isolated atolls in the North Central Pacific. Wake was bombed by planes and bombarded by heavy cruisers on 24 February, with one plane lost, while Marcus was hit by the same task force on 4 March. Both attacks achieved little, except to stir up the Japanese and place

Doolittle's B-25s crowd the flight deck. Their psychological impact far outweighed the minor damage they inflicted.

Japan on a nationwide alert for several days. Now it was Brown's turn.

Brown's Task Force, now reinforced by the *Yorktown*, was operating in Australian waters when he learned that the Japanese were landing troops on New Guinea on the north coast of that large island. Fuel considerations would allow for operations with both fleet carriers for only a limited period of time. Originally Brown intended to raid Rabaul, but with the invasion in progress at Lae and Salamaua on the northern New Guinea

160

coast, he decided to try an audacious surprise attack from the south coast with the planes flying overland, crossing a 7,500 foot pass in the 15,000 foot Owen Stanley Mountains, then roaring down on the assembled Japanese fleet. Captain Ted Sherman of the *Lexington*, who later in the war made the rank of admiral, was key in organizing the raid.

The attack took place on 10 March. The 104 aircraft involved were 18 Wildcats, 61 Dauntless dive bombers, and 25 Devastator torpedo planes. Because of the mountain pass, there was some concern that torpedo planes could not carry their loads that high. As a result, 13 were armed with torpedoes, and the other 12 with a lighter payload of two 500-pound bombs each. The strike departed at dawn, launching about 45 miles from Port Moresby in New Guinea, the key remaining Allied base there.

The Japanese had 16 ships present of which half were transports, the rest old destroyers except for the *Kiyokawa Maru*, a seaplane tender, and one very small cruiser, the *Yubari*, the flagship of Rear Admiral Kajioka who had led the Wake invasion. There was absolutely no air opposition to the attack and it was a surprise to the Japanese who had been busy unloading the previous two days.

Firing 50 caliber slugs into an old destroyer or transport can do serious damage. Thach led the fighters on strafing runs and dummy runs. The purpose of the latter was to race in, but not firing, to draw fire on a Wildcat rather than a slower, more vulnerable dive bomber or torpedo bomber. The other planes ranged up and down in the large bay attacking ships with bombs and torpedoes. With little opposition and the element of surprise, the U.S. planes hurt the Japanese while only losing one dive bomber in the attack. Only one Japanese plane rose, a Dave, and while brave, it was quickly shot down. Two transports and the armed merchant cruiser *Kongo Maru* (8,624 tons, four 5.5-inch guns, 18 knots) were sunk while the *Kiyokawa Maru* and one other transport suffered some damage. Other minor ship damage was inflicted and 375 Japanese were killed or wounded. Admiral Ugaki wrote of this attack that "It is extremely regrettable that again the enemy was able to escape unharmed."

The fleet carriers reported that losses inflicted on the Japanese were much higher, claiming that nine ships, including two heavy cruisers sunk. Overestimating damage in attacks to the enemy was a common problem for all navies throughout the war.

The next raid was the most dramatic of the war in the Pacific and put the icing on the cake as far as Yamamoto was concerned. The Doolittle Raid on Tokyo made a strike against Midway and a decisive battle against the U.S. Navy absolutely imperative to him. Appropriately on 1 April 1942, a strange sight greeted Captain Mitscher, officers, and men of the *Hornet* while the ship was at the Alameda Naval Air Station. Some 16 B-25s with 70 officers and 130 enlisted men started loading. What were army medium bombers doing on an American Navy aircraft carrier? The next day, the task force departed and proceeded west. Target: Tokyo.

In January of 1942, Admiral King discussed with Captain Francis S. Low possible diversionary raids to capture Japanese attention. Such an attack would be the first major retaliation for Pearl Harbor. They came up with the idea of launching Army Air Corps B-25s from carriers as they had the range to carry bombs to Japan, something that the navy planes could not do. While the B-25s could not land on a carrier, they could fly from it. With the enthusiastic support of General "Hap" Arnold, the commander of the Army Air Force, an idea to fly a bombing strike against Japan from the deck of the *Hornet* was born.

The *Hornet*'s trip across the Pacific was filled with planning and preparation for the pilots and air crews, including lectures on "how to make friends and influence Japs" if captured. Since the *Hornet* could not fly off her planes (the B-25s had to remain on the flight deck throughout the trip), Vice Admiral Halsey escorted the carrier with the *Enterprise* and other vessels. Destroyers were left behind because their limited fuel capacity would not enable them to make the long trek.

After one last refueling on 17 April, the carriers and cruisers pushed towards Tokyo, only 1,000 miles away. Planes were supposed to depart 500 miles from Tokyo and attack at night, but 700 miles away the task force ran into a picket line of small craft. Thus the raid was launched 668 miles from the heart of Tokyo, where most of the planes were bound. Three of the B-25s

*A Doolittle raider takes off from the **Hornet** with but a few feet to spare.*

were sent on separate missions to individually raid Osaka, Nagoya, and Kobe.

The raids hit Japan in the early afternoon, and while targets were military in nature, some civilians were accidently killed. Little real damage was done but the real impact of the attack was psychological. Captain Mitsuo Fuchida remarked on this raid that "at 1300, *Akagi* received a report that Tokyo had been bombed...such widespread enemy action came as a distinct shock, and we in the Nagumo force did not know what to make of it." Later, after he realized that these B-25s were carrier launched, Fuchida noted, "The Americans, with characteristic Yankee boldness and ingenuity, had evidently devised a means of launching heavy land-type aircraft from carriers and had employed this new stratagem to penetrate the Japanese defenses."

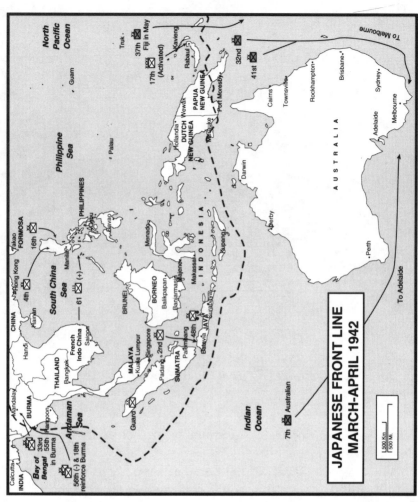

JAPANESE FRONT LINE
MARCH-APRIL 1942

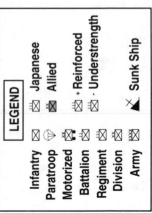

LEGEND

Infantry	⊠	Japanese	⊠
Paratroop	⟁	Allied	⊠
Motorized	⊠	+ Reinforced	⊠
Battalion	⊠	- Understrength	⊠
Regiment	⊠		
Division	⊠		
Army	⊠	Sunk Ship	⊠

Two planes failed to arrive at safe airfields or friendly areas of China, while a third landed in the Soviet Union where its crew was interned for the war. Eight prisoners were sentenced to die for killing civilians—three were killed while the other five had their sentences commuted. The more fortunate planes managed to crash land in China and eventually the crews made it to friendly havens. Colonel Doolittle later went on to command the Army Air Forces in North Africa as his reward for his daring raid.

What made this attack even more interesting, beyond the Allied propaganda value (including FDR's famous comment that the B-25s came from Shangri-la!) is the Japanese reaction to it. Doolittle's raid finally cemented the go-ahead for Operation MI. While Japanese plans for an attack against Midway (Operation MI) were well along, there were still two other schools of thought advocating further attacks against India and the physical linking up with the other Axis forces in the Indian Ocean, as well as an offensive to move down through the southwest Pacific to cut Australia off from her sea links to the West Coast of America. These were passed over for an operation which would ultimately doom the continuation of Japanese offensive operations in the Pacific.

Doolittle's raid also created a great deal of embarrassment for the Japanese army and the navy. The fighting services had an almost religious devotion to the Emperor and his safety, and an attack on Tokyo that brought danger to his person was thus a grave dereliction of duty.

What must be remembered, too, throughout this early period of the war, is that the Japanese maintained strong forces in Japan for her defense. At one point in February the aircraft carriers *Shokaku* and *Zuikaku* were in Japan, as well as the 21st Air Flotilla after her successes in Southeast Asia. The 26th Air Flotilla took over these duties after 1 April 1942. These measures were similar to the U.S.A.'s elaborate plans for defense of the West Coast in 1942, or the panicky reaction of one politician to Pearl Harbor, who advocated defense preparations in the Rocky Mountains to defend the rest of America after the West Coast fell to a Japanese advance!

CHAPTER XI

The Battle of the Coral Sea

3 - 10 May 1942

Before the decisive battle of Midway burst upon the Pacific, there was the first naval battle in history between two enemy fleets in which no surface ship came in sight of the enemy fleet. The battle was fought entirely with air units from opposing fleet carriers. The battle of the Coral Sea set the tone for many of the battles in the rest of the war. It was a curtain raiser for the battle of Midway and directly affected the fortunes of war for the South Pacific.

The immediate goal of the Japanese was to secure Port Moresby, thus completing the conquest of all of New Guinea, and move down the Solomons chain and establish an airbase in the southern portion of those islands. The importance of Port Moresby lay also in its ability to allow Allied airpower to range to and beyond Rabaul. If held by the Japanese, it would be an airbase from which Australia could be harassed. The seizure of all of the Solomons would also aid in future advances to isolate New Zealand and especially Australia. Australia was especially feared by the Japanese war planners as a potential base from which the Allies could counterattack the Japanese defensive perimeter.

The Allied goal was primarily to stop the Japanese advance. Secondly, it was to prepare bases for an advance sometime in the future. One of the key areas to be developed was the Tonga

Island chain where there was an excellent anchorage capable of holding the *entire* Allied fleet.

The Japanese plan called for reinforcing the 4th Fleet based at Rabaul with major warships, including at least one fleet carrier and launching amphibious operations against Tulagi and Guadalcanal in the Solomons and Port Moresby, with the main attack force: the ubiquitous South Sea Detachment. In the plan termed Operation MO, the Japanese hoped to seize these key positions and then move the major warships, especially the fleet carriers, back to Japan to prepare for the operation against Midway. The Japanese wanted to start the operation in early May and move their hopefully undamaged units back to Japan to be ready for operations in early June. It should be noted that the Japanese still were operating with little more than a rein-forced Army regiment and several Special Naval Landing Forces units in this part of the world, while the Allies were busily assembling divisions of infantry to hold the Japanese back.

Japanese carrier forces had three types of planes on the large fleet carriers: dive bombers, torpedo bombers, and fighters. Japanese light carriers (such as the *Shoho*, which was converted from a tanker) carried two types, fighters and either torpedoes or dive bombers. The *Shoho* was originally used only for ferrying aircraft, but was released for combat duties just before the battle of the Coral Sea.

The Val, or Japanese dive bomber (915 mile range, 3 MGs, 551-pound bombload, 240 m.p.h.) was similar to the American Dauntless. Normally 21 were carried on each carrier, three as spares, the other 18 organized into two *chutais* of nine planes each. Highly maneuverable, the Val was not as rugged as the Dauntless and also carried a smaller bombload.

The Kate, or Japanese torpedo bomber (1,237 mile range, 1 MG, 1,764-pound torpedo or bombload, 235 m.p.h.), occasion-ally used as a horizontal high-altitude bomber, was much superior to the American Devastator. The Kates had a three-man crew and were organized into six-plane chutais. As with the Val, 21 were carried on each large carrier except for the *Kaga* which carried a total of 30. An additional advantage over the Ameri-cans was the superior torpedo which allowed for release at a higher air speed (thus making the plane less vulnerable to damage or destruction just before the release point).

The Zero was the standard fighter. The normal complement was 21 planes organized into two nine-plane chutais with three spares. The Zero had a radius of about 300 miles when flying from a carrier and 500 miles when based on land. The difference was due to slower carrier flight deck operations, as well as over-water operations. A brilliantly designed highly maneuverable plane, along with all of Japan's aircraft it lacked armor and defensive protection. American pilots began using incendiary bullets to take advantage of the vulnerable fuel tanks on the Zero and other Japanese planes.

The standard Japanese fighter formation for cruising was three planes arranged as follows:

When combat was imminent they sometimes adopted a formation with 100 to 200 meters between planes looking somewhat like this, right or left echelon, with right echelon shown:

Usual Japanese fighter tactics called for the Japanese fighters to sweep down from above at the rear or side, firing at the target plane, then pulling up and away as the next plane came into the attack.

Japanese pilots were trained much differently than American pilots. Most were non-officers, i.e., enlisted men. In contrast, in the American Naval Air Corps in December of 1941, only about 13% were originally enlisted men. This was due in part to an

American law requiring naval aviators to command American carriers. Japanese training lasted about six months and the numbers graduated were quite small, which meant that it was very difficult to replace lost pilots during the war. Officers clocked about 400 hours of flying time while 254 hours was the minimum for enlisted graduates.

The big Japanese advantage at the start of the war was the combat training gained in the war against China. From 1937 on pilots received additional training through the fighting there. The extremely tough training methods of the Japanese allowed for only small numbers to be graduated from air schools. Once assigned to a frontline unit, pilots tended to remain there until killed in combat. Problems arose when an air unit took heavy losses and there were no replacements available to move directly on board a carrier. Thus, after the Battle of the Coral Sea, the *Zuikaku* had to rely on rookies straight out of school to replace lost pilots and thus could not take part in the operation against Midway.

The planes flown from the flight decks of American carriers were slightly inferior to their Japanese counterparts in some ways, but most would prove equal to the tasks required of them at Coral Sea and Midway. The early American successes in the Pacific can be credited to the Dauntless dive bomber (1345 mile range, 4 MGs, 1,200 pounds of bombs, 250 m.p.h.). Crewed by two men, this rugged plane could take a great deal of damage and was even sometimes used as a combat air patrol unit. Because of its range, it was also used for scouting purposes, although usually armed with just one 500-pound bomb in that role. The usual fleet carrier had two squadrons of Dauntless dive bombers: one was a bombing squadron while the second was designated for scouting. Almost 6,000 were built in the war years and they were given progressively more powerful engines. The SBD-3, introduced in March of 1941, had self-sealing fuel tanks, a great advantage in combat.

The Devastator torpedo plane (716 mile range, 2 MGs, 1 torpedo or 1000 pounds of bombs, 206 m.p.h.) was first built in 1937 and required a three man crew. By 1942, the Devastator was hopelessly outclassed and only 129 were built.

Devastators on board **Enterprise** *at the time of the Coral Sea engagement.*

The Wildcat fighter (770 mile range, 6 MGs, 318 m.p.h.) was not quite the equal of the Zero fighter. With self-sealing tanks introduced along with armor on the Wildcats shortly after the start of the war, the fighter could fly 816 miles at 150 m.p.h. In practical terms, that gave it a radius of action of about 200 miles; if land based, it would be about 250-300 miles. It should be noted that while the armoring was protection against the machine guns on Japanese aircraft, that same armor could not stop 20mm cannon fire from the Zero. The Wildcat pilots were well schooled in gunnery tactics, and the carrier pilots were particularly adept at firing at an acute angle to the enemy, called deflection shooting. This was a big advantage in dealing with the nimble

Zero, which only allowed time for a fleeting shot before it darted away from the slower and less maneuverable Wildcat.

The men flying the American planes ultimately made the difference between victory and defeat. The Americans primarily used officers for pilots, though Secretary of the Navy Josephus Daniels, under President Woodrow Wilson, had established a program, in 1917 allowing for enlisted men to undertake pilot training, a progressive and successful program. The majority of the fighter pilots on the *Lexington* were products of this program which gave it a unique esprit d'corps.

American pilots had received a great deal of flying time experience by the outbreak of war, though, like the Japanese, this declined as the war progressed. At the time of the battle of the Coral Sea, 27% of the fighter pilots on the fleet carriers had more than 1,000 flight hours, while 50% had 300 to 600. Unlike the Japanese, Americans pulled veteran pilots out of combat duty from time to time and rotated them back to training camps in America to impart their unique knowledge to new and upcoming trainees.

Before the development of the Thach Weave, at the time of Midway, the standard American fighter formation involved the six-plane division made up of two-plane sections. It looked something like:

The standard echelon formation was common to both navies at this time. It appeared something like:

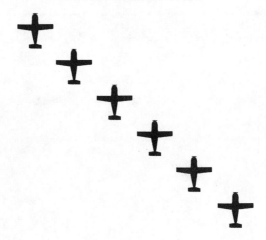

The problem faced by the American pilots was in devising a tactic that would permit combat with an enemy plane that was faster and more maneuverable than the Wildcat. The Thach Weave would eventually solve this problem.

The Japanese began Operation MO, by moving seaplane tenders and small craft into the northern and central Solomons. Seaplane operations began off of the Shortland Islands, near Bougainville in May. The purpose of these maneuvers was to extend the range of reconnaissance throughout the Coral Sea. As with so many Japanese operations, several different task forces were in motion at the same time, and the Allies usually knew in advance that the Japanese were in the vicinity. Because of the advance warning imparted by ULTRA, the Allies surprised the Japanese with an early reply and strong response to their attacks.

Action moved into second gear with Rear Admiral Shima landing an invasion force made up of part of the 3rd Kure Special Naval Landing Force at Tulagi Island, just off Guadalcanal, on the morning of 3 May. Rear Admiral Goto's warships protected this force by moving to the central Solomons. There was no opposition facing the Japanese on this island, only the growing Coastwatcher Program.

The offensive came sooner than Rear Admiral Frank Fletcher expected, and his refueling operations were not complete. The problem with fuel in this area was twofold. First, it had to be moved there by tanker. Secondly, while the larger warships

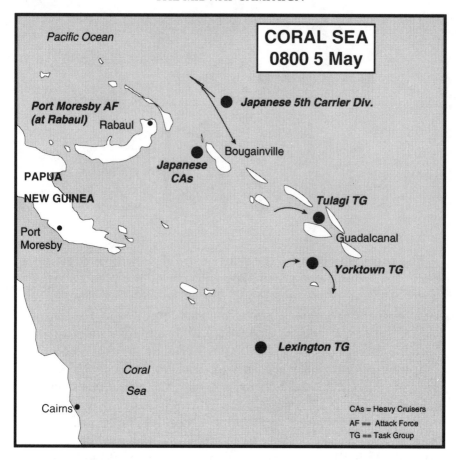

Pacific Ocean

**CORAL SEA
0800 5 May**

● *Japanese 5th Carrier Div.*

**Port Moresby AF
(at Rabaul)** Rabaul

Bougainville

● *Japanese
CAs*

PAPUA

NEW GUINEA

Tulagi TG ●

Guadalcanal

Port
Moresby

● *Yorktown TG*

● **Lexington TG**

Coral

Sea

Cairns ●

CAs = Heavy Cruisers
AF = Attack Force
TG = Task Group

could carry plenty of fuel, the destroyers used it up quickly in high speed operations. Both Fletcher and Rear Admiral Aubrey Fitch were slow in performing the refueling operation in the first days of May.

Fletcher decided upon an immediate strike, with the *York-town*, as he was unaware of the status of the *Lexington*, detached to the south to refuel though in reality capable of joining the *Yorktown*. This situation could not be clarified as radio communications would alert the enemy of the Allied presence. The *Yorktown* moved into position for a strike on the 4th, while Goto retired not expecting the Allies to attack since the island had just fallen to the Japanese. The assault was from attack planes, with no fighters, since it was unlikely the Japanese could deploy fighters that quickly to the area. The 28 dive bombers armed

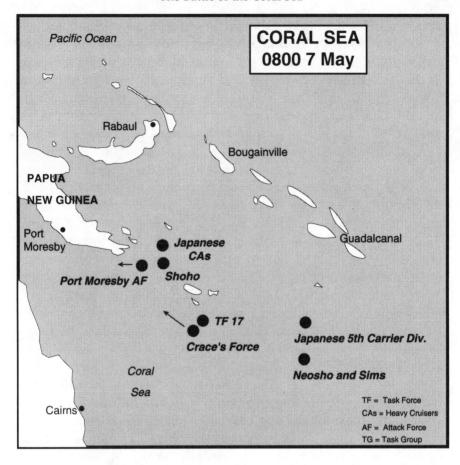

with 1,000-pound bombs and 12 Devastators laden with torpedoes went in.

At 0815 the *Yorktown*'s planes completed the sweep over
Guadalcanal's mountains and attacked a surprised, anchored,
and unloading Japanese force in clear weather. The dive bombers swooped down from 10,000 feet and should have hurt the
enemy badly, but at 7,000 feet the planes moved into a warm air
layer, which fogged the bombsights! All bombs from the dive
bombers missed. The flagship, the large minelayer *Okinoshima*
(5,000 tons, four 5.5-inch guns, 20 knots) received much of the
attention. Only one torpedo hit the fast transport *Kikuzuki* (1,913
tons, two 4.7-inch guns, six 24-inch torpedoes, 37 knots), which
sank. A second strike was ordered with 27 dive bombers and 11
torpedo planes. One group of dive bombers caught three con-

verted minesweepers near Savo Island (off Guadalcanal, and in the waters soon to be renamed Ironbottom Sound due to the tremendous number of ships sunk there); two ships were destroyed. The rest of the second strike sufficiently scared the Japanese ships and even shot down two Dave floatplanes, but missed all remaining ship targets.

Four Wildcat fighters went in afterwards and shot down three Pete floatplanes (460 mile range, 3 MGs, 230 m.p.h.) operating from the Shortlands. They also strafed the third minesweeper, the *Tama Maru*, already shaken up from the earlier attack by the dive bombers, and forced her to beach. The .50 caliber machine gun bullets could really damage a ship! Next they strafed the older destroyer *Yuzuki*, killing the captain, nine others, and wounding 20, forcing her to retire to Rabaul. A replacement destroyer was used for a later operation on 15 May for taking Nauru and Ocean islands near the Gilberts. Not a bad score! Unfortunately two Wildcats were lost when they ran out of fuel. As they approached Guadalcanal, the pilot of one, Scott McCuskey, radioed his wingmen, "Let's go native!" They were later both retrieved from the island.

A third strike by 21 dive bombers did little, though they managed to scare the flagship *Okinoshima* again. Ironically, after all this, the *Okinoshima* was sunk off Rabaul on 11 May by the submarine S-42. Obviously the pilots of the strike planes needed some target practice, and Nimitz later said that "The Tulagi operation was certainly disappointing in terms of ammunition expended to results obtained."

Fletcher retired and over the next two days completed refueling and prepared for the enemy advance. The Japanese obliged in part by moving the invasion force south from Rabaul towards the tail of New Guinea. They planned to establish a seaplane base there in the many islands present. Then, turning west, the Japanese planned to continue the advance on Port Moresby, while land based air from Lae pounded that port in preparation for the invasion. The wild card was the fleet carriers under Takagi. They were operating north of the Solomons and looped east coming around near the southern tail of the islands and then headed south, with the intention of smashing the American carrier task force.

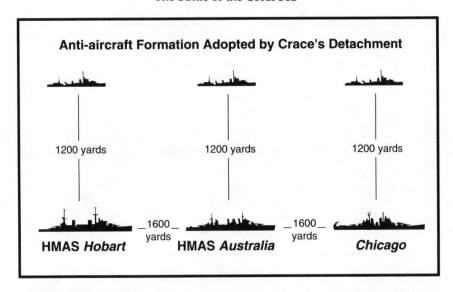

Anti-aircraft Formation Adopted by Crace's Detachment

1200 yards · 1200 yards · 1200 yards

HMAS *Hobart* — 1600 yards — HMAS *Australia* — 1600 yards — *Chicago*

Action began in earnest on the 7th of May with the detached oiler *Neosho* and escorting destroyer *Sims* retiring slowly to the south after successfully refueling the task forces. They were sighted and tracked by Japanese scout planes from the two fleet carriers. Unfortunately for everyone involved, they were reported as a carrier and a cruiser. Rear Admiral Hara, commander of the Japanese fleet carriers, accepted that report without reservation and ordered a total strike. Hara later said, "in the end it did not prove to be a fortunate decision." Hara's 5th Carrier Division launched a strike of 18 fighters, 24 torpedo planes and 36 dive bombers. It must be understood that the 5th Carrier Division was viewed by the other two Japanese fleet carrier divisions as the worst of the lot. After the battle, in which the Japanese thought they had possibly sunk both the *Lexington* and the *Yorktown*, the joke was that "Son of concubine gained a victory, so sons of legal wives should find no rival in the world." This misplaced case of optimism contributed to a bad case of Victory Disease.

Just as this strike went out, the real American task force was located to the west of the Japanese fleet carriers. But for the *Neosho* and the *Sims*, it was too late. The Japanese quickly found them, but delayed the attack while they searched for a nearby more worthwhile target. With fuel running low, they pounced on the vulnerable ships. The attack of such magnitude, even by

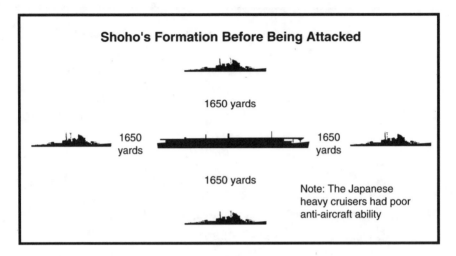

Shoho's Formation Before Being Attacked

1650 yards

1650 yards

1650 yards

1650 yards

Note: The Japanese heavy cruisers had poor anti-aircraft ability

the "son of a concubine," could only have one result. The *Sims* took three 500-pound bomb hits, and sank quickly. The *Neosho* took seven hits, including a kamikaze, and eight near misses. Yet this 8,000 ton, 553 foot long ship drifted for four days with engines knocked out before being sunk by a friendly destroyer that took off the remaining survivors. Losses were particularly heavy as the lieutenant in charge of radioing indicated the wrong location of the sinking *Sims* which delayed rescue operations.

The first American act of the day, beyond sending out scouting units at daybreak, was detaching Rear Admiral Crace's surface force to attack the invasion fleet. In this day of missed signals, the Americans located a small portion of the invasion fleet moving through the islands near the tail of New Guinea. It was erroneously coded, making Fletcher think that the Carrier Strike Force had been located. So at 0926 the *Yorktown* and the *Lexington* began launching a strike consisting of 18 Wildcats, 53 Dauntlesses, and 22 Devastators. By 1013 all planes were aloft. The torpedo planes were initially at wave top but rose to 4,000 feet, escorting fighters at 6,000 feet and dive bombers at 18,000 feet with additional escorting fighters. A textbook coordinated strike was going in.

By now the scouting pilot had reported back to the *Yorktown* and the error was corrected as best possible. Fletcher opposed the idea of calling back the strike and since the Army Air Corps had found the invasion fleet, the target would be the force going in. Ironically, the scouts had actually seen other Japanese forces in the area, not the force the navy planes would actually attack, the *Shoho* group. The strike from the *Lexington* and the *Yorktown* were the first American planes to locate the *Shoho* and her accompanying ships. Their main target was the light aircraft carriers whose air patrol was a mere one Zero and two Claudes.

The first attack was made by three Dauntlesses, the command group for the strike. All bombs missed, though one near miss literally blew five parked aircraft overboard. Next came 10 Dauntlesses of the scouting group armed with 500-pound bombs. They were to "soften" up the target while other dive bombers launched a coordinated strike with the Devastators. Two Claudes darted in and out of the diving Dauntlesses, pushing over at 12,000 feet to pull out at 2,000 feet, but the rapidly maneuvering *Shoho* avoided all hits. Doctrine called for the dive bombers to dive again at the supporting enemy ships and drop 116-pound underwing bombs. This proved impossible due to the persistence of the Japanese fighters. Contrast this with the efficiency of Japanese Vals against the *Dorsetshire* and *Cornwall* and one can get a sense of how good the Japanese training methods were.

The *Shoho* took this moment to launch three more fighters, but with the *Yorktown*'s planes also arriving, doom was upon her. The *Lexington*'s bombing Dauntlesses first scored with two 1,000-pounders hitting the *Shoho*'s poorly subdivided and unarmored decks from 2,500 feet. Lieutenant Commander Weldon Hamilton who led the group of dive bombers and scored the first hit remarked later that this was a "spectacular and convincing pageant of destruction." The torpedo planes from the *Lexington* had descended from 4,000 feet to 100 feet, dropping height for their torpedoes. They launched from both sides of the *Shoho*'s bow, and the attack paid off—five torpedo hits! Speed dropped and a list began.

The *Yorktown*'s planes went in against the sinking enemy ship. Possibly as many as 11 more bomb hits were scored and at least two more torpedo hits. The *Shoho* was the first of 12 carriers to be sunk by American airpower in the war, and the first of 20 carriers to be lost by the Japanese in the war. Lieutenant

Commander Robert E. "Bob" Dixon from the *Lexington* dive bomber group gave a prearranged signal to the carrier, "Scratch one flat top! Signed Bob."

Meanwhile Crace's force had also been attacked by 20 Nells armed with bombs, 12 Bettys armed with torpedoes and about 11 Zero fighters from Rabaul, which missed, though two sailors died and seven were wounded. Apparently four Bettys were shot down. Crace had been attacked by Allied planes as well, of Douglas MacArthur's command, though MacArthur attempted to cover up the incident by ignoring it and claiming it never happened. Crace remarked of the American Army Air Corps onslaughts, "Fortunately their bombing, in comparison with that of the Japanese formation a few moments earlier, was disgraceful." Admiral Crace, after the action, strongly advocated air support for such detached operations in the future. It should be noted that the Japanese were using new crews on the Nells which were not up to the pre-war training standards. This occurring so early in the war, with so few losses, was ominous for the future of Japan.

Admiral Fletcher was by no stretch of the imagination a brilliant admiral, but he was capable. After the return of the strike, and preparation for a second strike, Fletcher had to decide if a strike against the escorting ships of the *Shoho* was worthwhile. The Japanese escort was not important as long as the Carrier Strike Force had not been located. Weather conditions were deteriorating, and with early nightfall approaching (it was late fall in that part of the world), Fletcher decided to take a passive role and let land-based air locate the enemy.

Vice Admiral Inoue at Rabaul, learning of the loss of the *Shoho*, ordered the cruisers and destroyers escorting the transports to form a squadron for a night attack against the American surface fleet. This forced the transports to retire northward, and thus the Japanese invasion plans for Port Moresby unravelled further. To complicate matters, the Carrier Strike Force had to steam away from the American position to recover the straggling planes returning from the *Sims/Neosho* strike. Finally, the only sighting reports were of Crace's ships, and some were inaccurate, reporting the presence of carriers.

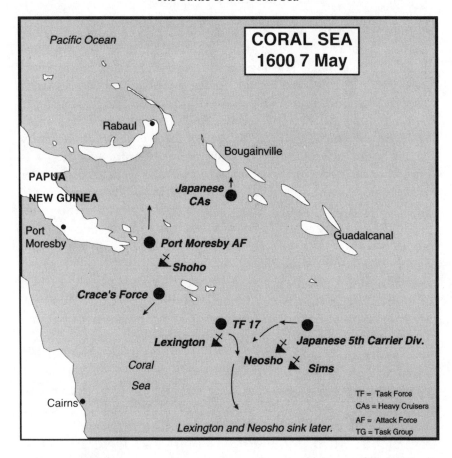

**CORAL SEA
1600 7 May**

Pacific Ocean

Rabaul

Bougainville

PAPUA

NEW GUINEA

Japanese
CAs

Port
Moresby

Port Moresby AF

Guadalcanal

Shoho

Crace's Force

TF 17

Lexington

Japanese 5th Carrier Div.

Neosho

Sims

Coral

Sea

Cairns

Lexington and Neosho sink later.

TF = Task Force
CAs = Heavy Cruisers
AF = Attack Force
TG = Task Group

The frustrated Japanese decided to gamble and launched a limited strike with their best night pilots. At 1815, 12 Vals and 15 Kates were in the air. They flew towards Crace's task force, but the *Yorktown*'s radar picked them up and the carrier's fighter director Frank F. Gill sent in four Wildcats on a long range interception. Meanwhile, the existing air patrol of eight planes was reinforced so that eventually 30 Wildcats were aloft.

The four Wildcats surprised the Japanese formation since the Japanese did not have radar on ships, let alone on planes at this stage of the war. Diving down, the lead Wildcat opened fire at 700 yards and before pulling out of its dive knocked down two Kates. One Wildcat got another confirmed kill, while another Kate was damaged. Due to rain, the Kates had closed their canopies and so their 7.7mm machine guns were not even

181

deployed. Over the next 30 minutes, Wildcats came across more isolated Japanese strike groups, primarily the Kates, and disrupted their attacks. The Japanese strike dispersed in all directions. When it finally returned to the *Zuikaku* and the *Shokaku*, seven Kates and one Val had been lost, for the loss of two Wildcats (one piloted by Leslie Knox, a native of Brisbane, Australia). Ironically, two groups of three Vals each actually slipped over the American Task Force. Confused, the Vals actually signalled the *Yorktown* to land! A Japanese pilot later wrote that, 'As the lead plane, with its flaps down and speed lowered, drifted toward the carrier deck to land, the pilot discovered the great ship ahead was an American carrier!" The Vals in question did not attack (they had dropped their bombs earlier when they thought they were heading home) and returned to their proper carrier. Another group of Vals at 2057 did the same thing with the *Lexington*! Needless to say, by this time the ships in Task Force 17 were nervous and began firing at any planes aloft, including friendly returning Wildcats. One additional Wildcat was lost that night when it was unable to find and return to the carriers.

The Japanese, with the returning strike coming back at about 2200, deployed in a unique pattern with support ships close by. Then, with the returning planes overhead, all ships switched on searchlights aimed into the sky to illuminate the carriers and facilitate safe landings, permitting all but one plane to land safely over the next two hours. At 2200 the two enemy task forces were the closest they had been all day to each other—100 miles separated them.

The morning search pattern for Task Force 17 was of 360 degrees. Normally a search pattern covered sectors up to 180 degrees since commanders usually assumed that there would be no enemies to the rear, but this was not so on the morning of 8 May in the Coral Sea.

Admiral Inoue decided to cancel his night strike, although he did order the heavy cruisers *Furutaka* and *Kinugasa* to reinforce the Carrier Striking Force. They joined up in the night and operated at the rear of the Japanese formation. Inoue also delayed the invasion of Port Moresby by two full days to 12 May. By now Admirals Takagi and Hara knew from the returning night strike where the American carriers were and could prepare for them in the morning. They, like the American admirals, also decided to scout 360 degrees early the next day.

After the early morning departure of scouting planes (most departing at 0600), the Japanese and American fleet carriers readied early morning strikes. The Japanese made use of their island based planes extensively, although the rain soaked runways on Rabaul tended to reduce the effectiveness of that base.

The big advantage that morning lay with the Japanese who were under cloud cover, while Task Force 17 was outside of the front under clear skies. However, the Americans got lucky and a Dauntless scout located the enemy force at 0820. At 0822, a Kate, piloted by First Class Petty Officer Mamoru Kanno, radioed the Carrier Strike Force, "Have sighted the enemy carriers." It appeared that a straight-up knock-down fight was about to begin.

The Japanese quickly organized a strike, under the command of Lieutenant Commander Kakuichi Takahashi, and at 0915 18 Zeros, 33 Vals and 18 Kates were on their way. Takagi ordered his Carrier Strike Force to follow his planes in at 30 knots. The decision was an error since the distance between the enemies was about 210 miles at this time, well within the range of the Japanese aircraft but practically out of range for some of the American aircraft, especially since the Devastators had notoriously short legs. Any advantage the Japanese had due to their long range aircraft was further nullified by the American decision to close with the Japanese due to the long distance of the contact made by the American scouting plane with the enemy forces.

Because of the poor atmospheric conditions, the American sighting report was not clear, but the Americans had overheard the reports of the Japanese Kate scouting Task Force 17. Though the message from the enemy plane could not be understood, Fletcher knew he did not want a strike force loaded with weapons and fuel sitting on his decks with an enemy force approaching, so a launch was ordered, despite the incomplete information. Task Force 17 dispatched 15 Wildcats, 39 Dauntlesses, and 21 Devastators, divided into two groups (the

Yorktown's strike departed 10 minutes earlier than the *Lexington*'s strike), and were on their way by 0925.

At this point in the war a strike from an American fleet carrier went in by itself as a tactical unit and was not coordinated with that from another carrier—the early departing group from the *Yorktown* went in first against the Japanese fleet.

Japanese air patrol doctrine at this point in the war was based on prewar practices. Due to the advantage of radar, the Americans could "see" an approaching strike well before it came in range for an attack, while the Japanese had to visually sight the approaching enemy. On 8 May, the Japanese maintained a small high altitude air patrol of six Zeros, one flown by an ace from the war with China. The patrol was to operate against dive bombers, while low altitude patrols operated against torpedo planes. On the decks sat reinforcing Zeros with engines warmed up and running and pilots in the cockpits. The weather helped the Carrier Strike Force by hiding it from enemy planes. When the carriers were finally discovered by the enemy, the advantage switched to the attacker because reinforcing Zeros on the deck could not rise until the enemy planes were visually sighted. If attacked from high enemy planes (such as dive bombers coming in at 17,000 feet), they would be hampered by a limited climbing ability.

The American attack was aided when the *Shokaku* was sighted in the open with the Japanese Task Force somewhat scattered due to recent landing of air patrol planes needing fuel. The *Zuikaku* was sighted, but ran under the overcast, which was probably a help to the Americans as the *Yorktown*'s strike was now concentrated against only one target (with the poor American aim displayed in these early carrier actions, it was an advantage to concentrate). Seven Zeros were launched when the *Yorktown*'s group was sighted.

Seven dive bombers went in first only to have their attacks handicapped by fogged bombsights, the same problem that plagued them during the attack at Tulagi (Nimitz's staff labeled this the "outstanding material defect" of the battle). No hits were scored, but no planes were lost, although several Dauntlesses were shot up.

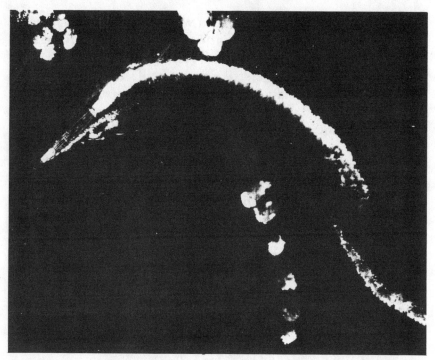

The Japanese carrier Zuikaku *proves to be elusive during the Battle of the Coral Sea.*

The remaining planes now went in with the dive bombers leading off while lumbering torpedo planes moved into position. One hit was scored forward on the *Shokaku* by a 1,000-pound bomb. Lieutenant John J. Powers earned a posthumous Medal of Honor for taking his plane down, damaged by anti-aircraft fire, to 200 feet, instead of the usual 2,000 to 1,500 feet, before releasing his 1,000-pounder. He did not survive the blast from the bomb as it tore up the deck of the *Shokaku*, putting her temporarily out of action and afire but still steaming at 34 knots (about 39 m.p.h.). Two dive bombers were lost, that of Powers and one other to a Zero.

The torpedo planes were escorted in by four Wildcats. The Wildcats were effective in occupying the Japanese air patrol, and shooting one Zero down in the process, while the torpedo planes deployed in a line abreast and went into the attack at about 125 miles an hour. Dropping point was 1,000 to 2,000 yards from the target. The attack failed to score any hits, the Japanese remark-ing afterwards that the Devastators launched "slow torpedoes [at] long range. We could turn and run away from them."

Most of the *Lexington*'s strike was unable to find the target with approximately half of the total aircraft (virtually all of the dive bombers) of the strike failing to locate the enemy carriers. Four dive bombers attacked in the teeth of 11 Zeros on air patrol. Three were lost, but one more hit was scored on the *Shokaku*. The torpedo planes attacked bravely, two launching torpedoes from 600 yards out, but though five hits were claimed, none actually scored. However, the third bomb hit sent the *Shokaku* on her way back to Japan for repairs, and during the voyage she almost capsized.

Now it was the Japanese turn. As the late Professor Paul S. Dull remarked of the incoming Japanese strike, "Despite their fewer planes (69) the Japanese had the advantage, since their air strike force had a good balance of plane types and clear idea of where the American ships were. They also had experience in battle. The American carriers fighter protection (CAP) was inadequate and poorly placed."

There were several false alarms that morning as returning scout planes triggered excitement in Task Force 17. A giant Mavis flying boat, vectored to the task force from the earlier sighting by the Kate, came, but was quickly shot down. Tension that morning continued to build. Frank F. Gill, the fighter direction officer, made some errors in his dispositions of the air patrol, including putting some Wildcats too far out at too low an altitude. Japanese torpedo planes came in at 10,000 feet and dropped down to attack, unlike American doctrine, which kept them much lower on the run in towards the target. Further, some overcast was present, and the pilots were probably, naturally, looking down for torpedo planes instead of up.

As the Japanese approached, the Kate that had been on duty watching Task Force 17 was running low on fuel and began to return to the Carrier Strike Force. She sighted the incoming Japanese strike, joined with it and flew along until the strike sighted the American fleet, then with the gratitude of all, headed back to home. That Kate, piloted by the brave Kanno, was shot down during its flight home by Wildcats in the returning American strike.

The torpedo planes went in first, dropping down from 10,000 feet to 4,000 feet. A Wildcat got one. Two more were shot down by Dauntlesses deployed on the bow of the *Lexington* as an anti-torpedo patrol, however, two Dauntlesses also went down. The Japanese came in closer, flying faster than American torpedo bombers because of their superior planes, and launched their weapons at 500 to 1,400 yards out from their target ship. The attack on the *Lexington* was assisted by the fact that the ship required 1,500 to 2,000 yards to turn a circle. The *Yorktown*, a full 100 feet shorter and a newer and lighter design, required much less room to do so, a vital consideration when several torpedoes are approaching from different angles and directions. Finally the Japanese Kates launched a proper anvil attack, calling for torpedoes coming towards the bow, on both sides. If the target ship turns one way to show its bow towards the torpedoes, it exposes its long vulnerable side to the other incoming torpedoes. Thus the *Lexington* took two torpedo hits at 1120. The *Yorktown* was luckier and managed to avoid being hit. The speed of the two ships during the actual attack was 32-33 knots.

The first torpedo hit was thought to have been the least damaging. However, one of the rooms evacuated due to gas fumes and malfunctioning ventilation had electric motors powering the Internal Communications Center, an extensive system on a large ship—these engines were left running.

The dive bombers came in the last moments of the torpedo plane attack and the escorting Zeros kept the Wildcats away from them. The rapidly maneuvering *Lexington* took only two hits, and several damaging near misses. Even the vaunted Japanese accuracy had its off days, or possibly these "sons of concubines" were not as good as the pilots on the other four fleet carriers. It is possible that the Japanese also suffered from fogged bombsights. These two hits killed and wounded many men in the anti-aircraft batteries (which got one of the attackers), but did little vital damage.

The *Yorktown* only took one hit, a 551-pound bomb that went down through four decks before exploding, so much of the damage was internal. About seven near misses shook her up, but

Escorting ships come to the aid of the stricken **Lexington.**

she survived. The Japanese reported both the *Yorktown* and the *Lexington* as being crippled and sinking. Although the Japanese flight leader, Takahashi, stayed in the area to watch the *Lexington* sink, she did not oblige him. Takahashi sent a new report in, "Cancel sinking report on *Saratoga* (The *Lexington* was of the *Saratoga* class). He, too, died on his return to the Japanese fleet carriers.

The withdrawing forces from each strike suffered losses on the way home to their respective carriers. Planes engaged in dogfights at different altitudes on the way back. The Japanese lost 19 planes directly, and 12 were so heavily damaged that they were jettisoned into the sea. American losses were equally heavy.

Things looked good for Task Force 17 until disaster struck the *Lexington* at 1247. Gas fumes from leaking fuel tanks had built up around the electric motors still running in the Internal Communication Center causing a massive explosion that ripped through the bowels of the *Lexington,* igniting fires, and sending up a cloud of smoke that almost engulfed the entire ship. The carrier was doomed. The order to abandon ship was given and performed sadly, but smartly. She continued to burn furiously and was sunk by torpedoes that evening, with her Captain, Frederick C. Sherman, being the last to leave the *"Lady Lex."*

The problem for Task Force 17 was twofold at this point. First, the *Yorktown,* with some orphan planes from the *Lexington,* many of which were damaged, had only seven torpedoes left in the magazine for the Devastators and had only 31 planes total by the afternoon of 8 May capable of forming a strike. Secondly, Fletcher had intelligence that the *Kaga* was in the enemy's lineup, a report that was seemingly confirmed when a land based scout reported another fleet carrier present. Finally, Nimitz ordered a retirement to conserve his fleet carrier strength, thinking the attack on Port Moresby had been turned back. As Nimitz said later, "inflicting damage on your enemy is no compensation for being sunk yourself."

The Carrier Strike Force had only 39 planes immediately available, most of which were Zeros. Admiral Takagi, who was not one to press home a success as shown at the Battle of the Java Sea, agreed with his orders from Inoue to retire to Truk. It should be noted that Japanese naval officers tended to be physically overweight as a rule and out of shape. This physical state may have affected their work, as several times during the war many higher Japanese officers tended not to perform their duties with vigor. Inoue issued these orders because he felt he needed more than one partially equipped fleet carrier to support the invasion fleet off Port Moresby due to Allied land based air in the area. Admiral Yamamoto was furious when he learned of this retirement. To him the failure to pursue a hurt enemy force and complete its destruction was a cardinal error in warfare. Yamamoto ordered the Carrier Striking Force to pursue the enemy, but 9 May was spent in refueling and by the 10th it was too late. Task Force 17 was gone, ending the first sea battle in history in which enemy ships did not see each other during the battle.

Although there were still officers on board when this photograph was taken, not a single crewman of the **Lexington** *was lost.*

It is difficult to assign a victor to the Battle of the Coral Sea. While the U.S. lost more tonnage than the Japanese in this battle, they did manage to halt the invasion of Port Moresby. The Americans also learned more from the battle than their adversaries; they improved their air doctrine and started the process by which more fighters would be included in the future on board fleet carriers. The Americans also improved damage control on their ships so the fate of the *Lexington* would never occur again. While the U.S. Navy lost the *Lexington*, its leaders gained valuable experience for the future. Samual Eliot Morison, chronicler of the exploits of the American navy in World War II wrote of the Battle of the Coral Sea,

> There is no greater teacher of combat that can even remotely approach the value of combat itself; call Coral Sea what you will, it was an indispensable preliminary to the great victory of Midway.

The morale value of the battle to all Allied nations, coming as it did immediately after the surrender of Corregidor, was immeasurable. Captain Sherman's statement (during the court martial always held when a ship is lost), articles by shipboard correspondents and numerous interviews with survivors printed in their home-town papers told a story of cool efficiency, relentless action, superb heroism and determination. That story of the last fight of "Lady Lex," her calm abandonment, the devotion of her crew to their ship and their captain, transcended mere history; the American people took it to their hearts and stored it up in the treasury of folk memory.

CHAPTER XII

Midway, The Turning Point

3 June - 6 June

At the time of the Battle of the Coral Sea, Admiral Nimitz wanted most of his firstline fleet carriers in the South Pacific, maintaining communication to Australia—his intelligence service indicated that the Japanese did not intend any action against the Allies in the Central Pacific. However, this was shortly to change.

A Magic intercept revealed that the Japanese were planning to launch a major assault against the island of Midway (called Operation MI). Nimitz reasoned that if Midway were reinforced and prepared to defend against such an assault that it could be repulsed. He also decided that if he could ambush the approaching Japanese forces, especially when they did not expect to encounter U.S. fleet carriers, that he could gain a favorable result: a victory that could halt the continuing Japanese advances. What Nimitz ended up gaining was a victory beyond his hopes and dreams! Still, American intelligence in Washington and Hawaii was not altogether convinced that Midway was the Japanese target. Some felt Hawaii or even the West Coast, where blackout precautions were in effect during the Midway operation, would be attacked.

Yamamoto was faced with three possible courses of action before deciding to undertake Operation MI. One was to continue attacks in the Indian Ocean with the seizure of Ceylon and a possible link-up with the European Axis forces. This option, surprisingly, had the least support within Japan's military, in part due to the view that the U.S.A. was the main enemy. Furthermore, the Japanese army wanted to commit troops to Burma, and not to Ceylon. Exercising this former option could have forced Great Britain out of the war, or at minimum turned the Indian Ocean into an Axis lake. Coming on the heels of the surrender of Singapore, the fall of Ceylon might have caused intense turmoil in India. The effect of this uproar on the British 8th Army (facing the Axis army under Rommel) in Egypt could have been catastrophic.

A second course, strongly supported by the Japanese chief of staff, was to advance through New Caledonia, Fiji, and Samoa, with the idea of cutting off Australia from the U.S.A. Yamamoto did not discount this approach, but decided to wait until after the Midway operation to pursue such an advance. The big advantage of this approach was that both Japan and the U.S. would be operating far from home bases; the operation against Midway was advantageous to the Americans because it would take place close to Hawaii but far from Japan. Further, the Japanese would have been within range of their own land-based aircraft, something they did not possess in regards to an attack on Midway. In passing it should be noted that a discussion for invading Australia was broached in early 1942. The Japanese army did not want to undertake such an operation against the Australian mainland, due to a perceived lack of troops.

The third option, the one Yamamoto wanted to adopt, was an advance against Midway. It was an operation that would include a diversionary action against Alaska and occupation of two islands in the Aleutian Island Chain. It was an offensive that would use more fuel than the Japanese fleet used in an entire year during peace time. Yamamoto perceived that by advancing against Midway, he would force the American fleet to react, as the island was a post threatening Pearl Harbor and if conquered would represent Japan's first base on the eastern side of the International Date Line. The Japanese admiral assumed that a surprise attack against Midway would bring the American fleet onto the scene within one to three days. By then the invasion would have occurred and a mighty Japanese fleet would be assembled in the area for a decisive battle with the much

Admiral Chuichi Nagumo, commander of the Japanese fleet at Midway. His pre-war career had little involvement with aircraft carriers or naval aviation.

reduced American naval forces probably with but two fleet carriers. The destruction of the American carrier force would bring America closer to the negotiating table. The point that must be made is that Yamamoto did not expect to see any American fleet carrier force until the Japanese had reduced Midway and captured it. They certainly did not expect to see the U.S. Navy in force before the landing on Midway. Still, Yamamoto told Nagumo, the commander of the Japanese fleet carriers, that half of the air units on board the fleet carriers were to be armed with anti-ship armaments (torpedoes and armor piercing bombs) and not ground attack weapons (high-explosive bombs). The violation of this directive was one of the key failures of the Japanese at Midway.

As with too many Japanese strategic plans, the plan called for complex and involved maneuvering of several fleets. The motion of these fleets in several areas of the central and northern Pacific was on a rather tight schedule.

The first move would be a submarine reconnaissance of Alaska while long-range seaplanes refueled in French Frigate Shoals (an uninhabited lagoon in the Central Pacific) from

Rear Admiral Raymond Spruance, American commander at Midway. He was able to overcome his lack of aviation experience to become one of the war's great naval commanders.

submarines for a mission to fly over Pearl Harbor to assess the situation there. A similar air operation by Japan had been performed on 3-4 March and 10 March of 1942, but had achieved little. Additional scouting operations were to be undertaken from Paramushiro (in the Kuriles), Wake, and Marcus Islands. The second move called for the Second Carrier Striking Force to launch an air raid on Dutch Harbor, on the island of Unalaska, on 3 June. This diversion was to cover a landing of 1,550 troops on Attu and Kiska. It would also throw off the American response to the main Japanese offensive. Just after that attack, the First Carrier Striking Force would bomb Midway on 4 June and stand ready to attack any American naval forces that appeared, while the Second Fleet Strike Force, covering the invasion fleet, approached Midway. Next, 1st Fleet, Battleship Division 1, would hurry to the area to help complete the destruction of the weakened American fleet. The older battleships in Battleship Division 2 sailed with the *Yamato*, eventually turning to the northeast to support the Second Carrier Strike Force in its attack against Alaska. On the 5th of June the Japanese would invade Midway with the Second Fleet Strike Force, capture it, and establish an air and seaplane base.

Japan was using all but two fleet carriers, five heavy cruisers, and ten light cruisers of their major combat ships. All in all, 113 warships and 16 submarines were involved in this operation.

Nimitz placed both Alaska and Midway on alert and rushed as many reinforcements to each area as possible. Midway received between May and early June: radar, over 20 additional anti-aircraft guns, a hodge-podge of 121 aircraft from the Army, Navy, and Marines, PT boats, five Stuart tanks, as well as two rifle companies of the Second Marine Raider Battalion. This augmented the original prewar garrison of 834 men of the Sixth Marine Defense Battalion. The problem with this force was that it was thrown together from several sources, especially the air units, and so could not be properly coordinated and, in the case of some of the pilots, included new recruits. Secondly, Midway was an extremely small island and there were, in effect, no fallback positions. It was a tiny atoll and all of it would have to be defended.

Twenty-six submarines were deployed by Nimitz although in the course of the battle of Midway they proved largely ineffective. During the battle of Midway, the sub *Nautilus* fired three torpedoes at a sinking and stationary *Kaga*, but scored only one hit and it was a dud.

Nimitz next organized his fleet carrier task force. Built around the *Enterprise* and *Hornet*, it was normally commanded by Vice Admiral Bill Halsey but he was ill with a skin disease and unable to leave the hospital. Halsey suggested his cruiser commander to replace him; a man from the gun school and not a flyer, Rear Admiral Raymond Spruance. Nimitz accepted this recommendation and so to the fore came America's most thoughtful and brilliant fighting admiral of World War II.

Spruance kept Halsey's staff together, and took orders from the commander of the other task force built around the damaged *Yorktown*, Rear Admiral Jack Fletcher, who was hurrying north after the Battle of the Coral Sea. The *Yorktown* needed a full month of repairs to reach 100% efficiency from the damage suffered at Coral Sea—as she limped into Pearl on 27 May, she was trailing an oil slick. Over the period of three days, emergency repairs, involving 1,400 workmen, were performed to put her back in the line.

Fletcher planned to use his flagship, the *Yorktown*, as both the reserve fleet carrier and the fleet carrier offering scouting duties to the other task force. The *Hornet* and the *Enterprise* were then

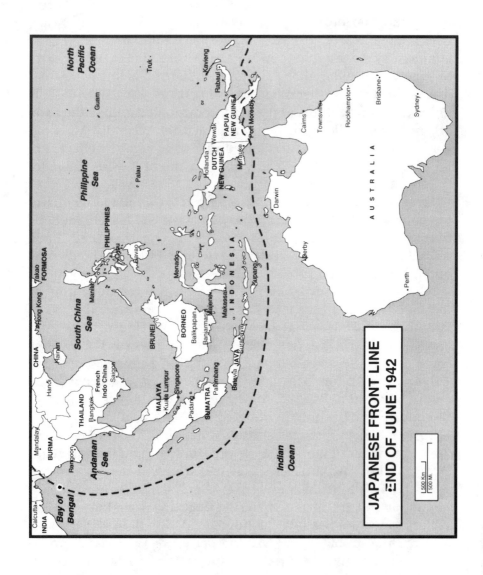

JAPANESE FRONT LINE
END OF JUNE 1942

free to launch all their planes in air strikes. Ideally, they would be in position to the northeast of Midway to launch an airstrike against the Japanese main carrier force when least expected.

Rear Admiral Robert A. Theobald was given a small surface fleet and was rushed northward to be available for possible attacks against the Japanese diversionary operations in the Aleutians.

America's battleship fleet did not participate in the Midway operation due to the Japanese battleship fleet being concentrated in the same harbor in Japan with the fleet flagship, the *Yamato*. Since no radio communications to transmit plans from the flagship *Yamato* were necessary, Nimitz did not know that the Japanese were employing all their battleship strength— He assumed it was in port. Through his intelligence, Nimitz thought that only two or four of the *Kongo* class fast battleships were being used by the Japanese in the operation. Further, since the American battleships used an incredible amount of fuel oil, Nimitz stationed the American battleship fleet in San Francisco. It did sortie during the operation, but was too distant to offer real support.

Finally, the *Salt Lake City* and seaplane tender *Tangier* were planted in the South Pacific to simulate radio traffic of an aircraft carrier task force. Surprisingly, the Japanese on the *Yamato* did not fall for this trick, but did note unusually heavy radio traffic from Pearl Harbor including much in a high priority code. There was suspicion on board the *Yamato* that an American carrier force was operating from Pearl Harbor before the Japanese struck at Midway. However, they could not alert Nagumo in the 1st Carrier Strike Force because the *Yamato* had already gone to sea and was maintaining radio silence.

On 26 May the Japanese submarines arrived at French Frigate Shoals to prepare for the launching of six seaplanes for reconnaissance. Present were the American seaplane tenders *Ballard* and *Thorton*. This, and other American air and sea activity, kept the Japanese seaplanes from their operation. ULTRA had alerted the American Navy and she had responded by this move. The first act of the unfolding drama spoke of trouble for the Japanese.

In early June, Rear Admiral Kakuta took his Second Carrier Strike Force against the Aleutians, masked by the fog, under the American air-reconnaissance and through a line of picket ships without being sighted. On 3 June 1942 Admiral Kakuta launched the first attack on schedule. He was able to send off the air attack from 165 miles away towards Dutch Harbor, believed to be the only airbase that the Americans had in the area. Due to bad weather, only the *Ryujo*'s small strike of 12 planes got through. Fine weather over Dutch Harbor did not help much as no ships were damaged and while some fuel tanks were hit, only 25 soldiers and sailors died in the attack. One Japanese plane was lost.

A second strike was launched against Commander Craig's destroyer strike force stationed near Dutch Harbor when it was sighted by a returning airplane. This force, normally nine destroyers, but only six destroyers at the time of the airstrike, was to provide direct defense of the area around Dutch Harbor. Ideally, they would attack an invasion fleet at night. Fortunately, though, the second airstrike failed to find them and lost two planes shot down, and two others heavily damaged when P-40s from a base unknown to the Japanese (Otter Point) ripped into the flight.

The Japanese carriers were only 130 miles south of Dutch Harbor and they still had not been positively sighted. That night Kakuta moved towards Adak Island, which he was to "soften up," but bad weather precluded this, so once again he moved in towards Dutch Harbor. Another strike against Dutch Harbor yielded a few more dead and a few more buildings damaged and destroyed. Meanwhile, an army airstrike finally went in against the Japanese carriers, scoring no hits, although a B-26 and a B-17 were lost. A few other planes were lost by both sides in this desultory battle, altogether a very minor operation for all involved, due in part to the bad weather.

In the course of the next few days Kakuta was called south after the disaster at Midway. Then he was ordered north, again by Yamamoto, to proceed with the capture of Kiska and Attu. Kakuta and Vice Admiral Hosogaya (the overall commander in the north) were even given additional reinforcements, the principal ones being the fleet carrier *Zuikaku*, the light carrier *Zuiho*, battleships *Kongo* and *Hiei*, as well as heavy cruisers *Myoko*, *Haguro*, *Tone*, and *Chikuma*. The campaign ended with the withdrawal of the naval units after the bloodless capture of Attu and Kiska.

An important footnote to the action in the Aleutians tells of Petty Officer Tadayoshi Koga from the *Ryujo* who had his Zero hit by one bullet, causing the oil pressure gauge to drop, though no actual fuel was being lost. Koga brought his plane down on Akutan Island in an emergency landing on an island. While the Japanese pilot did very little damage to his plane, he broke his neck during the rough landing on marshy ground. Five weeks later, Koga's Zero was sighted from the air. Shipped to San Diego by October of 1942, a full report on the Zero aided in devising tactics against the plane and pointed the way for its eclipse as the supreme fighter in the war in the Pacific.

Meanwhile during late May and early June, lumbering PBYs (also known as Catalinas) and occasional B-17s on patrol left Midway every morning searching for approaching enemy forces. In the last few days PBYs tangled with Mavis flying boats from the Japanese islands. While none were lost, several PBYs were shot up. Surprisingly, the Japanese did not seem suspicious of the increased radio traffic from Pearl and Midway, nor of the extra-long range patrols or Japanese submarine reports of extensive activity both day and night on Midway. Overconfidence brought on by the fever of victory was taking its toll.

Ensign Jack Reid, piloting a PBY on 3 June 700 miles from Midway, turned to his copilot Ensign Hardeman at 0925 and asked, "Do you see what I see?" Hardeman looked over and said, "You are damned right I do." Commander Toyama on the light cruiser *Jintsu* later recalled that on that day he was pleased that the lumbering transports were keeping station when suddenly a destroyer on the port side hoisted a signal and fired a smokeshell. There, in the distance, out of range of guns, hovered a PBY. Reid saw 27 ships and reported, erroneously, "Main Body." This led to some confusion, but Nimitz radioed his fleet that these were obviously not enemy fleet carriers, which were to the north while this sighting was from the southwest where the invasion fleet was coming after lifting anchor from Saipan. The invasion force had departed Saipan on 28 May, while

Nagumo's carrier force left Japan the day before. The carriers were hurrying east to soften up Midway before the invasion force arrived on the scene.

The Second Fleet was attacked twice that day, once by a flight of B-17s dropping bombs from great altitude—all missing—and the second from an unusual source, three PBYs out of Pearl. Along with a fourth flying boat, these planes were all armed with torpedoes and with radar to guide them home at night. Three managed to find the transports and launched an attack at 0100 on 4 June. Pushing these lumbering birds at full throttle into the midst of an enemy fleet only 50 feet off the water was quite a feat. One PBY almost broadsided an enemy destroyer! The PBYs achieved surprise and each plane launched torpedoes at about 1,000 yards at a sea of targets. A participant in the attack, Lieutenant Hibberd, remembered one crewman yelling at him, "Drop that damn thing and let's get the hell out of here!" But he held on a bit longer, released the torpedo, and heard an explosion as he roared towards home with tracer bullets peppering his plane. A torpedo hit the forward section of the tanker *Akebono Maru*, killing 13 and wounding 11. Surprisingly, the tanker was not badly hurt and could still maintain 12 to 14 knots, so she kept station and the invasion fleet plodded on.

Meantime Nagumo with the 1st Carrier Strike Force was approaching Midway Island. He was moving in under a heavy cloud cover and it was unlikely he would be sighted. Yamamoto decided that he should not report the attacks on the invasion fleet to Nagumo, so not to give its position away.

On Midway, the pilots all knew that the enemy was approaching and they would see a lot of action on the 4 June.

Normally Commander Mitsuo Fuchida would have been leading the first raid against Midway on the morning of 4 June, but he was recovering from an appendicitis operation. Lieutenant Joichi Tomonaga of the *Hiryu* was picked to lead the first wave instead and this quiet hard-drinking officer looked forward to the operation. The first strike consisted of 108 planes, 36 Vals from the *Akagi* and *Kaga*, 36 Kates from the *Hiryu* and the *Soryu*, and nine fighters from each of the four carriers. The Kates were carrying 1,770-pound type 80 general purpose bombs, while the dive bombers were armed with 532-pound type 25

The powerful Japanese aircraft carrier **Kaga.** *Although built in 1935, she still had some of the features of the early, improvised carriers.*

general purpose bombs. By 0445, the planes had moved to launching stations, started their engines, launched, formed up, and the first wave was on its way to Midway.

Nagumo also launched at 0430 seven scout planes from the various cruisers and battleships to search the east for possible enemy ships, out to a range of 300 miles. The 300 miles was plenty of distance because, as a rule, American planes could not have the range of the Japanese planes, especially the American torpedo planes. The heavy cruiser *Tone* had trouble launching one of her planes and it was not until 0500 that the last one from her went out. Nagumo also ordered the second strike to be brought up from below on all four fleet carriers and to be armed and readied with anti-ship weapons. The Japanese admiral wanted to be ready for possible contacts with any American ships early that morning, no matter how unlikely the possibility of such an occurrence. Some 24 fighters were placed on combat air patrol over the fleet. Nagumo would have liked more fighters on hand, but believing the U.S. Navy would not be present in strength, he made do with what he had.

Lieutenant Ady on a PBY saw a small seaplane whip by on an opposing course at 0510; it was one of the scout planes sent out from the Japanese support warships. He radioed that contact when he saw at 0530 two Japanese fleet carriers through a break in the clouds. He had to be careful to not be jumped by enemy fighters that could easily bring him down, so he stayed in the clouds as he reported "5:34, enemy carriers"..."5:40, ED 180, sight 320 degrees"..."5:52, two carriers and main body of ships, carriers in front, course 135, speed 25." On the American carriers there was some confusion as other reports were arriving. Also, the message mentioned only two carriers, and Fletcher knew that there were more than two out there. Where were those others?

Lieutenant William Chase in his PBY had just seen at 0540 a huge formation of fighters and bombers. Chase did not bother with encoding this message and sent en clair. "Many planes heading Midway bearing 320, distance 150 miles."

The message did not get things moving as quickly as it should have, even though the commander of Midway, Captain Simard, U.S.N., did not want his planes caught on the ground as they were at both Pearl and the Philippines. It was not until radar picked the planes up 93 miles from the island at about 0555 that orders to get the planes airborne were finally given. B-17s, which had already been armed and launched to attack the enemy force sighted the previous day, were ordered to change course and attack this new enemy force. PBYs had already been sent off on search missions that morning, but, on the island there were still over 60 aircraft needing to be launched, many of which were Buffalo fighters. It required time for fighters to reach altitudes high enough for proper attacks against enemy planes.

As the Japanese approached the island, an interesting foot-note to history was in the making. Film director John Ford had arrived a few days previously from Pearl Harbor. He had been brought into Nimitz's office and asked if he wanted to witness a battle though he was not told when or where. When Ford accepted, he was whisked off to Midway to film the Japanese attack. He picked up some shrapnel in his shoulder in the course of the day, but did get some great action shots.

The fighting opened with American fighters knocking down two Kates in an attack from above. Most of the Marine fighters got in one pass before the escorting Zeros roared into them. Unfortunately for the Marines that day, they learned that the Wildcat might be an equal to the formidable Japanese fighter, but the lumbering overweight Buffalo was an all too easy target for the enemy. Lieutenant Charles Hughes said of the Buffalo fighters that it "looked like they were tied to a string while the Zeros made passes at them." Of the 25 fighters that rose that morning, six struggled back to base, the rest being victims of America's inability to be prepared for war or to avoid it. The Japanese lost 11 aircraft to all causes in the airstrike against Midway.

At 0631 the guns on the island opened up on the attackers. Anti-aircraft accounted for a few planes, but hangers, buildings, fuel tanks were all hit. Zeros came down to strafe after that, wreaking havoc everywhere. On the ground 11 died and 18 were wounded.

The Japanese felt that with such stiff resistance another strike was warranted to "soften" the target. Lieutenant Tomonaga radioed the First Carrier Strike Force that, "There is need for a second attack."

Nagumo was faced with a difficult decision. If he launched a second strike at Midway, he had to rearm the planes currently on deck for land based targets. In doing so, he would have no effective force to confront any naval force that the Americans might have in the area until the first strike returned to the carriers and were refueled and rearmed. As Professor H.P Wilmott put it, "The problem, dodged by Yamamoto...(with his splitting up of Japan's aircraft carriers in to various forces, instead of a massive concentration) was how the First Carrier Strike Force in the absence of a reserve, was to operate against one target while safeguarding against the possibility of encountering an enemy task force at sea."

Nagumo decided that since most of the scouts had been out for some time and reported no significant enemy opposition, the American navy was probably not around. Also, the first American planes from Midway were about to attack, a trigger to influence Nagumo to attack Midway with a second strike.

Six Avenger torpedo planes and the four Army B-26 bombers sighted the Japanese fleet and launched an immediate, uncoordinated attack. The Avengers were immediately jumped by Zeros and all but one were lost. While the Avenger was brand new and would shortly replace the Devastators from all the aircraft carriers, both planes shared one fatal weakness: speed at which a torpedo had to be dropped was quite slow.

Characteristics of American, Japanese, and British Air Launched Torpedoes in 1942.

	SIZE	EXPLOSIVE CHARGE	DROPPING SPEED
U.S.A.	22.4-inch	600 pounds of Torpex	110 knots
Japan	17.7-inch	331 pounds of Type 97	260 knots
Britain	17.7-inch	388 pounds of TNT	145 knots

Captain Collins led in the four B-26s armed with torpedoes at 200 feet. He remembers that after racing through a curtain of anti-aircraft fire to get a good position for the final attack run on the *Akagi*, one of the planes broadcast by radio, "Boy, if mother could see me now!" Of the four bombers, the last two were lost though the second one managed to incur some damage when bombardier Lieutenant Russ Johnson actually strafed the carrier deck with the nose gun! The *Akagi* lost two men, had the No. 3 anti-aircraft gun placed out of action, and the transmitting antenna cut from the strafing.

At 0715, this American first strike was over and the order to rearm planes went out to the carriers. Midway would be attacked a second time. Planes were sent below where plane crews scurried to remove torpedoes and armor-piercing bombs while additional general purpose bombs came up from the magazines below.

At 0728 the late departing scout plane from the *Tone* reported, "Sight what appears to be ten enemy surface ships in position bearing 10 degrees distance, 240 miles from Midway. Course 150 degrees, speed over 20 knots." They were within striking range. And Nagumo's fleet was dispersed due to rapid maneuvering during the last air attacks. Back on the *Yamato*, Yamamoto felt that the presence of the American fleet was a surprise, but was not concerned since it would mean a victory that much earlier. Admiral Yamamoto had not yet become suspicious of the fact that the Americans were not reacting to the Japanese, but were acting on their own plan.

Again, when every minute counted, Nagumo discussed what to do with his staff, and at 0748 ordered, "Prepare to carry out

Dauntless dive bombers at Midway. They were slightly outdated, but could absorb a lot of punishment.

attacks on enemy fleet units. Leave torpedoes on those attack planes which have not as yet changed to bombs."

Starting at 0755 16 Dauntless dive bombers under Major Loften R. Henderson from Midway "glidebombed" (the pilots were too inexperienced for proper divebombing) the *Hiryu* and *Soryu*. The Japanese received a good scare, but all bombs missed. Henderson died in the attack, but lived in immortality by having an airfield on Guadalcanal named after him. Eight Dauntless failed to return. It was all over for them by 0812.

The *Tone*'s searchplane was still reporting, but was a very poor scout. It did not send in many messages, and the ones that were dispatched were not very accurate. At 0809 it reported the composition of the enemy fleet to the Japanese carrier force, "Enemy is composed of five cruisers and five destroyers." None of the American carriers had been seen.

At 0814 the next attack came in from the B-17s that had been diverted from their early morning run against the invasion fleet. Instead of 8,000 feet, as the day before, they came in at 20,000 feet. By 0820 the *Soryu* and *Hiryu* had been bombed again, and missed again. Some Zeros made a few half-hearted passes at the B-17s, but out of respect they did not press home their attacks, for the bomber was too big and a difficult target to bring down. By now things were getting even more complicated for the Japanese as their strike against Midway had returned and was trying to land. With the B-17 attack in progress, the returning planes milled around waiting for a break in the action to land. At 0820 the *Tone's* scout plane sent a message to the commanders standing on the *Akagi's* bridge: "The enemy is accompanied by what appears to be a carrier." At 0830 the scout plane reported two enemy cruisers on the horizon, implying the presence of a second task force.

Next up were the 11 old and slow Vindicator dive bombers that had been unable to keep up with the Dauntlesses. Only two were lost because they did not attack the carriers, but opted for the battleship *Haruna*, which they missed. This was the last attack from Midway.

Nagumo now had a difficult decision. The first wave was running out of fuel and needed to land. The combat air patrol was also low on fuel and some of the fighters were out of ammunition. The torpedo planes were still below decks and many planes still were armed with ground attack armaments. At 0830 Rear Admiral Yamaguchi signaled from the *Hiryu*, "Consider it advisable to launch attack force immediately." Normally, it was highly unusual for a Japanese commander to signal their impatience to a superior.

Nagumo decided that the best course of action was to recover the first strike and air patrol fighters that needed to land. The decks of the Japanese carriers needed to be cleared. Due to the constant changing of armaments, bombs and torpedoes had not been returned to the magazines and were literally lying around because of the need for speed and the element of command confusion that had manifested itself. All Nagumo needed was time, but as Commander Fuchida later said, "Victory in battle does not always go to the stronger; it often goes to the side which is quicker to react boldly and decisively to unforeseen developments, and to grasp fleeting opportunities."

By 0830, Nagumo knew that his position had been known to the enemy for at least two hours and had had plenty of time to put together and launch an attack. Considering the superior range of Japan's planes, following Yamaguchi's suggestion made the best sense. There were bound to be enemy incoming planes at this point. To clear the decks of the planes already on the decks, with their weapons, forming up over the First Carrier Strike Force and lashing out at the American carriers seemed to be the best course. Some of the congestion on the decks would have been relieved and enough damage might have been done to the Americans to force a retreat or disrupt further attacks.

Spruance, with the two carriers that were to make the main strike, wanted to close the enemy to within 100 miles, but that would mean delaying an attack until 0900. The only report Spruance had was from 0602 and by postponing an attack, he might learn more and better intelligence. It would not be until 0838 that further data locating the enemy would arrive. Part of the problem was that Midway's radio traffic was on another frequency and could not be heard on board the *Enterprise* or *Yorktown*. His chief of staff, the difficult Captain Miles Browning from Halsey's staff, urged that the attack be launched quickly at 0700, although that meant the planes would be flying 155 miles and would have little fuel for a margin of error. Browning was obsessed with the element of surprise, and rightfully so. Spruance went with his man, and made a second important decision: he launched everything he could when only two Japanese carriers had been sighted.

First off were 16 fighters for the combat air patrol, being launched one every 20 to 30 seconds. High patrols operated with eight of the 16 at 18,000 feet for the *Hornet* and *Enterprise*; the others would operate as lower. The *Hornet* next launched 10 fighters for escort, and 34 Dauntless dive bombers, half armed with a single 500-pound bomb, and the rest with 1,000-pound bombs. Then 15 Devastator torpedo planes rose from the *Hornet*. The dive bombers steadily climbed to 18,000 feet, with their escort about 2-3,000 feet above that. The *Hornet*'s strike went out separately from the *Enterprise*'s strike, due to delays getting the planes off the deck.

The *Enterprise* began launching 33 dive bombers at 0706, 15 armed with 1,000-pounds, six with 500-pounds, and nine with 500-pound bombs and two 100-pounds bombs each, three unknown. After a delay until 0806, the *Enterprise* launched 10 fighters, and 14 torpedo planes. The delay on the deck of the *Enterprise* caused Lieutenant Commander Wade McClusky to take his dive bombers off separately. McClusky had started the war as a flight leader for Wildcats but had been transferred to the Dauntless just before this battle. He took his planes up without fighter escort and headed out.

The formation adopted by the dive bombers was, as described by Lieutenant Clarence E. Dickinson, "six wedge-shaped sections, inverted Vs, three planes in a section..." somewhat like this:

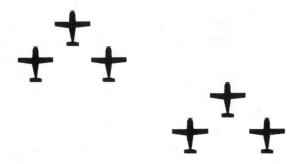

The planes in the sections flew at various altitudes as they were "stepped down" in their six wedge-shaped sections.

Uncoordinated with Spruance's strike, the *Yorktown* began launching at 0830. Twelve Dauntlesses went up first, and cruising at 100 knots, headed off towards the enemy. Following them, at 130 knots, went 17 Dauntlesses armed with 1,000-pounders. The dive bombers from the *Yorktown* had some quick surprises after launch. There was a new device on the planes that allowed pilots to electronically arm their bombs when in flight. Several of the fliers used the device only to discover that instead of just arming the bombs (which apparently it did), it released them as well! The commander of *Yorktown*'s flight broke radio silence to warn all his other pilots not to use the new device. Six fighters went last as an escort as they were fast enough to catch up to the two departed forces. Fletcher was a little more deliberate in his attack and did not commit all his forces, due to the lesson learned at the Battle of the Coral Sea where he attacked on the first sighting, and missed the main enemy force.

America was still new to carrier warfare, and, frankly, this attack was uncoordinated, the various plane types ending up going off separately and largely unescorted. Commander Waldron of the *Hornet* was first to sight the enemy. He had deployed his planes in a long line—part of the line sighted the outer ring of the Japanese carrier force. He sent a sighting report, but it was not picked up by the *Hornet*.

At 0918 Nagumo recovered his planes, but in the course of the morning lost three planes overhead, along with 11 at Midway. He was getting ready for his planned 1030 strike against the enemy carriers when the heavy cruiser *Chikuma* reported enemy torpedo planes approaching.

Waldron thought about attacking from two directions, but the Zeros were so thick and deadly that he decided to concentrate his force in a spearhead aimed at the enemy carriers. None of the torpedo planes survived. One man, Ensign George Gay, launched his torpedo at 800 yards at the *Soryu* and was struck by a bullet in his upper left arm shortly thereafter. "He shifted the stick to his left hand, ripped his sleeve, pressed a machine gun slug from the wound with his thumb. It seemed like something worth saving, so he sought to put it in the pocket of his jacket. When he found his pocket openings held shut by his safety belt and parachute straps and life jacket, he popped it into his mouth." Gay's plane went down with his rear gunner dead, but the pilot survived in the water. There he watched the middle innings of this battle unfold, as the power hitters came up for a swing.

The torpedo planes from the *Enterprise* went in next. Ten were shot down while the other four managed to return home. No hits were scored on their targets, the *Kaga* and *Akagi*. No fighter escort helped them, although the *Enterprise*'s escort had been present at 22,000 feet, reporting the total absence of Japanese air patrol at that altitude. These fighters had not heard over the

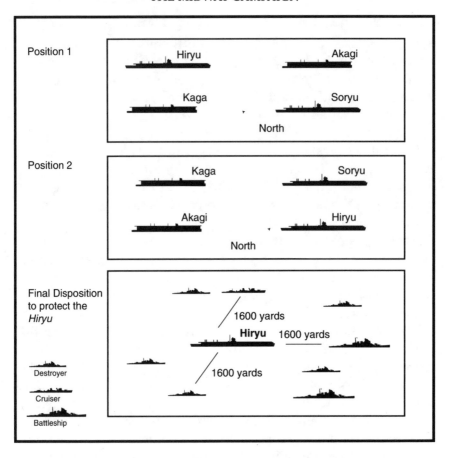

radio the call for them to come down and help the torpedo planes, who naturally felt betrayed.

Where were the dive bombers that had left first and were faster, but had not attacked? *Hornet*'s dive bombers never found the enemy, and with fuel dwindling quickly, were forced to abort. They had proceeded to an area where earlier reports placed the Japanese fleet, to the south. When they failed to find them, several planes ditched, but most landed safely on Midway, refueled, and returned to the *Yorktown* later in the day. McClusky's group from the *Enterprise* was also running low on fuel, but he took a guess and headed north. Up ahead, he sighted the wake of a speeding destroyer. It was the detached *Arashi* that had attacked the submarine *Nautilus* when it had been sighted lurking near the First Carrier Strike Force. McClusky pointed the dive bombers in the direction the Japanese destroyer was steaming. At 1002, 28 minutes before the Japanese strike was to take off, McClusky sighted the enemy and made a report. McClusky was at about 20,000 feet, while Lieutenant Dickerson, leading a division (two sections of three each), was at about 15-16,000 feet so he did not see the Japanese carriers until about five minutes after McClusky first sighted them. On the *Enterprise* Captain Browning immediately shouted into the microphone, "McClusky, attack, attack immediately!"

The dive bombers from the *Yorktown* had been droning alone at 15,000 feet with their 1,000-pound bombs. On their first leg out (they had started later than the *Enterprise*'s planes) they sighted the Japanese at 1003. Incredible accidental timing? Nagumo was about to be attacked with virtually everything on his fleet carrier decks, littered with weapons and lines filled with aviation gas.

The first phase of the action saw the fighter escort for the torpedo planes from the *Yorktown*, four Wildcats, take on about 20 Zeros. All but two came in a string formation, to make a firing pass. It appeared something like:

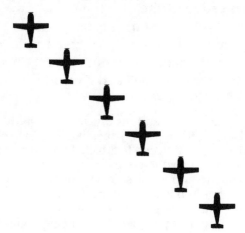

The group was commanded by the legendary Lieutenant Commander John Thach, inventor of the "Thach Weave" to defeat the Zero. The Weave demanded teamwork with planes literally weaving in and out in opposite directions, somewhat like passing a ball in football. The plane coming in would take out the Zero chasing the first American plane. The key feature of the move was that planes did not fly all in formation, but interacted. It was at Midway that the Thach Weave received its debut in this action. Unfortunately the rearmost plane was lost by two rogue Zeros surprising Thach's formation from the rear. Thach shot one fighter down, tried his weave and came head on from below on another enemy. Thach said later that, "I was so mad that I was determined that I was going to run into this bastard because he jumped my poor, little inexperienced wing-man." Thach got three that day while one or two Zeros were shot down by the remaining two wingmen.

Two other escorts, operating closer to the torpedo planes, became involved in a fierce battle with the Zeros; eventually the torpedo planes were attacked, but ended up attacking the *Hiryu*, the only planes to do so during this part of the action. Only two torpedo planes from the *Yorktown* survived to return, but this action had sucked down all the Japanese air patrol, which ended up numbering, with fighters landing and taking off during the entire morning, 41 Zeros, 11 which were shot down in the course of this attack by the Americans.

Poised overhead were the dive bombers of the *Enterprise* and the *Yorktown*. The moment of truth had arrived when McClusky's group of dive bombers sighted all four fleet carriers. He felt that he could handle two of them. McClusky's squadron pushed over towards the *Kaga* and *Akagi*. Lieutenant Dickerson described the dive bomber attack:

> Right after the skipper and his division had started I kicked my rudders back and forth to cause a ducklike twitching of my tail. This was the signal for my division to attack. In my turn I pulled up my nose and in a stalled position opened my flaps. We always do this, throw the plane up and to the side on which we are going to dive, put out the flaps as brakes and then peel-off...as I put my nose down I picked up our carrier target below in front of me....
>
> The carrier was racing along at thirty knots, right into the wind. She made no attempt to change course. I was coming at her a little bit astern, on the left-hand side. By the time I was at 12,000 feet I could see all planes ahead of me in the dive...the target was utterly satisfying...near the dropping point I began to watch through my sight. As I was almost at the dropping point I saw a bomb hit just behind where I was aiming, that white circle with its blood red center [on the *Kaga*'s deck]...I saw the deck rippling and curling

back in all directions exposing a great section of the hanger below. That bomb had a fuse set to make it explode about four feet below the deck.

Four bombs slammed onto the crowded decks of the *Kaga* immediately igniting a furnace of death and destruction. At 1025, just as the *Akagi* was in the act of launching Zeros, two 1,000-pound bombs hit the deck. Both carriers were mortally wounded.

A total of 18 of the dive bombers failed to return to the *Enterprise*. Most were lost due to a casual attitude and lack of planning towards the return flight to the carrier after action. Most ditched into the sea due to a lack of fuel.

The dive bombers from the *Yorktown* began pushing over towards the *Soryu*. Three 1,000-pound bombs of the 13 dropped ripped open the vitals of this fleet carrier and wrecked 27 bombers and torpedo planes, fueled and ready for launching, which added to the inferno on board. The damage was so obviously severe that several of the final dive bombers went after a battleship and a destroyer, but missed their targets. Three fleet carriers down and one to go!

The *Akagi* would not sink until 5 June, the coup de grace being delivered by Japanese destroyers. She lost only 221 men killed. The *Kaga* sank at 0925 after two violent internal explosions. She lost about 800 killed, many from the engine rooms. The *Soryu*, totally on fire, sank at 2115, and at 2120 was rent by a tremendous internal explosion underwater. At least 718 went down with the ship. All three lost their captains, the *Kaga* by a bomb blast during the attack, the other two when their ships sank. The Japanese carriers had been designed for quick handling of aircraft and not for defensive qualities. With the added disadvantage of having "readied" aircraft parked on deck and in the hangers, probably nothing could have saved the Japanese carriers. The most grievous loss to the Japanese were the highly trained air crews. In this one blow, the Japanese edge in naval combat was wiped out. While not all the pilots and crews would be lost, their overall numbers were devastated.

On board the *Hiryu*, need for an airstrike seemed obvious to Rear Admiral Yamaguchi. If he delayed attack, he could mount a full strike, and he reasoned another attack from the U.S. could be some hours away. But Yamaguchi launched 18 Vals and six Zeros by 1040. Twelve of the Vals had 551-pound semi-armor piercing bombs, while the other six had general purpose bombs that would normally have been used against Midway. The attack was led by Lieutenant Michio Kobayashi.

Kobayashi followed home a flight of *Yorktown*'s planes at 13,000 feet. However, as he neared the American Task Force, the *Yorktown* directed in by radar 12 Wildcats that tore through Kobayashi's formation, immediately knocking down six Vals. The *Yorktown*'s returning flight had not been aware that it was being followed. However, the American radar had an IFF capability which informed the *Yorktown*'s operators at 65 miles distance that an enemy formation was present with the *Yorktown*'s planes.

Meanwhile, the *Yorktown* had launched additional scouting planes at 1150, as Fletcher was still concerned about other enemy carriers. Eventually it was this scouting group that located the *Hiryu*. With the knowledge of an incoming strike, the *Yorktown* took defensive measures in securing the deck and hangar space. About 800 gallons of aviation fuel were thrown overboard. Speed was worked up to 30 knots. Returning dive bombers were waved off, and most flew onto the *Enterprise* for a safe landing, although some even tried to join up with the friendly air patrol. Eventually a staff officer came to Admiral Fletcher and reported, "The attack is coming in, sir." Fletcher replied, "Well, I've got on my tin hat. I can't do anything else now."

The escorting Zeros were poorly handled that day and gave little assistance to Kobayashi's Vals. Still, Kobayashi bored in on his target determined to hurt the *Yorktown* and regain the balance needed for any sort of a Japanese victory. He died in the attack. Only seven Vals made it through the fighters and the flak. Bombs were released at 1,000 feet beginning at 1210. Of these seven—only one bomb clearly missed—three were near misses and three scored hits on the *Yorktown*. Two hits caused little real damage, although the first one exploded on the deck killing many men. The third bomb penetrated to the second deck where it exploded near the boiler uptake. For some reason, Lieutenant Charles Cundiff had a premonition down in emergency boiler

Yorktown *and its escorts throw up an impressive anti-aircraft umbrella.*

control and shouted, "Hit the deck," just before the explosion. His men obeyed and none were hurt. The bomb blast literally blew out most of the fires in the boiler room and brought the *Yorktown* to a dead stop. The loss of power was serious, but damage control parties went to work immediately. Thirteen Vals and three Zeros failed to return.

Yamaguchi, on the *Hiryu*, now launched a second attack. He had six Zeros and 10 Kate torpedo planes ready for launching at 1510. Tomonaga led this attack. Yamaguchi knew the number of

Crewmen on the listing flight deck of the Yorktown, *when it was still thought the stricken ship could be saved.*

enemy carriers he was facing, as a scout plane (the new experimental Judy dive bomber of which there were two on the *Soryu* at the start of the day) had reported all three. Also, a pilot from the *Enterprise* torpedo squadron had been captured earlier that day and had revealed that there were three American fleet carriers on the scene. This unfortunate flier would later be executed while still on board the destroyer; his crime apparently being a participant in the American victory.

Tomonaga led his planes out at 13,500 feet at 1530. He sighted the *Yorktown* at 1630, but thought it was a different carrier than the one Kobayashi had attacked as it looked in fine condition, proof of how efficiently America's damage control worked. Spruance was just over the horizon and he had reinforced Fletcher's task force with two cruisers and two destroyers. Tomonaga decided to execute a standard split attack which involved five planes coming in from two directions (90 degrees)

The destroyer **Hammann** *is sunk while coming to the aid of Yorktown.*

on the *Yorktown*. Two torpedoes scored on the *Yorktown*, jamming her rudder, causing a list to the port, and further explosions and fires. The *Yorktown* was out of action.

The *Yorktown* eventually was abandoned. The following day there was discussion and attempts to bring her into port with a small salvage party. Progress was being made when the Japanese sub *I-168* fired four torpedoes. One missed, two went under the destroyer *Hammann* lying alongside and hit the *Yorktown*. The last one hit the *Hammann*, which sank within three minutes. The hero that day was Seaman Berlyn M. Kimbrell who set all the depth charges on the *Hammann* to "safe" (this would keep them from exploding at pre-set depths when the *Hammann* sank), put life jackets on all the men gathered on the fantail, pushed them into the water, and left last. Kimbrell died in the underwater explosion that occurred when the *Hammann* finally sank. The *Yorktown* lingered on until 0600 on 7 June when she rolled over and sank. Earlier, Fletcher had decided he could no longer command the carriers with the *Yorktown* disabled and handed over command to Spruance.

The Japanese First Carrier Strike Force had several important events occur in the late morning and early afternoon of the 4th. Nagumo had been transferred off the *Akagi* and handed over command to Rear Admiral Abe on the *Tone*. Abe informed Yamamoto of the losses. The shock was only dimly felt on the *Yamato* that morning. The invincible Japanese fleet had been defeated, and losses had obviously been catastrophic.

Yamamoto, after some discussion, ordered all his units to move to assist the First Carrier Strike Force. The transports were given light protection and moved to an area about 500 miles from Midway so they could either go in for the invasion later or else retreat, but they would not be in danger. Kondo was ordered to take most of the powerful surface ships from this group and hurry to help Nagumo. Kondo had already acted on his own and was moving with 23 ships toward Nagumo. Kondo was ordered to detach a force to attack Midway with gunfire. He thought about detaching his battleships, but their limited speed would cause them to arrive off Midway not at night, but in the morning. So Kondo sent in the escorting ships of the Second Fleet, Occupation Support Force, the heavy cruisers *Kumano*, *Mogami*, *Mikuma*, and *Suzuya*, with two escorting destroyers. The *Yamato* itself and the entire First Fleet under Yamamoto were also moving to aid Nagumo. Finally, Yamamoto ordered the carriers of the Second Carrier Strike Force to move south from the Aleutians. Since this force needed to refuel and could not be in the area until 7 June, too late to influence events, the order was shortly countermanded.

Nagumo's force was informed that the American fleet was only 90 miles away in the late morning so he, now with his flag (and back in command) transferred to the light cruiser *Nagara*, ordered surface combat ships to form line of battle with destroyers in the van. Nagumo feared that the American fleet would finish off the cripples with gunfire. Based on prewar doctrine, this was a logical concern, and if the Americans possessed a more powerful surface force, a real danger. Later reports showed the American task forces moved away, recovering and launching aircraft. Nagumo formed a formation around the *Hiryu* for her last stand.

After the *Hiryu*'s two strikes against the *Yorktown*, she had hardly anything left. Six fighters, five dive bombers, and four torpedo planes were all that remained for a third strike, with some additional Zeros deployed for air patrol, and one Judy as scout. The crews were exhausted, but the planes could have been launched at 1830. Instead the men were given dinner and told that the strike would be at 2000. An excellent example of the way the Japanese command structure thought in terms of what they wanted the enemy to do, instead of what the Americans were capable of doing.

At 1903 the *Hiryu*'s watch shouted "Enemy dive bombers directly overhead." Twenty dive bombers dropped down out of the sun against the *Hiryu* while four others dived down on the escorting ships. The attack came as a surprise although the Japanese air patrol did engage the dive bombers in their dives. The first 13 dive bombers missed. Then the first hit landed squarely on the forward elevator platform, hurling it back against the ship's island, and breaking every window on the bridge. Three more bombs ripped through the *Hiryu* with the rest missing. Once again intense flames roared through the ship, although her speed was virtually unaffected. Eventually the fires reached the engine room where the engine gangs continued to perform their duty while the deck literally melted above them. Virtually everyone there died on the *Hiryu* that day.

Air units on Midway made additional attacks during the afternoon, which accomplished little except disrupting futile attempts to save the *Hiryu*.

Rear Admiral Yamaguchi went down with the *Hiryu*, sending a message to Nagumo just before his death, "I have no words to apologize for what has happened. I only wish for a stronger Japanese Navy—and revenge." Four hundred and sixteen men died on the *Hiryu*.

The greatest error made after the loss of the first three Japanese fleet carriers was not withdrawing the *Hiryu* to the west. This would not have ended the action, but would have lengthened the distance between the two enemies. The Japanese, with greater range in their aircraft, might have been able to hit the American force and prevented damage to themselves. If the Americans pursued, then they would have been closer to the other converging Japanese surface forces who were attempting to force a night surface engagement with superior forces.

In pursuing this strategy, the forces under Kondo deployed in a long line. Rear Admiral Tanaka, who would make his reputation with the Tokyo Express off Guadalcanal later in the year, deployed his destroyers to the right, while the other destroyers and light cruisers deployed to the left. There was a ship spaced every four miles. The battleships *Kongo* and the *Hiei* were six miles astern of the flagship *Atago* which was deployed to the right of the center of the line. Nagumo's surface forces were to sweep down from the north towards the southeast.

However, Admiral Spruance had not obliged the Japanese. He ordered a withdrawal to the east until morning air units could locate and identify the enemy forces still facing him. Early on the morning of the 5th, Yamamoto realized the game was up and ordered the Japanese navy to retire.

One final act remained. Kurita's bombardment force was less than 90 miles from Midway, when it was ordered to retire. Earlier as an almost pathetic token gesture, the submarine *I-168* was ordered to surface and fire on Midway. The vessel fired eight rounds which all fell into the lagoon. Shore batteries forced the submarine to dive and it managed to get away, later torpedoing the *Yorktown*.

The American submarine *Tambor* was near Kurita's force and running on the surface. She sighted Kurita's cruisers, but at such a distance, it was not possible to be certain what ships they were; the captain of the *Tambor* made a sighting report stating, "many unidentified ships," which was a poor report in that neither speed nor heading direction was mentioned. The *Tambor* followed on the surface, finally closing the range to identify the distinctive *Mogami*. The Kurita force saw the *Tambor* at the same instant. Flagship *Kumano*, leading the line, immediately turned

45 degrees away and flashed a warning down the line of the following ships. The cruisers were arranged in a line with the *Kumano* leading, then the *Suzuya*, the *Mikuma*, and the *Mogami*. Unfortunately for the Japanese, the navigating officer on the last ship, the *Mogami*, mistook the *Suzuya* for the *Mikuma* and turned too soon. At 26 knots speed, the *Mogami* rammed the rear of the *Mikuma*, crumpling the bow of the *Mogami* and slowing her to 12 knots. The *Mikuma*, with fuel tanks damaged, began trailing an oil slick. Kurita decided to split off his two undamaged cruisers and leave his two escorting destroyers with the two cripples. Both forces, at best speed, headed back towards Nippon.

The *Tambor* failed in her attack, but on 5 June the Midway air units finally did get their first blood in a dramatic way that pointed to the future in an ironic twist. Spruance and the carriers were on a false scent to the north looking for Nagumo's carriers, now all sunk. Midway directed a strike of six Dauntlesses and six Vindicators towards the two crippled heavy cruisers steaming west. They literally followed the trailing oil slick to the targets, and once again the Dauntlesses dived, while the Vindicators glide-bombed the heavy cruisers which were putting up a tremendous volume of anti-aircraft fire. All bombs missed, but Captain Richard E. Fleming of the lead Vindicator, when hit with anti-aircraft at the drop point for his bomb, deliberately crashed his plane into the *Mikuma*, a forerunner of the kamikaze attacks to occur late in the war. Commander Fuchida's account of that crash states the pilot "attempted a daring suicide crash into *Mikuma*'s bridge. He missed the bridge but crashed into the afterturret, spreading fire over the air intake of the starboard engine room. This caused an explosion of gas fumes below, killing all hands working in the engine room."

Spruance found an empty ocean, except for the destroyer *Tanikaze* retreating from the now sunk *Hiryu*. In the course of the afternoon the destroyer had 56 bombs from B-17s dropped on her. All missed. Returning Dauntlesses, unable to find a suitable target, also attacked, and failed to hit, though a near miss killed six crewmen and damaged a turret. Another flight of B-17s attacked, and missed again. In the course of this skirmish, a dive bomber and two B-17s were lost.

U.S. aircraft gets close-up shot of the flaming **Mogami.**

Finally, on 6 June, with the Japanese navy all but withdrawn, Spruance got his last lick in by attacking the two retiring crippled enemy heavy cruisers. Spruance's carriers scored six bomb hits on the *Mogami*, and at least five on the *Mikuma*, plus one bomb each on both destroyers. Only the *Mikuma* sunk, largely due to the fact that most of the bombs dropped were not armor piercing—they lacked delayed action fuses and exploded immediately. Thus, no underwater damage could be inflicted by near misses, and the bombs tended to pound and smash the superstructure, but not do severe damage in the bowels of the ships hit. The main blow against the *Mikuma* was caused when her torpedoes were hit by a bomb, setting off a tremendous explosion. The *Mikuma* lost 648 men dead, while the *Mogami* lost about 300 dead and would be under repair until July of 1943.

So ended the battle. As Admiral Spruance said after the action, "Towards sundown on June 4th I decided to retire to the

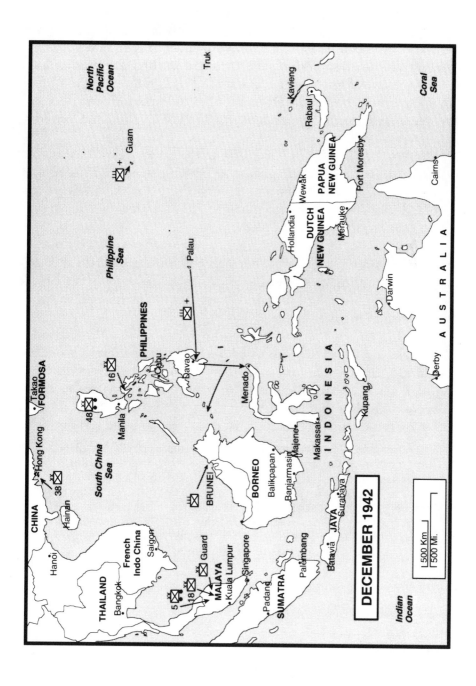

eastward to avoid the possibility of night action with superior forces....the Japanese did order a night attack. When the day's action on June 6th was over...we were short of fuel, and I had a feeling, an intuition perhaps, that we had pushed our luck as far to the westward as it was good for us...." It is interesting to note that Yamamoto had some ships proceed to Wake to try to decoy, by radio traffic, the Americans into range of the land based planes present there.

Finally, the *Saratoga* was pulling in from the West Coast and joined the *Enterprise* and *Hornet*. All three considered heading north to engage the Aleutian diversionary force, but it was decided that it was too late to do so. Thus ended the decisive battle, the turning point, of Midway.

Japan's loss of four fleet carriers could never be fully compensated, but more importantly, her valuable pilots, the best in the world for fighting at sea, suffered devastating losses. This first major naval defeat for Japan in World War II was the end of the first phase of the war at sea.

With the end of the first phase, the Allies, led by the United States, would begin the long road back. Ultimate victory would be ours, and the price for Japan's attack on Pearl Harbor would be paid back in full. But let us not forget the sacrifice of the torpedo bombers that day. Of the 41 torpedo planes from those three carriers, only six returned. Gary North summed it up with,

> It is here that Midway's supreme lesson appears in all its harshness: some men die without seeing their dreams achieved, yet their supreme sacrifice makes possible the fulfillment of those dreams. American torpedo bombers from Midway and from the carriers saw their best efforts fail. Most of them did not live to tell about it. Their planes were poor; their torpedoes missed their mark; and it looked as though all was in vain. But within 30 minutes, their sacrifice was to pay enormous dividends.

Orders of Battle

PEARL HARBOR

Japanese Air Attack

Of 185 planes scheduled for the attack in the first wave, 183 took off. They were:

43 Zero Fighters
49 Kate Horizontal Bombers (armed with 800 Kg armor piercing bombs)
51 Val Divebombers (250 Kg land target bomb)
40 Kate Torpedo bombers (torpedoes)

Two additional fighters tried to take off, but one crashed on launch and a second one was forced back due to engine trouble.

The second wave launched:

36 Zero Fighters
54 Kate Horizontal Bombers (mixed selection of bombs)
79 Val Divebombers (250 Kg land target bomb)

One Val had to return to the carriers due to engine trouble. Fighters were always the first to lead, while the torpedo bombers were always the last to rise from the deck.

U.S.A. Land Based Aircraft	**Quantity**
Modern Bombers	
B-17C and B-17D	12
A-20A	12
Obsolete Bombers	
B-18A	35
A-12	2
Modern Fighters	
P-40 A, B, C, & E	99
P-36	39
P-26	14
Miscellaneous Army	
Cargo, Transport, Observation Etc.	22
Navy Landbased Aircraft	
At Kaneohe airfield	
PBYs	36
Some few miscellaneous craft	
At Ford Island - misc. -	
including shipboard scout planes	33
At Ewa Marine Airfield	
Wildcats	11
Vindicator SB2U-3s	32
Miscellaneous aircraft	6

PHILIPPINE INVASION

Japanese Land Forces

This is the Japanese Order of Battle directed towards the Filipino-American army under General Douglas MacArthur in the first five months of the war, mainly detailed for the invasion force landing on Luzon. From the first air raids on December 8, 1941, to the fall of Corregidor Island, the long and bloody struggle for control of the Philippine islands consumed blood, time, and treasure. Yet, the Japanese mustered an army and air force that was not all first rate, but in actuality a mixed force of first, second, as well as third rate units.

14th Army Headquarters

The Japanese 14th Army Headquarters consisted of about 1,021 men
48th Division
(Lt. General Yuichi Dobashi - about 350 men at the Headquarters)
    1st F Infantry Regiment (each with three infantry battalions)
    2nd F Infantry Regiment
    47th Infantry Regiment
48th Reconnaissance Regiment
    1st Company (motorized infantry)
    2nd Company (motorized infantry)
    3rd Company (type 97 armored car)
    4th Company (type 97 armored car)
48th Artillery Regiment
    1st Battalion (motorized)
    2nd Battalion (motorized)
    3rd Battalion (motorized)
    4th Battalion (horsedrawn)
    Entirely 75mm mountain artillery, though one battalion may have had howitzers.
    Engineer Regiment (with three motorized companies)

The 48th was an elite division and was considered by Japanese standards to be a motorized unit. As with the 16th and other divisions, each regiment had an infantry artillery company (four 75mm field guns) and a light artillery company (usually 37mm guns, which was considered Anti-Tank by the Allies but not designated by the Japanese as such).

Each infantry battalion in the 48th had *four* infantry companies, one machine gun company and one battalion artillery platoon (two 70mm howitzers - they fired a 8.3 pound high explosive shell to a maximum range of 3,000 yards). The 48th could move one third of her infantry by truck, one-third by bicycle, while the final third marched. Wartime strength in the invasion of the Philippines was 15,663. It was later used in the invasion of Java and spent the rest of the war there.

Support units include transport, medical, ordnance, water purification, headquarters (usually 300 men), and veterinary.

F=Formosa

16th Division
(Lt. General Sususumu Morioka - about 240 men at the Headquarters)
    9th Infantry Regiment (each of three infantry battalions)

20th Infantry Regiment
33rd lntantry Regiment
Each regiment had a company of infantry artillery and a company of
  light artillery as above.
16th Reconnaissance Regiment
  1st company (motorized infantry)
  2nd company (motorized infantry)
  3rd company (type 97 armored car)
  4th company (type 97 armored car)
22nd Field Artillery Regiment
  1st Battalion (motorized)
  2nd Battalion (horse drawn)
  3rd Battalion (horse drawn)

Numbering about 2,000 men, the 1st had twelve 75mm field guns with a
range of 13,300 yards firing high explosive, armor piercing, shrapnel, or
smoke. The 2nd and 3rd had 12 105mm howitzers each with a range of
14,200 yards, firing high explosive only.

16th Engineer Battalion (with two companies, one motorized, the second on foot)

Each infantry battalion in the 16th had *three* infantry companies, one machine gun company, and a battalion artillery platoon, the latter containing
two 70mm howitzers. One battalion of each regiment was mounted on bicycles. One battalion of the 33rd regiment was used in the initial landing at
Davao on Mindinao and was not present on Luzon.

Consider the armament of the 16th as typical for a normal Japanese Division.

Please note that the reconnaissance regiment and engineer regiment were
regiments in name only and in actual size were much smaller in size. The former numbered either 440 or 650 men (sources vary - it could be the 48th was
the latter, while the 16th would be normal for the former). Each infantry regiment in the 16th had 2,850 men each.

Type 97 armored car or tankette, weighed 4.25 tons, had one 37mm, 4mm to
12mm of armor, 26 m.p.h., and a crew of two.

Later, in February, after General Homma was stalled in front of Bataan, the
Japanese Imperial General Headquarters sent the 4th Infantry Division, and
more independent units to aid General Homma. The 4th had been at Shang-
hai under the direct command of Imperial General Headquarters, before being attached to the 14th Army. The 4th was poorly equipped (note the
cavalry in the reconnaissance regiment), and may have been somewhat un-
derstrenght (11,000 men?) Apparently the Japanese Official History, the *Senshi Sosho* does not indicate that the 4th was an inferior division, but General
Homma testified that it arrived with 11,000 men only, and was short of
equipment (including two of its four assigned Field Hospitals). Was this an
apology for his delay in achieving the conquest of the Philippines? One
should note that the *Senshi Sosho* is not considered one of the most accurate
of the Official Histories of the various nationalities that fought in World War
II. For example, I refer the reader to Arthur Marder's discussion in *Old
Friend, New Enemies* of the sinking of the Prince of Wales and Repulse where
the *Senshi Sosho* is in great error as to the accuracy of the Japanese air attack
on those two Capital ships.

At this time 7,000 replacements for the 16th Division and the 65th Brigade also arrived.

4th Division
(Lt. General Kenso Kitano)
  8th Infantry Regiment (each of three Infantry Battalions)
  37th Infantry Regiment
  61st Infantry Regiment
  Each regiment had a company of infantry artillery only.
4th Cavalry Regiment
  1st company
  2nd company
  Machine-gun platoon
  Armored car "group" - a few (?)
4th Field Artillery Regiment
  1st Battalion (horse drawn -75mm field guns)
  2nd Battalion (horse drawn -75mm field guns)
  3rd Heavy Howitzer Battalion (horse drawn)

Each Infantry Battalion has three Infantry Companies, one Machine-gun Company, and one Battalion Artillery Platoon. Official strength was 12,379 men, with each regiment having 2654 men. The Headquarters, howitzers, and the 61st regiment arrived on 27 February, 1942, the 8th Infantry Regiment on 5 March, 1942, the 37th Infantry Regiment and the rest of the artillery on 15 March, 1942. The cavalry arrived on 3 April, 1942.

65th Brigade
  122nd Infantry Regiment (two infantry battalions)
  141st Infantry Regiment
  142nd Infantry Regiment
  Each regiment, (note only two battalions) had a field-gun company,
    and a light artillery platoon. Equipment would tend to be older
    marks. Each battalion had three infantry companies and a ma-
    chine gun company.
  65th Engineer "Group" (one company)

The 65th was a garrison brigade and would resemble a *landwehr* unit. The 65th numbered about 7,300 and was entirely on foot. Though a second line unit, it was used heavily at Bataan after the 48th division was withdrawn for operations in the Dutch East Indies.

Additional Ad Hoc Infantry units
  21st Infantry Division (Nagano Detachment named for its commander,
    Major General Kiichi Nagano and numbered about 4,000 men)
  62nd Infantry Regiment
  3rd battalion of the 51st Infantry Artillery Regiment
  one company of the 21st Engineer Regiment
    Used starting 26 February, 1942.
  56th Infantry Division (Sakaguchi Detachment named for its commander,
    Major General Shizuo Sakaguchi and numbered about 5,000 men)
  146th Infantry Regiment
    Used with a minor armor unit, a battalion of the 16th division, and one
      battalion of divisional artillery it was employed in the southern
      Philippines. Arrived from Palau in December and was part of 16th
      Army moving south into the Dutch East Indies.

18th Infantry Division (Kawaguchi Detachment named for its
commander, Major General Kiyotake Kawaguchi and numbered
4,852 men)
124th Infantry Regiment
Used some support units from 14th Army and was employed in the southern
Philippines. Employed starting 1 April, 1942. This unit would end up
on Guadalcanal.
5th Infantry Division (Kawamura Detachment named for its commander,
Major General Saburo Kawamura and numbered 4,160 men)
41st Infantry Regiment
Used some support units from 14th Army and was employed in the southern
Philippines. Employed starting 5 April, 1942.
10th Independent Garrison Group (five battalions, each with 762 men)
This unit was essentially an occupation unit, lacking artillery and
other support elements. One battalion served at Manila and two
on the front line at Bataan during the fighting while the other
two arrived later.

Independent Japanese Units
4th Armor Regiment (with three companies)
Each company had about ten tanks each. Type 95 light tanks (6.7 tons,
one 37mm gun, two 7.7mm MG, 6mm to 12mm of armor, 28
m.p.h., and a crew of three.)
7th Armor Regiment (with three companies)
Each company has about ten tanks each. Type 89 MK 11, medium tank
(12.1 tons, one 57mm gun, two 7.7mm MG, 10mm to 17mm of armor, and a crew of four.)

Independent Artillery
1st Artillery Headquarters
This was the command unit for all artillery units of the 14th Army, primarily utilized during the siege of Bataan and Corregidor, arrived on 28 March, 1942.
1st Heavy Feild Artillery Regiment (with two battalions)
Each battalion had six companies, armed with two 240mm howitzers.
This unit was motorized and arrived on 28 March, 1942.
8th Heavy Field Artillery Regiment (with two battalions)
The 8th had a total of sixteen horse-drawn 100mm field guns.
21st Heavy Field Artillery Regiment
Part only is present armed with 150mm field guns and arrived 1 April,
1942.
3rd Independent Infantry Gun Regiment (essentially an Anti-tank unit of
two battalions)
Each battalion has two companies, each company has four 37mm Type
94 guns. The type 94 has a range of 5,500 yards, fires both High
Explosive and Armor Piercing, and has a muzzle velocity of
2,300 feet per second. Arrived 27 February, 1942.
20th Independent Infantry Gun Regiment (another Anti-tank unit of three
battalions
Each battalion has three companies, each company has four 37mm
Type 94 guns and arrived 5 April, 1942.
1st Heavy Artillery Regiment motorized with two battalions)
Each battalion has two companies, each company has two 240mm howitzers

(firing a High Explosive shell to a maximum range of 11,000 yards. Designed in 1912, it required ten trucks to move each piece).

9th Independent Heavy Field Artillery Battalion (two motorized Companies)
    Each company armed with two 150mm type 89 guns.
2nd Independent Heavy Field Artillery Company
    Two 150mm type 89 guns arrived 14 February, 1942.
3rd, 8th, 9th, and 10th Independent Light Artillery Company
    Each of these companies had three to four 37mm guns.
40th Anti-Aircraft Artillery Battalion (three companies)
45th Anti-Aircraft Artillery Battalion (three companies)
47th Anti-Aircraft Artillery Battalion (two companies)
48th Anti-Aircraft Battalion (three companies)
    Each of the above four units had a company with four 75mm type 88 anti-aircraft guns.
30th and 31st Independent Anti-Aircraft Companies used in the rear areas for air base defense.
3rd Mortar Battalion (three companies)
    Each company had twelve 81mm mortars (fires a seven pound shell 2,000 yards) arrived 19 March, 1942.
2nd Independent Howitzer Battalion (three companies)
    Each company had four 150mm howitzers (really mortars) firing to a maximum range of only 2,100 feet and throwing a high explosive shell weighing just over 50 pounds.
14th Independent Howitzer Battalion
    Each company had 300mm howitzers (really mortars) arrived 20 March, 1942.
15th Independent Howitzer Battalion
    Possibly 250mm short ranged howitzers (?), definitely the short range type which was essentially a mortar.

Independent Engineers

3rd Independent Engineer Regiment (three companies)
    Combat engineers, utilizing horses for equipment movement and numbering a total of 1055 men.
21st Independent Engineer Regiment (two companies)
    Conventional engineers, used primarily in river crossings. This unit organized the three gun boat Task Forces using 3-4 boats each and one Special Task Force using captured American craft with ten landing boats. The 21st was used in the landing on Corregidor.
3rd Independent Engineer Company - Conventional engineers.
23rd Independent Engineer Regiment (four companies)
    Conventional Engineers, this unit arrived 20 March, 1942. The 23rd was used in the landing on Corregidor.
6th, 10th, 28th Independent Engineer Regiments, and one company of the 26th Independent Engineer Regiment - the regiments each had four companies and these unit were used for amphibious operations.

Japan was the first nation to develop specific craft for amphibious operations. During the Lingayen Gulf landing the Japanese employed 184 various landing craft, of which the Type A Daihatsu, with bullet proof gunwales, and a landing ramp, was the middle sized type. It could carry alternatively 70 men (up to 120 if a short haul), 10 to 15 tons of supplies, or a tank. As the war progressed several upgraded versions of this workhorse would appear. It was 46 foot long, steel made, diesel powered and could make eight knots. It had a minimum armament of two machine-guns.

Japan also employed three ton craft which were used to move key personal about the invasion beach.

1st Kure Special Naval Landing Force (three rifle companies and one machine gun company, strength 820 men) Landed at Legaspi.

2nd Kure Special Naval Landing Force was used in the Southern Philippines.

These are typical units used in the Philippine campaign by Japan. Note that not all sources agree. For example, some show the 1st heavy field artillery as having twenty-four 150mm howitzers. The gun data is largely from A.J. Barker's *Japanese Army Handbook (1979)*.

5th Air Division (Lieutenant General Hideyoshi Obata)

4th Air Brigade

50th Air Regiment (3 fighter squadrons)
36 Nates (390 mile range, 2 MGs, 292 mph - obsolete)

8th Air Regiment (1 reconnaissance squadron and 3 light bomber squadrons)
9 Babs (1,491 mile range, 1 MG, 298 mph)
27 Lilys (1,230 mile range, 3 MGs, 661 pound bombload, 298 mph) 2 Dinahs (1,537 mile range, 1 MG, 375 mph - reconnaissance)

16th Air Regiment (3 light bomber squadrons)
27 Anns (1,056 mile range, 2 MGs, 661 pound bomb load, 263 mph - older than the Lily)

14th Air Regiment (3 bomber squadrons)
18 Sallys (932 mile range, 6 MGs, 1,653 pound bomb load, 268 mph - Hurricanes and P-40s had advantage on Sally)

Attached to 5th Air Division

24th Air Regiment (3 fighter squadrons)
36 Nates

76th Independent Air Squadron
9 Babs

10th Independent Air Unit
52nd Independent Air Squadron
9 Somas (660 mile range, 3 MGs, 441 pound bomb load, 263 mph - popular well protected ground support aircraft - Japanese Stuka!)

74th Independent Air Squadron
12 Marys (826 mile range, 2 MGs, 661 pound bomb load, 263 mph - obsolete. This unit converted to the Ida army co-operation light bomber by March of 1942. Ideal for rugged short runways, it operated up close to the frontline. 767 mile range, 2 MGs, 330 bombs (ten small ones), 216mph)

11th Air Fleet

21st Air Flotilla (based on Formosa)

Kanoya Air Group (bombers)

27 Bettys (3,749 mile range, 3 MGs, 1 20mm cannon, 1,764 pound bomb load or torpedo, 266 mph)

1st Air Group (bombers)

36 Nells (2,722 mile range, 3 MGs, 1 20mm cannon, 1,764 pound bomb load, or torpedo, 232 mph - older verson of Betty. Design initiated by Yamamoto in 1933), the long range of the Nell was a real surprise to the Allies.

Higashi-ko Air Group (reconnaissance)

27 Mavis—based at Palau (2,981 mile range, 3 MGs, 1 20mm cannon, 211 mph - extended range to 3,779 miles)

1001 1st Air Unit (transports)

25 Tina (Nell style) transports - for Yokosuka Special Naval Landing Force (SNLF = Japanese Marines) paratroops (1 MG, 216 mph)

23rd Air Flotilla

Takao Air Group (bombers)

54 Bettys

Thainan Air Group (Fighters)

54 Zekes (better known as the Zero, it had a 1,160 mile range, 2 MGs, 2 20mm cannon, 331.5 mph - the Zero was the best with an extended range of 1,930 miles. Some 837 were build by March of 1942.)

6 Claudes (746 mile range, 2 MGs, 270 mph - the plane the Zero replaced. The light aircraft carriers Ryujo, Hosho, and Zuiho and garrison areas began the war with this plane.)

(reconnaissance)

8 Babs

3rd Air Group (fighters)

45 Zekes

7 Claudes

(for reconnaissance)

7 Babs

The main body of the 11th Air Fleet moved to the Dutch East Indies by 26 December, 1941. The Takao and the 1st Air Group departed with about 100 aircraft aftcr 7 January, 1942. A few aircraft remained, mostly at Legaspi, but no operations involving naval aircraft were conducted on Luzon after 24 January, 1942.

The radius of action for a warplane is not simply the dividing of the range in two equal parts. The combat radius (airbase to target) must also include factors such as forming up of the attack force or wave, as well as obtaining the most optimum altitude and air speed to obtain maximum flight time. Combat must be assumed which will use up fuel at an alarming rate. It is not uncommon to take 1/3rd of the normal radius of an aircraft and throw it out, then divide in half.

Below are the combat radius of action for Japanese planes as defined by Japanese sources. Note that the Zero was given an additional 50 miles of radius then shown below by careful husbanding of fuel and rigorous practice.

Sally	530 miles
Babs	440 miles
Lily	440 miles
Ann	380 miles
Sonia	310 miles

Nate	160-220 miles
Betty	650 miles
Nell	650 miles
Mavis	800 miles
Zero/Zeke	500 miles

Filipino And U.S. Land Forces

US Army Unit
Philippine Division (10,233 troops - as 30 November 1941) HQ had about
211 men
31st Infantry Regiment (only American unit - 1,729 men)
45th Philippine Scouts Infantry Regiment (2,435 men)
57th Philippine Scouts Infantry Regiment (2,435 men)
12th Field Artillery Brigade
24th Artillery Regiment (two motorized battalions with British
75mm guns of 843 troops)
one battalion of the 23rd (2.95" mountain guns Artillery Regiment
with 401 men)
14th Engineer Regiment (894 men)

Independent USA Units
43rd Intantry Regiment (328 men)
Independent 26th Cavalry (two squadrons with three troops each
numbering 842 men).
86th Philippine Scout Field Artillery Regiment (395 men)
88th Philippine Scout Field Artillery Regiment (538 men)
192nd Tank Battalion (54 Stuart Tanks - 588 men)
194th Tank Battalion (54 Stuart Tanks - 410)

The Stuart tank, weighed 12.3 tons, had one 37mm, 51mm of frontal armor, 36 m.p.h., and a crew of four.

Of the several provisional units formed in the coming battle were two battalions of 75mm guns mounted on trucks and used as a poor man's self-propelled artillery substitute. This was a technique quite commonly used in the North African fighting by the Commonwealth and the Italians.

4th Marine Regiment.

Philippine Commonwealth forces (120,000 men)

Regular Army
1st Regular Division (1st, 2nd, and 3rd regiments). No organic artillery as
of 19 December, but a unit with a high degree of *elan*.
2nd Regular Division (made up of the 1st, 2nd, and 4th Constabulary
Regiments, formed at the start of the war).

Ten Reserve Corps were to be mobilized. Unfortunately the mobilization began only in September of 1941, with one of the three regiments in each division. This mobilization would continue into the invasion of the Philippines so it was never complete. The 11th, 21st, 31st, 41st, 51st, 71st, and 91st served on Luzon, while the 61st, 81st, and the 101st served in the rest of the Philippines. The 71st and 91st left there 3rd regiment in the south where they first mobilized.

A typical division was the 31st (on paper numbering 7500 men), with one regiment (the 31st) first mobilized on 1 September. The 32nd regiment fol-

235

lowed on 1 November, the 33rd regiment on 25 November. Between 18 and 30 November the service units and Headquarter company were mobilized. The motor transport company consisted of five trucks and command cars (!). The division also had an engineer battalion and a signal company. The anti-tank battalion was not formed for any of the reserve units.

Each regiment had two .50 caliber machine-guns and six 3-inch trench mortars. Each company had one browning automatic rifle, and there were eight Browning .30 caliber machine-guns in each machine gun company.

The regimental artillery, the 31st artillery regiment, began mobilizing on 12 December, and was of two battalions. Each battalion was to have three batteries of four guns each (World War I 75mm Field guns), on paper that is, in reality it received only eight guns and without sights.

To the best of my knowledge no thorough study has been written on the strength and deployment of the Filipino-American army in 1941-42. Comparing and contrasting the results of this early fighting with the Malayan, Burma and Dutch East Indies native contingents would be quite interesting. The fact that thousands of the Filipinos fought and died at Bataan and beyond is much different from much of the conduct of the Malays, Burmese and especially Indonesians.

Filipino-American aircraft strength in the Philippines
As of December 1, 1941.
35 B-17s C's and D's (many based at Mindanao)
18 B-18s (obsolete)
 9 A-27s
12 B-10s (obsolete)
107 P-40E (the latest fighters went to the Philippines, older versions to Pearl)
16 P-26As (belonged to the Filipino air force)

MALAYA

Japanese 25th Army
Lieutenant General Tomoyuki Yamashita
5th Mechanized Division (15,342 men, 1,008 vehicles, no horses)
 9th Infantry Brigade
  41st Infantry Regiment
  11th Infantry Regiment
 21st Infantry Brigade
  21st Infantry Regiment
  42nd Infantry Regiment
 5th Field Artillery Regiment
 5th Engineer Regiment
 5th Reconnaissance Regiment
Imperial Guard Division (12,649 men, 914 vehicles, no horses)
 3rd Guards Regiment
 4th Guards Regiment
 5th Guards Regiment

Guards Field Artillery Regiment
Guards Engineer Regiment
Guard Reconnaissance Regiment
18th Infantry Division (22,206 men, 33 vehicles, 5,707 horses)
  23rd Infantry Brigade
    55th Infantry Regiment
    56th Infantry Regiment
  35th Infantry Brigade
    114th Infantry Regiment
    124th Infantry Regiment
  18th Mountain Artillery Regiment
  12th Engineer Regiment
  22nd Cavalry Battalion
Attached to 25th Army:
  3rd Tank Group HQ (5 medium, 5 light tanks)
  1st Tank Regiment (37 medium, 20 light tanks, 91 vehicles)
  6th Tank Regiment (37 medium, 20 light tanks, 91 vehicles)
  14th Tank Regiment (45 light tanks, 48 vehicles)
  1 Light Tank Company (10 light tanks, 8 vehicles)

3rd Air Division (used for Malayan operation)
Attached: 12th and 20th Anti-aircraft Regiments
3rd Air Brigade
  59th Fighter Regiment (3 fighter squadrons) (745 mile range, 2 MGs,
    308 mph - the best Japanese Army fighter)
  27th Light Bomber Regiment (3 light bomber squadrons)
  75th Light Bomber Regimemt (3 light bomber squadrons)
  90th Light Bomber Regiment (3 light bomber squadrons)
7th Air Brigade
  64th Fighter Regiment (3 fighter squadrons)
  12th Heavy Bomber Regiment (3 heavy bomber squadrons)
  60th Heavy Bomber Regiment (3 heavy bomber squadrons)
  98th Heavy Bomber Regiment (3 heavy bomber squadrons)
12th Air Brigade
  1st Fighter Group (2 fighter squadrons)
  11st Fighter Group (2 fighter squadrons)
  81st Reconnaissance Regiment
15th Independent Air Group (this force would normally operate close to
  the front)
  71st Independent Reconnaissance Squad
  73rd Independent Reconnaissance Squad
  89th Independent Reconnaissance Squad

11th Air Fleet
22nd Air Flotilla (based near Saigon)
  Genzan Air Group
  Takao Air Group detachment
  Mihoro Air Group
Detached from the 21st Air Flotilla
  Kanoya Air Group
Detached from the 23rd Air Flotilla
  Tainan Air Group Detachment (Yamada Unit)
Stationed at Rong Sam Lem Bay (near the Thailand border) were the three

seaplane tenders Kimikawa Maru (15 seaplanes), Sanyo Maru (8 seaplanes), and Sagara Maru (8 seaplanes). The various additional ships operating in the area carried another 25 scout planes.

Allied Naval Strength in the Far East on December 17, 1941

Eastern Fleet Based At Singapore
Vice-Admiral Tom Phillips, commanding
Battleships
Prince of Wales
Battle Cruisers
Repulse
Light Cruisers
Danae, Dragon, Durban, with the Mauritius refitting at port
Destroyers
Electra, Express, Tenedos, Vampire, Scout, Thanet, with the Encounter, Jupiter, Stronghold, Vendetta, Iris refitting at port

East Indies Squadron (Indian Ocean)
Vice-Admiral Geoffrey Arbuthnot, commanding
Battleships
Revenge
Light Aircraft Carriers
Hermes refitting
Heavy Cruisers
Exeter
Light Cruisers
Enterprise refitting

Australian And New Zealand Squadrons
Rear Admiral John Crace, commanding
Heavy Cruisers
Canberra (Australia on route from South Atlantic)
Light Cruisers
Adelaide, Perth, Achilles, Leander, with the Hobart en route from the Mediterranean
Destroyers
Le Triomphant (Free French) and the Stuart and Voyager refitting

Netherlands East Indies Fleet
Vice-Admiral Conrad E.L. Helfrich, commanding
Light Cruisers
De Ruyter, Java and Tromp (Sumatra was out of commission at Surabaya)
Destroyers
Van Nes, Bankert, Witte de With, Kortenaer, Piet Hein, Evertsen, and van Ghent

United States Asiatic Fleet Based In The Phillipines
Admiral Thomas C. Hart, commanding
Heavy Cruisers
Houston
Light Cruisers
Boise and Marblehead
Destroyers

Pope, John D. Ford, Paul Jones, Stewart (which was captured at Surabaya in March 1942 and served as a Japanese warship), Bulmer,
Barker, Parrott, Whipple, Alden, Edsall, John D. Edwards, with
the Peary and Pillsbury refitting.
Additionally, the British had 1 submarine refitting, the Dutch 14 (one refitting) and the Americans 29 (four refitting)

Commonwealth Order of Battle in Malaya on 7 December, 1941
(Lieutenant General A.E. Perceval)

Army Reserve: 12th Indian Infantry brigade
Singapore Fortress
    1st Malaya Infantry Brigade
    2nd Malaya Infantry Brigade
    Coast Battery Forces
8th Australian Division
    22nd Australian Infantry Brigade
    27th Australian Infantry Brigade
III Indian Corps
    11th Indian Division
        6th Indian Infantry Brigade
        15th Indian Infantry Brigade
    9th Indian Division
        8th Infantry Brigade
        22nd Infantry Brigade
    Corps Reserve
        28 Indian Brigade (three battalions of Gurkha troops)
    Attached:
        Penang Fortress force
        three airfield defense forces
        Singapore Straits Volunteer Force (forming)

Commonwealth Order of Battle in Malaya on 8 February, 1942
(Lieutenant General A.E. Perceval)

Army Reserve: 12th Indian Infantry brigade
Singapore Fortress
    1st Malaya Infantry Brigade
    2nd Malaya Infantry Brigade
    Singapore Straits Volunteer Force Brigade
    Coast Battery Forces and one field battery
8th Australian Division
    22nd Australian Infantry Brigade
    27th Australian Infantry Brigade
    44th Indian Infantry Brigade
    Attached: Area Troops (three odd companies and special reserve battal-
        ion of Australians)
III Indian Corps
    11th Indian Division
        8th Indian Infantry Brigade
        28th Indian Infantry Brigade
        53rd Infantry Brigade (detached from 18th British Division)
    18th British Division

54th Infantry Brigade
55th Infantry Brigade
Corps Reserve
15 Indian Brigade +2 battalions

Note reinforcements and the destruction of various units in the time frame above. The forces huddled in Singapore by this point were to a great degree demoralized.

DUTCH EAST INDIES

Japanese 16th Army for Employment in the Dutch East Indies
2nd Infantry Division
  4th Infantry Regiment (three battalions),
  16th Infantry Regiment
  29th Infantry Regiment
  2nd Field Artillery Regiment of three battalions
  2nd Recon regiment (motorized)
  support troops
38th Infantry Division after used for capture of Hong Kong
  228th Infantry Regiment
  229th Infantry Regiment
  230th Infantry Regiment
  38th Mountain Artillery Regiment of three battalions
  support troops - it may have lacked the usual Recon regiment.

The Japanese often employed mountain artillery with their army units used in amphibious operations as they were lighter and more maneuverable than regular field artillery. In 1941 they recommended to the Italians the employment of mountain troops in the proposed Axis invasion of Malta.

48th Mechanized Division after employment with the 14th Army in the
    Philippines
56th Regimental Group (Sakaguchi Detachment)
2nd Tank Regiment
4th Tank Regiment

21st Air Flotilla
23rd Air Flotilla
3rd Air Division

1st Kure Special Naval Landing Force (3 rifle companies and 1 machine
    gun company, strength 820 men)
2nd Kure Special Naval Landing Force (3 rifle companies, 1 machine gun
    company, 1 anti-aircraft battery, strength 1,000 men) 1st and 2nd
    Sasebo Special Naval Landing Force (each consisted of 3 rifle
    companies and 1 machine gun company, 800 men each and
    employed as a combined unit)
1st Yokosuka Special Naval Landing Force (paratroop unit organized as
    an HQ company and 3 rifle companies, 519 men, plus 1 machine
    gun company, about 800 men)
2nd Yokosuka Special Naval Landing Force (HQ company, 3 rifle
    companies, 1 machine gun company, strength 28 officers, 1,150 men)

3rd Yokosuka Special Naval Landing Force (paratroop unit consisting of 3 rifle companies and 1 machine gun company, strength about 1,000 men)

Japanese Invasion Force: Third Fleet, Dutch Indies Force (Java Invasion)

Direct Support Force (Both East And West Java Invasions)
Vice Admiral Ibo (Sources vary, but it is Ibo) Takahashi, commanding
Heavy Cruisers
    Ashigara, Myoko
Destroyers
    Asashio, Oshio, Arashio, Kawakaze

Western Java Invasion
Rear Admiral Takao Kurita, commanding
Heavy Cruisers
    Mikuma, Mogami, Kumano, Suzuya (Chokai attached in earlier invasions)
Destroyers
    Amagiri, Asagiri, Yugiri

Third Escort Force
Rear Admiral Kenzaburo Hara, commanding
Light Cruisers
    Natori and Yura
Destroyers
    Asakaze, Harukaze, Hatakaze, Natsukaze, Fubuki, Shirayuki, Hatsuyuki, Satsuki, Minazuki, Nagatsuki, Shirakumo, Murakumo, Hibiki, Akatsuki, Hatsuharu

First Air Group
Rear Admiral Kakuji Kakuta, commanding
Light Aircraft Carriers
    Ryujo (22 Claude Fighters, 18 Kate torpedo planes and strength at start of war)
Transport Force
    Fifty-six transports (including two Japanese army airplane transports, one of which was lost in Battle of Sunda Straits)

Eastern Java Invasion Force Support Group
Rear Admiral Takao Takagi, commanding
Heavy Cruisers
    Nachi, Haguro
Destroyers
    Ikazuchi, Akebono

First Escort Force
Rear Admiral Shoji Nishimura, commanding
Light Cruisers
    Naka
Destroyers
    Murasame, Harusame, Yudachi, Samidare, Asagumo, Natsugumo, Minegumo, Yamakaze

Second Escort Force
Rear Admiral Raizo Tanaka, commanding
Light Cruisers
Jintsu
Destroyers
Kuroshio, Oyashio, Hayashio, Hatsukaze, Yukikaze, Amatsukaze,
Sazanami, Ushio, Tokitsukazc

First Base Force
A rear force not employed directly, in the final attack on Java
Light Cruisers
Nagara
Destroyers
Hatsharu, Nenohi, Wakaba

Second Base Force
Seaplanes tenders Chitose, Mizuho, Sanyo Maru, Sanuki Maru (latter two
are capable of operating eight planes each)

Transport Force
Forty-one transports

ABDA Combined Strike Force For The Defense of East Java
Rear Admiral Karel Doorman, commanding
Heavy Cruisers
Houston (USN) and Exeter (RN)
Light Cruisers
Java (RNN), de Ruyter (RNN), Perth (RAN)
Destroyers
John D. Edwards, Paul Jones, John D. Ford, Alden, Pope (all USN);
Electra, Jupiter, Encounter (RN); Witt de With, and Kortenaer
(RNN)

ABDA Western Striking Force
Captain H.L.Howden (RAN) commanding
Light Cruisers
Hobart (RAN), Dragon, and Danae (RN)
Destroyers
Scout, Tenedos (RN), and Evertsen (RNN)

The Allied-Dutch Army on Java, March of 1942
West Java Command
1st Infantry
1st Infantry Regiment
2nd Infantry Regiment
1st Artillery Regiment
1st Cavalry Regiment
5th Cavalry Company
1st Motorized Cavalry Company
Scattered through Java were six Landstorm garrison units of doubtful quality
Black Force
2/3 Australian Machine Gun Battalion
2/2 Australian Pioneer Battalion

Australian Engineer Company
King's Own Hussars Light Armor Company
131st Artillery Battalion (USA)

Central Java Command
4th Infantry Regiment
2nd Motorized Cavalry Company
Twelve 75mm Artillery field pieces
Zuid Reserve Group Regiment
Composite garrison unit at Tjilatjap (battalion strength)

Eastern Java Command
3rd Infantry Division
  6th Infantry Regiment
  2nd Artillery Regiment
  3rd Motorized Cavalry Company
Dutch Marines at Surabuya (small composite unit)
Barrisan Corps
  Madoera Island detachment composite unit of about 3 battalions
Two companies of infantry
21st Light Anti-Aircraft Battalion
77th Heavy Anti-Aircraft Battalion

(The 2nd Dutch Artillery includes 1 battery of the 131st American)

INDIAN OCEAN

Japanese Carrier Strike Force
Vice-Admiral Chuichi Nagumo, commanding
  Aircraft Carriers
    Akagi, Hiryu, Soryu, Shokaku, Zuikaku
  Battleships
    Haruna, Kirishima, Hiei, Kongo
  Heavy Cruisers
    Tone, Chikuma
  Light Cruiser
    Abukuma
  Destroyers
    Tanikaze, Urakaze, Isokaze, Hamakaze, Arare, Shiranuhi, Kasumi,
      Kagero, Maikaze, Hagikaze, Akigumo

British Eastern Fleet, 26 March 1942
Vice-Admiral James Somerville, commanding

Force A (Fast)
  Aircraft Carriers
    Indomitable (12 Fulmar fighters, 9 Sea Hurricane fighters, 24 Albacore
      torpedo planes) and Formidable (12 Martlet fighters, 21 Albacore
      torpedo planes)
  Battleships
    Warspite
  Heavy Cruisers
    Dorsetshire, Cornwall
  Light Cruisers
    Enterprise, Emerald

Destroyers
  Napier, Nestor, Paladin, Panther, Hotspur, Foxhound
Force B (Slow Class)
Vice-Admiral Algernon Willis, commanding
  Light Aircraft Carrier
    Hermes (12 Swordfish torpedo planes)
  Battleships
    Resolution, Ramillies, Royal Sovereign, Revenge
  Light Cruisers
    Caledon, Dragon, Heemskerk (RNN)
  Destroyers
    Griffin, Norman, Arrow, Decoy, Fortune, Scout, Vampire (RAN), Isaac
      Sweers (RNN)

Ceylon Based Air Units

The Royal Air Force had two squadrons of Hurricanes based at Colombo, and one at Trimcomalee. One additional fighter squadron made up of Fulmars was based at Trimcomalee. One RAF squadron of Blenheim bombers was based at Colombo along with some Catalina flying boats.

The Royal Navy had two squadrons of Fulmars based at Trimcomalee, along with one squadron of torpedo planes there consisting of Swordfish and Albacore.

British Airplane Characteristics

Fulmar (820 mile range, 8 MGs 253 mph)

Hurricane MKII (480 mile range without tanks, 12 MGs, 4 cannon, 342 mph)

Albacore (521 mile range, 2 MGs, 1 torpedo or 1500 lbs., 163 mph)

BURMA

Japanese 15th Army
  (Lieutenant General Yojiro Iida)
    33rd Infantry Division
      213th Infantry Regiment
      214th Infantry Regiment
      215th Infantry Regiment
      33rd Mountain Artillery Regiment of three battalions
      33rd Engineer Regiment
      support troops
      (the 213th first went to Bangkok with a portion of the 33rd's artillery
        and arrived in Burma in March. There was no Recon unit).
    55th Infantry Division
      112th Infantry Regiment (two battalions)
      143rd Infantry Regiment (two battalions)
      55th Mountain artillery regiment of three battalions (two present)
      55th Cavalry Regiment
      55th Engineer Regiment
      support troops
      (Its 144th regiment was absent with the ubiquitous "South Sea Detachment").

Attached to 15th Army:
4th Independent Engineer Regiment
20th Independent Engineer Regiment

Reinforcements after March 4, 1942:
18th Infantry Division, after employment with the 25th Army in Malaya, arrived in mid-March at Rangoon.
56th Division
  Two regiments, the 113th and 148th with motorized 56th Reconnaisance regiment, 56th Field Artillery regiment, and 56th Engineer Regiment.
  Elements including the 146th regiment were absent in Java with the 56th Regimental Group (Sakaguchi Detachment).
1st Tank Regiment
14th Tank Regiment
18th Heavy Field Artillery Regiment
21st Heavy Field Artillery Regiment
21st Independent Artillery Brigade

5th Air Army (at start of campaign)
4th Air Corps
  50th Fighter Group   Nates
  8th Light Bomber Group   Lily, Sally, & Dinahs
  14th Heavy Bomber Group   Sallys
10th Air Corps
  31st Light Bomber Group   Anns
  62nd Heavy Bomber Group   Sallys
  77th Fighter Group   Nates
Attached:
  70th Independent Squadron - a mixed force of Oscars and Nates

Reinforcements,
  After 9 February, 1942
    47th Independent Fighter Squadron   Tojo
      (575 mile range, 2 MGs & 2 cannons, 360 mph - a new plane with teething problems - not all sources agree and this *may* have been an Oscar squadron)
  After 22 February, 1942
    71st Independent Recon Squadron   Sonias
  After 7 March, 1942
    15th Independent Air Group
      50th Independent Squadron   Nates
      51st Independent Squadron   Nates
    12th Air Corps
      1st Fighter Group (-1 sqd.)   Nates
      11th Fighter Group (-1 sqd.)   Nates
    7th Air Fleet
      64th Fighter Group   Oscars
      12th Heavy Bomber Group   Sallys
      99th Heavy Bomber Group   Sallys
      20th Anti-aircraft Regiment
  After 3 April, 1942
    89th Independent Squadron   Idas
    91st Independent Squadron   Idas

After 16 April, 1942
27th Dive Bomber Group   Sonias
81st Recon Group, 1st Squadron   Babs & Dinahs

Army of Burma (27 December, 1941)
1st Burma Division
Major General J. Bruce Scoff
1st Burma Brigade (three battalions)
2nd Burma Brigade (seven battalions + 2 companies & a battery of 12th
    Indian Mountain Artillery)
13th Indian Brigade (three battalions)
16th Indian Brigade (three battalions)
Rangoon garrison of two battalions (- two companies)
support troops

Chinese Expeditionary Force In Burma Order of Battle
Winter - Spring of, 1942 (Lieutenant General Lin Wei)
V Army
22nd division (three regiments)
96th division (three regiments)
200th division (three regiments)
Training depot with two reserve regiments
Attached:
cavalry regiment
artillery regiment
armored regiment
motor regiment
engineer regiment
VI Army
49th division (three regiments)
55th division (three regiments)
93rd division (three regiments)
Attached:
one battalion of the 13th artillery regiment
transport battalion
engineer battalion
LXVI Army
28th division (three regiments)
38th division (three regiments)
29rd division (three regiments)
Attached:
one battalion of the 18th artillery regiment
Note: A division is the equivalent of a regiment and not all troops had rifles.

Army of Burma Corps (Burcorps)
19 March, 1942 (Lieutenant General W.J. Slim)
1st Burma Division
1st Burma Brigade (four battalions)
2nd Burma Brigade (three battalions)
13th Indian Brigade (one battalions)
Attached:
27th Indian Mountain Regiment

four Frontier Force battalions
8th Indian Anti-tank battery
two batteries of Indian mountain guns
17th Indian Division (much reduced in combat)
   16th Indian Brigade (four battalions - 2,500 men)
   48th Indian Brigade (equivalent to four battalions - 2,500 men)
   63rd Indian Brigade (four battalions - 1,700 men)
Attached:
   1st Indian Field Regiment
   two Frontier Force battalions + three small detached Frontier Force
      units
   three infantry battalions
   one battalion of Burma Military Police
   8th Indian Anti-tank battery
   one battery of Indian mountain guns
   two batteries of Indian field guns
   Royal Marine River Patrol (Force Viper)

Attached to Corps:
7th Armoured Brigade Group
   7th Hussars
   2nd Royal Tank Regiment
   414th Royal Horse Artillery
   one Anti-tank battery
   one infantry battalion
   Attached:
      one battery each of heavy and light anti-aircraft guns one battalion
      of Indian Engineers

Attached to the Army:
eight various strength battalions
1st Heavy Anti-Aircraft Regiment
detachment of Rangoon Field Brigade field artillery
In the Rear:
   nine garrison companies
   14 battalions
   2nd Indian Anti-tank Regiment with no guns and shy two companies
   8th Indian Anti-Aircraft battery
   one troop of light Anti-Aircraft guns

By April the continuing Japanese advance through Burma and closer to India, the Commonwealth formed two armies in India. By 21 April, 1942 the Eastern Army under Lieutenant General Sir Charles Broad consisted of the 14th, 26th, and 23rd Indian Divisions and the British 70th Infantry Division, with a reserve force of the Assam Division. The 26th Indian Division was stationed at Calcutta. The Southern Army was under General Sir Brodie Haig. It consisted of the 19th and 20th Indian Division (stationed at Madras and Bangalore respectively), and two armored brigades, one the 50th Army Tank Brigade and the 251st Indian Armoured Brigade.

The depleted BurCorps was down to an average of 400 men a battalion, but was still in the field.

CORAL SEA

Japanese Forces

Carrier Strike Force

Vice-Admiral Takeo Takagi, commanding (promoted for his victory at The Java Sea)
Aircraft Carriers
   Zuikaku (20 Zero fighters, 22 Val divebombers, 20 Kate torpedo
      planes) and Shokaku (18 Zero fighters, 21 Val divebombers, 19
      Kate torpedo planes)

It should be noted that the Zuikaku had their spare Zero fighters, and the Shokaku five that were without pilots destined for the Rabaul garrison. Takagi would be delayed 24 hours on 2 May due to bad weather by the need to fly these planes to Rabaul, an operation that would not be completed during this battle.

Heavy Cruisers
   Haguro and Myoko (flagship)
Destroyers
   Ushio, Akebono, Ariake, Yugure, Shigure and Shiratsuyu Fleet Train:
      one oiler

Port Moresby Invasion Force

Rear Admiral Koso Abe, commanding
Tsugaru
   Twelve transports carrying the main portion of the 3rd Kure SNLF and
      most of the 144th Infantry regiment of the South Seas Detach-
      ment (three battalions), auxiliary craft, and two oilers

Attack Force

Rear Admiral Kakuji Kajioka, commanding
Light Cruisers
   Yubari (flagship)
Destroyers
   Oite, Asanagi, Mutsuki, Mochizuki, and Yayoi

Close Cover Force

Rear Admiral Kuninori Marumo, commanding
Light Cruisers
   Tenryu (flagship) and Tatsuta
   Seaplane carrier Kamikawa Maru
   Three gunboats

Close Support Force

Rear Admiral Goto, commanding
Light Aircraft Carriers
   Shoho (8 Zero fighters, 4 Claude fighters, 6 Kate torpedo planes)
Heavy Cruisers
   Aoba (flagship), Kako, Kinugasa, and Furutaka
Destroyers
   Sazanami

Tulagi Invasion Force

Rear Admiral Kiyohide Shima, commanding
M L (Minelayer)
   Okinoshima (flagship)

Destroyers
  Yuzuki
APD (Fast Attack Transport)
  Kikuzuki

One transport and auxiliary craft carrying part of the 3rd Kure SNLF. There were approximately 6 fighters at Lae, 57 at Rabaul, and 86 bombers at Rabaul.

Japanese army strength in the South Pacific did not get a real boost until May of 1942 when the 17th Army was activated under General Hyakutake. It initially consisted of nine infantry battalions, drawn from several formations.

Allied Fleet at Coral Sea

Task Force 17 was broken into parts. Overall command was Rear Admiral Frank Jack Fletcher

Task Group 17.2

Rear Admiral Kinkaid, commanding
  Heavy Cruisers
    Minneapolis (flagship), New Orleans, Astoria, Chester, and Portland
  Destroyers
    Phelps, Dewey, Farragut, Aylwin, and Monaghan

Task Group 17.3

Rear Admiral Crace RN, commanding
  Heavy Cruisers
    HMAS Australia and Chicago
  Light Cruisers
    HMAS Hobart
  Destroyers
    Perkins and Walke (the Farragut was detached to 17.3 when it operated separately during the battle)

Task Group 17.5

Rear Admiral Fitch, commanding
  Aircraft Carriers
    Lexington (21 Wildcat fighters, 36 Dauntless divebombers, and 13 Devastator torpedo planes) and Yorktown (17 Wildcat fighters, 35 Dauntless divebombers, and 12 Devastator torpedo planes). Planes available at dawn on 7 May, 1942
  Destroyers
    Morris, Anderson, Hammann, and Russell

Task Group 17.6

Captain Philips, commanding
  Two oilers
  Destroyers
    Sims and Worden
    The seaplane tender Tangier was at Noumea with 12 Catalina flying boats

Allied Land Based Air

There were 19 B-25s, 19 A-24s, and 14 A-20s at Charters Towers, 12 B-25s and 80 B-26s at Townsville, with about 50 P-39 fighters. There were about 50 P-

39 fighters in New Guinea at Port Moresby. 48 B-17s were at Cloncurry and Darwin had 90 P-40s while Sydney had 100 P-39s.

Both sides had submarines in the area but neither side achieved much with them. The Americans had 11 subs, the S-37 through the S-47. These were older subs. The Japanese had seven, the I-21, I-22, I-24, I-28, I-29, RO-33, and the RO-34. After the Battle of the Coral Sea, the I-22-, 1-24 and 1-27 took on midget submarines and attacked Sydney Harbor in the so called "Battle of Sydney." The midget subs had a near miss on the heavy cruiscr Chicago and sank the barracks ship HMAS Kuttabul. All midgets were eventually sunk and the commander of one became the only Japanese in the war to be elevated to "War God" status, an unusual and a very rare honor in the tradition of Japan.

MIDWAY

Japanese Forces at Midway

First Fleet
Admiral Isoroku Yamamoto, commanding
Light Aircraft Carrier
  Hosho (9 Claude fighters, 6 Jean B4Y torpedo planes - 978 mile range, 1 MG, 173 mph, 1 torpedo or 1,102 pounds of bombs)
Battleships
  Yamato (flagship), Nagato and Mutsu
Light Cruiser
  Sendai
Destroyers
  Fubuki, Shirayuki, Murakumo, Hatsuyuki, Isoname, Uranami, Shikinami, Ayanami and Yukaze

First Mobile Force, Carrier Strike Force
Vice-Admiral Chuichi Nagumo, commanding
Aircraft Carriers
  Akagi (flagship) (18 Zero fighters, 18 Val bombers, and 27 Kate torpedo planes)
  Kaga (18 Zero fighters, 18 Val bombers, and 27 Kate torpedo planes)
  Hiryu (18 Zero fighters, 18 Val bombers, and 18 Kate torpedo planes)
  Soryu (18 Zero fighters, 18 Val bombers, and 18 Kate torpedo planes and 2 experimental Judys used for scouting)

It should be noted that in actual numbers at Midway, these four CVs carried between them 73 fighters, 74 Vals, and 81 Kates, as well as 21 Zero fighters of the 6th Air Group intended to garrison Midway. One Kate each on the Kaga and the Akagi were delegated to scouting purposes only.

Japanese Fleet Carrier Characteristics
  Akagi (41,300 tons, six 8-inch guns, twelve 4.7 inch anti-aircraft guns, 91 aircraft, 31 knots)
  Kaga (42,541 tons, ten 8-inch guns, sixteen 5-inch dual purpose guns, 90 aircraft, 28 knots)
  Hiryu (20,250 tons, twelve 5-inch dual purpose guns, 73 aircraft, 34 knots)
    Soryu (18,800 tons, twelve 5-inch dual purpose guns, 71 aircraft, 34.5 knots)

Battleships
   Haruna and Kirishima
Heavy Cruisers
   Tone and Chikuma
Light Cruiser
   Nagara
Destroyers
   Makigumo, Yugumo, Isokaze, Hagikaze, Hamakaze, Arashi,
      Kazegumo,
   Urakaze, Tanikaze, Nowaki, and Maikaze
Fleet Train
   Akigumo, eight tankers

Second Fleet, Strike Force, Support Force, Main Body
Vice-Admiral Nobutake Kondo, commanding
   Light Aircraft Carriers
      Zuiho (12 Claude fighers, 12 Jean torpedo planes)
   Battleships
      Hiei and Kongo
   Heavy Cruisers
      Atago (flagship), Chokai, Myoko, and Haguro
   Light Cruiser
      Yura
   Destroyers
      Murasame, Yudachi, Harusame, Samidare, Asagumo, Minegumo, Nat-
         sugumo, and Mikazuki
   Fleet Train
      four tankers

Second Fleet Escort Force
Rear Admiral RaizoTanaka, commanding
   Light Cruiser
      Jintsu (flagship)
   Destroyers
      Kuroshio, Oyashio, Hatsukaze, Tokitsukaze, Amatsukaze, Yukikaze,
         Kasumi, Kagero, Arare, and Shiranuhi
   Patrol Boats
      Three subchasers, and four minesweepers and No. 1, 2, and 34 carry-
         ing troops. Twelve transports with 5,000 troops (Ichiki Detach-
         ment, Kure & Yokosuka 5th Special Naval Landing Force, and
         two construction battalions) and one tanker. Patrol Nos 1, 2 and
         34 were old Japanese destroyers converted to troop carrying.

Second Fleet Occupation Support Force
Rear Admiral Takeo Kurita, commanding
   Seaplane Tenders
   Chitose (7 Alfs and 16 Daves)
   Kamikawa Maru (8 Daves and Jakes- 460 mile range, 230 mph, 3MGs, two
      132 pound bombs), 4 Pete scout planes)
   Heavy Cruisers
      Kumano (flagship), Mogami, Mikuma, Suzuya
   Destroyers
      Arashio, Asashio, and Hayashio

251

Patrol Boat No. 35 with 550 troops. This force was detailed for the occupation of Kure Island and setting up of a seaplane base.

Special Duty Force
Captain Harada
Seaplane Carriers
Chiyoda and Nisshin (modified to carry 8 midget submarines, and 5 motor torpedo boats respectively. To be deployed around Midway after its capture to attack Allied ships)

First Supply Force
Destroyer
Ariake
Two freighters
12 submarines supporting Midway operation
3 "refueling" submarines supporting seaplane operation

First Fleet, 2nd Battleship Division
Vice-Admiral Shiro Takasu, commanding
Battleships
Hyuga (flagship), Ise, Fuso, and Yamashiro
Light Cruisers
Kitakami and Oi (special ships armed with 40 Long Lance 24-inch torpedoes each and retaining four 5.5" guns from their original armament)
Destroyers
Asagiri, Yugiri, Shirakumo, Amagiri, Umikaze, Yamakaze, Kawakaze, Suzukaze, Ariake, Yugure, Shigure and Shiratsuyu
Fleet Train
two oilers

Second Strike Force, Carrier Force
Rear Admiral Kakuji Kakuta, commanding
Light Aircraft Carrier
Ryujo (flagship) (12 Zero fighters, 18 Kate torpedo bombers)
Aircraft Carrier
Junyo (18 Zero fighters, 15 Val divebombers)
Heavy Cruisers
Maya and Takao
Destroyers
Akebono, Ushio, Sazanami, and Shiokaze
Fleet Train
one oiler

Fifth Fleet, Main Body
Vice Admiral Boshiro Hosogaya
Heavy Cruiser
Nachi (flagship)
Destroyers
Inazuma, Ikazuchi, two oilers and three supply ships

Attu Occupation Force
Rear Admiral Sentaro Omori, commanding
Light Cruiser
Abukuma (flagship)
Seaplane Tender
Kimikawa Maru (8 Jakes, through capable of operating 12)

Destroyers
> Hatsuharu, Hatsushimo, Wakaba, and Nenohi
> one minelayer
> one transport with 1,200 men of the Army North Sea Detachment under Major Hozumi

Kiska Occupation Force
Captain Taken Ono, commanding
Light Cruisers
> Tama and Kiso (flagship)

Destroyers
> Akatsuki, Hibiki, and Hokaze
> three minesweepers

Armed Merchant Cruiser
> Asakamaru
> two transports with 550 troops of the Maizuru 3rd Special Naval Landing Force and 700 pioneers under Lieutenant Commander Mukai
> 6 submarines supporting Aleutian operation

American Forces At Midway

Task Force 16
Rear Admiral Raymond Spruance, commanding
Aircraft Carriers
> Enterprise (flagship) (27 Wildcat fighters, 33 Dauntless divebombers, 14 Devastator torpedo planes) and Hornet (27 Wildcat fighters, 34 Dauntless divebombers, 15 Devastator torpedo planes)

Heavy Cruisers
> New Orleans, Minneapolis, Vincennes, Northampton, and Pensacola

Light Cruiser
> Atlanta (a new class of anti-aircraft cruiser armed with sixteen 5-inch guns)

Destroyers
> Balch, Conyngham, Benham, Ellet, Maury, Phelps, Worden, Monaghan, Aylwin, Dewey, and Monssen (the latter two destroyers were covering two oilers.)

Task Force 17
Rear Admiral Frank Jack Fletcher, commanding
Aircraft Carriers
> Yorktown (flagship) (25 Wildcat fighters, 34 Dauntless divebombers, 12 Devastator torpedo planes)

Heavy Cruisers
> Astoria and Portland

Destroyers
> Hammann, Hughes, Morris, Anderson, Russell, and Gwin

Note: Plane totals are for operational planes available. Thirteen planes were under repair or inoperable.

Fleet Train
Destroyers
> Blue, Ralph Talbot
> One oiler

Guarding Western Minor Islands Of The Hawaiian Group, Especially The French Frigate Shoals
Destroyers
  Clark
  One tanker,two auxiliary seaplane tenders,some minor craft

Task Force 1
Vice-Admiral William Pye, commanding
  Aircraft Carrier and Scout
    Long Island (12 Wildcat fighters, 8 fixed wheel SOC-3 Seagull Recon planes) The SOC-3 was used primarily as a cruiser-launched seaplane, 679 mile range, 2 MGs, 165 mph, 650 pounds of bombs)
  Battleships
    Maryland, Pennsylvania, Tennessee, Colorado, New Mexico, Mississippi, and Idaho
  Eight destroyers

Midway Island Defenses
Captain Cyril Simard, commanding
    6th Marine Defense Battalion, 2 companies of the 2nd Battalion of Marine Raiders detachment 3rd Marine Defense Battalion
    8 PT boats, 4 small patrol craft
    2 PT boats at Kure Island
    Shore Based Air- (these are operational totals - there were a few additional planes present but not operational) USN contingent 32 PBY long range scout planes, 6 Avenger torpedo planes.
    Marine contingent - 20 Buffalo fighters, 7 Wildcat fighters, 11 Vindicator divebombers, 16 Dauntless divebombers
    Army Air Corps contingent - 4 Marauder B-26 medium bombers, 19 B-17 bombers

Task Force 7 - Submarines
  12 submarines in support of Midway
  3 submariens patrolling east of Midway
  3 submarines patrolling north of Oahu

U.S. Forces In The Aleutian Action

Task Group 8.6
Rear Admiral Robert A. Theobald, commanding
  Heavy Cruisers
    Indianapolis and Louisville
  Light Cruisers
    Nashville (flagship), St. Louis, and Honolulu
  Destroyers
    Gridley, Gilmer, McCall, and Humphreys

Task Group 8.1
Captain Leslie Gehres, commanding
  Seaplane Tenders
    Williamson, Gillis, and Caco servicing 20 PBYs and one B-17.

Task Group 8.2
Captain Ralph Parker, commanding
  Gunboat
    Charleston

Fourteen patrolcraft
Five Coast Guard cutters
One tanker

These ships were placed in an offshore line for search purposes (similar to the Japanese patrol line that the Doolittle raid surface force ran into and alerted), but did not sight the Japanese ships during the action.

Task Group 8.3

Brigadier General William 0. Butler, commanding
    Cold Bay, 21 P-40 fighters, 12
        B-26 bombers, 2 B-18 bombers
    Point Otter on Umnak: 12 P-40 fighters
    Kodiak: 15 P-39 fighters, 17 P-40 fighters, 5 B-17 bombers, 2 LB-30
        bombers
    Anchorage: 25 P-38 fighters, 15 P-39 fighters, 4 P-36 fighters, 7 B-17
        bombers, 5 B-18 bombers, 12 B-26 bombers, and 2 LB-30 bombers.

Task Group 8.4

Commander Wyatt Craig, commanding
    Destroyers
        Case, Reid, Brooks, Sands, Kane, Dent, Talbot, King, and Waters named
        "Destroyer Striking Force".

Task Group 8.5

Six submarines (S type)
    present and ineffective

Task Group 8.9 - Fleet Train

Two tankers
One freighter

Selected Bibliography with Commentary

Below is a select list of major sources used in the writing of *The Midway Campaign*. Please note that it is not a complete list, but should lead to further reading on the topic.

Cohen, Stan. *East Wind Rain, A Pictorial History of the Pearl Harbor Attack*. Pictorial Histories Publishing Co. Homespun style with some nice pictures.

Deacon, Richard. *Kempei Tai*. Berkeley. History of the Japanese Secret Service.

Drea, Edward J., MacArthur's ULTRA. University Press of Kansas. Quite good, but especially for the latter part of the war.

Dull, Paul S. *The Battle History of the Imperial Japanese Navy (1941-1945)*. USNI. Unexciting, but excellent for Order of Battle.

Evans, David C., The Japanese Navy in World War II. 2nd edition, United States Naval Institute. A quite well edited and interesting series of articles by former Japanese officers.

Firkins, Peter. *The Australians in Nine Wars*. Pan. General history of the Australian Army.

Francillon, Rene J. *Japanese Aircraft of the Pacific War*. USNI. Excellent.

Gill, Hermon G. *Royal Australian Navy 1939-1945*. Two volumes. Australian War Memorial. Solid, though with some errors on the Japanese.

Hara, Tameichi. *Japanese Destroyer Captain*. Ballantine. Good for Japanese point of view, but has many battle errors.

Jentschura, Jung, and Mickel. *Warships of the Imperial Japanese Navy, 1869-1945*. Standard work on the subject.

Lord, Walter. *Day of Infamy*. Holt. Based on a series of interviews with a multitude of individuals at Pearl Harbor on 7 December. Extremely entertaining.

Lord, Walter. *Incredible Victory*. Harper & Row. More scholarly than the above, but not as entertaining. Very good for Japanese point of view.

Lundstrom, John B. *The First South Pacific Campaign*. USNI. Dry, but excellent history of December of 1941 to June of 1942 in the South Pacific.

Lundstrom, John B. *The First Team: Pacific Naval Air Combat From Pearl Harbor to Midway*. USNI Press. Simply brilliant. Lundstrom goes beyond the easily available sources for the best view of naval air combat, from the American perspective.

Marder, Arthur. *Old Friends, New Enemies: The Royal Navy and the Imperial Japanese Navy*. Oxford University Press. Simply the best. Vol. II is not by Marder and weaker.

Morison, S.E. *History of the United States Naval Operations in World War II*. Atlantic Little Brown. Very readable and good.

Morton, Louis. *The Fall of The Philippines*. Government Printing Office. An excellent study. The Army Green Series (named for the color of this multivolume series) has a warranted reputation as one of the most honest of the various official histories.

Muir, Malcolm Jr. *The Capital Ship Program in the United States Navy, 1934-1945*. University Microfilms International (300 N. Zeeb Rd., Ann Arbor, MI, 48106) Good thesis.

Muir, Malcolm Jr. *The Iowa Class Battleships*. Blandford Press. Best operational history of these ships.

Prange, Gordon W. *At Dawn We Slept*. McGraw Hill. Very good study on Pearl Harbor, but should be read in conjunction with Admiral Layton's *I Was There*.

Prange, Gordon W. et. al., *Dec. 7, 1941*. McGraw Hill. If you enjoyed Walter Lord's *Day of Infamy*, you will like this updated version with many new reminisces from both sides of the attack on Pearl Harbor.

Rohwer, J. and Hummelchen, G. *Chronology of the War at Sea, 1939-1945*. Arco. Excellent.

Smith, S.E. *The United States Navy in World War II*. Ballantine. Very good first person history of the naval war from the U.S. point of view.

Stillwell, Paul, ed. *Air Raid: Pearl Harbor Recollections of a Day of Infamy*. USNI. Solid first person stories to add to Walter Lord's book.

United States Naval Institute Proceedings, various articles. While primarily containing articles on the modern navy, it does have some historical gems from time to time, often dealing with some small incident or aspect of the war. The Institute must really be complimented for publishing over the years some very interesting and yet not necessarily commercially successful books. Well done!

Wilmott, H.P. *Empires in the Balance.* USNI. Very good for a synthesis that is well written, but some technical errors creep in and suffers from a lack of Japanese source material.

Wilmott, H.P. *The Barrier and the Javelin.* USNI. Volume II in the series takes one through Coral Sea and Midway. Considers Admiral Yamamoto to have been a poor strategist at Midway.

Index